S0-CMR-041

JOURNEY TO MOTHERHOOD

JOURNEY TO MOTHERHOOD

Great writings on pregnancy-
from a woman's first love
to her baby's first day of life

Compiled by Emanuel Martin Greenberg, M.D.

ST. MARTIN'S PRESS
NEW YORK

St. Martin's Press, Inc., 175 Fifth Avenue, New York, N.Y. 10010.
Manufactured in the United States of America
Library of Congress Catalog Card Number: 78-3985

Library of Congress Cataloging in Publication Data
Main entry under title:
Journey to motherhood.
1. Pregnancy—Literary collections.
2. Childbirth—Literary collections. 3. Pregnancy—Addresses, essays, lectures. 4. Childbirth—Addresses, essays, lectures. I. Greenberg, Emanuel Martin.
PN6071.P62J6 808.8'99287 78-3985
ISBN 0-312-44506-7

ACKNOWLEDGMENTS

Grateful acknowledgment is made for permission to reprint the following material:

Excerpts from *Anne of The Thousand Days,* by Maxwell Anderson, copyright © 1948 by Maxwell Anderson. Reprinted by permission of William Morrow & Co., Inc.

"Should Breast Feeding Be Encouraged?" by Hugh R. K. Barber, M.D., *The Female Patient,* March 1977. Reprinted by permission of Hugh R. K. Barber, M.D.

"Love Came By From The Riversmoke," from *John Brown's Body,* by Stephen Vincent Benet; Holt, Rinehart and Winston, Inc. Copyright © 1927, 1928 by Stephen Vincent Benet. Copyright renewed © 1955, 1956, by Rosemary Carr Benet. Reprinted by permission of Brandt & Brandt.

Quotation from *This Is My Beloved,* by Walter Benton. Copyright © 1943 by Alfred A. Knopf, Inc. and renewed 1971 by Walter Benton. Reprinted by permission of Alfred A. Knopf, Inc.

"A Man Child!" from *The Good Earth* by Pearl S. Buck (John Day). Copyright © 1931, 1949 by Pearl S. Buck; renewed 1958 by Pearl S. Buck. Reprinted by permission of Harper & Row, Publishers, Inc.

Excerpts from *Safe Convoy: The Expectant Mother's Handbook,* by William J. Carrington, M.D. Copyright © 1944 by William J. Carrington. Reprinted by permission of J. B. Lippincott Company.

Excerpt from *The Scandals of Clochemerle,* by Gabriel Chevallier. Copyright © 1937, 1965 by Simon & Schuster, Inc. Reprinted by permission of Simon & Schuster, a Division of Gulf & Western Corporation.

"Birth," from *The Citadel* by A. J. Cronin, copyright © 1937 by

A. J. Cronin. Reprinted by permission of Little, Brown and Co.

"It was Just a Habit," from *The Autobiography of Will Rogers,* edited by Donald Day, copyright © 1949 by Rogers Company, copyright renewed 1977 by Donald Day and Beth Day. Reprinted by permission of Houghton Mifflin Company.

Excerpts from pp. 1-3, 4-5 in *Childbirth Without Fear,* by Grantly Dick-Read, copyright © 1944 by Grantly Dick-Read. Reprinted by permission of Harper & Row, Publishers, Inc.

"Midwifery 1977," by Thomas F. Dillon, M.D.; Barbara A. Brennan, R.N., C.N.M.; John F. Dwyer, M.D.; Abraham Risk, M.D., M.P.H.; Alan Sear, PH.D.; Lynne Dawson, M.P.H., R.N., and Raymond Vande Wiele, M.D., *American Journal of Obstetrics and Gynecology,* April 15, 1978; Vol. 130, pp. 917-921. Courtesy of Thomas F. Dillon, M.D.

Excerpts from *Expectant Motherhood,* by Nicholas J. Eastman, copyright © 1940 by Nicholas J. Eastman. Reprinted by permission of Little, Brown and Co.

"The First Test Tube Baby," by Edward Edelson from The New York *Daily News,* July 27, 1978. Copyright © 1978 by N. Y. News, Inc. Reprinted by permission.

"Childbirth Through the Ages," by Solveig Eggers, *Private Practice,* October 1973. Reprinted by permission of *Private Practice.*

Excerpt from pp. 158-159 in *The Man From Nazareth,* by Harry Emerson Fosdick. Copyright © 1949 by Harper & Row, Publishers, Inc. Reprinted by permission of Harper & Row, Publishers, Inc.

Excerpt from *Good Night, Sweet Prince,* by Gene Fowler. Copyright © 1944 by Gene Fowler, © renewed 1972 by Gene Fowler, Jr., Jane Fowler Morrison, and Will Fowler. Reprinted by permission of The Viking Press.

Excerpt from *Mr. Adam,* by Pat Frank. Copyright © 1946 by Pat Frank. Copyright © renewed 1974 by Patrick Frank. Reprinted by permission of J. B. Lippincott Company.

Excerpt from pp. 59-61 in *Infant and Child in the Culture of Today,* Rev. Ed., by Arnold Gesell, Frances L. Ilg, and Louise Bates Ames. Copyright © 1974 by Gesell Institute of Child Development. Reprinted by permission of Harper & Row, Publishers, Inc.

Quotation from *The Prophet,* by Kahlil Gibran, reprinted with permission of the publisher, Alfred A. Knopf, Inc. Copyright © 1923 by Kahlil Gibran, renewal copyright © 1951 by Administrators C.T.A. of Kahlil Gibran Estate and Mary G. Gibran.

Margaret Shea Gilbert, *Biography of the Unborn,* 1st edition. Copyright © 1938, The Williams & Wilkins Co. Reproduced by permission.

Excerpts, abridged from Chapter 13, "Have You Seen the Latest Model?" from *Cheaper by the Dozen,* by Frank B. Gilbreth, Jr. and Ernestine Gilbreth Carey (Thomas Y. Crowell). Copyright © 1948,

1963 by Frank B. Gilbreth and Ernestine Gilbreth Carey. Reprinted by permission of Harper & Row, Publishers, Inc.

"A Sixteenth-Century Birth," from *Into This Universe,* by Alan F. Guttmacher. Copyright © 1937, © 1965 by Alan F. Guttmacher. Reprinted by permission of The Viking Press.

Excerpt from *A Farewell to Arms,* by Ernest Hemingway, reprinted by permission of Charles Scribner's Sons. Copyright © 1929 Charles Scribner's Sons.

Chapter One in *Brave New World,* by Aldous Huxley. Copyright © 1932, 1960 by Aldous Huxley. Reprinted by permission of Harper & Row, Publishers, Inc.

"History of Frozen Semen," Idant Laboratories. Reprinted by permission of Idant Laboratories.

"Childbirth Center Responds to Demands for More Family Participation", *Hospitals, Journal of the American Hospital Association,* September 1, 1976; Vol. 50, No. 17, pp. 11-12. Reprinted by permission of the Maternity Center Association.

From *Painless Childbirth,* by Fernand Lamaze. Reprinted by permission of Contemporary Books, Inc.

Excerpt from *Birth Without Violence,* by Frederick Leboyer, translation copyright © 1975 by Alfred A. Knopf, Inc. Reprinted by permission of Alfred A. Knopf, Inc.

"What Happens to Your Newborn Baby?" by Amelia Lobsenz, *Today's Woman,* October 1951 (Fawcett). Reprinted by permission of CBS Publications.

"Developing Maternity Services Women Will Trust," by Ruth Watson Lubic, *American Journal of Nursing,* October 1975, Vol. 75, No. 10. Reprinted by permission of the Maternity Center Association.

"The Natural Childbirth Illusion," by Theodore Mandy, M.D., Robert Farkas, M.D., Ernest Scher, M.D., and Arthur Mandy, M.D., *Southern Medical Journal,* June 1951, Vol. 44, pp. 527-534. Reprinted by permission of the authors.

Excerpt from *The Magic Mountain,* by Thomas Mann. Copyright © 1927, renewed 1955, by Alfred A. Knopf, Inc. Copyright © 1952 by Thomas Mann. Reprinted by permission of Alfred A. Knopf, Inc.

Excerpt from "Bliss," from *The Short Stories of Katherine Mansfield,* copyright © 1920 by Alfred A. Knopf, Inc. and renewed 1948 by J. Middleton Murry. Reprinted by permission of Alfred A. Knopf, Inc.

"Compulsory Rooming In," by Angus McBryde, *Journal of the American Medical Association,* March 3, 1951; Vol. 145, No. 9, p. 625. Copyright © 1951, American Medical Association. Reprinted by permission of *Journal of the American Medical Association.*

"Human Cloning: Reality or Ripoff?" from Medical World News, April 3,

1978. Reprinted by permission of *Medical World News,* a McGraw-Hill Publication.

Excerpts from *Tales of the South Pacific,* by James Michener. Copyright © 1946, 1947, The Curtis Publishing Company. Copyright © 1947 by James Michener, renewed 1975 by James Michener. Reprinted with permission of Macmillan Publishing Co., Inc.

"Having a Baby at Home," by Myryame Montrose, from *American Baby Magazine,* July 1978. Reprinted by permission of American Baby Inc.

Quotation from *The Face is Familiar,* by Ogden Nash, copyright © 1940 by Ogden Nash. Reprinted by permission of Little, Brown and Co.

"First Child Probably Boy," August 25, 1951, © 1951 by The New York Times Company. Reprinted by permission.

"Maternity Dress Her Specialty," September 28, 1951, © 1951 by The New York Times Company. Reprinted by permission.

"A Note on the Stork," June 24, 1950, © 1950 by The New York Times Company. Reprinted by permission.

"I Worked Till My Baby Was Born," by Ellen Raymond, *Today's Woman,* January 1951 (Fawcett). Reprinted by permission of the author.

"Obstetrics in Primitive Peoples," by Duncan Reid and Mandel Cohen, *Journal of the American Medical Association,* March 4, 1950, Vol. 142, No. 9, pp. 616-618. Copyright © 1950, American Medical Association. Reprinted by permission of *Journal of the American Medical Association.*

Excerpt from *In His Image: The Cloning of a Man,* by David Rorvik, copyright © 1978 by David Rorvik. Reprinted by permission of J. B. Lippincott Company.

"Procreation without Sex," by Albert Rosenfeld, *Physician's World,* May 1973 issue. Reprinted by permission of Albert Rosenfeld and PW Communications, Inc.

Excerpt from *Songs for Patricia,* by Norman Rosten, copyright © 1951 by Norman Rosten. Reprinted by permission of the author.

Excerpt from *Abraham Lincoln: The Prairie Years,* Volume One, by Carl Sandburg, copyright © 1926 by Harcourt Brace Jovanovich, Inc., renewed 1954 by Carl Sandburg. Reprinted by permission of the publishers.

Excerpt abridged from *The New You and Heredity,* by Amram Scheinfeld. Copyright © 1965, 1961, 1950 by Amram Scheinfeld. Reprinted by permission of J. B. Lippincott Company.

"Factors Influencing Sex Ratios," by Landrum B. Shettles, M.D., *International Journal of Gynaecology and Obstetrics,* September 1970. Re-

CONTENTS

PREFACE

This book had its origins early in my obstetrical practice, when I distributed a "Suggested Readings List" to expectant mothers. That was more than thirty years ago, and just as some of the babies whom I delivered then have now gone on to give birth to babies of their own, so has the list of readings continued to grow and develop.

There was a rich and vast literature to choose from—the subject of childbirth has inspired writers for thousands of years—and the selections in JOURNEY TO MOTHERHOOD include prose and poetry, fiction and practical writings, works as ancient as the Bible, as nostalgic as early twentieth-century obstetrics, and as new as cloning and test-tube babies. In reading this book, an expectant mother can gain a sense of what the experience of giving birth has meant to women throughout time and throughout the world.

JOURNEY TO MOTHERHOOD really explores several journeys: the journey to parenthood of a man and a woman, the journey of a sperm and an egg to a full-term, healthy baby—even the journey of obstetrical practice from its first primitive days to the atomic age.

All of these journeys add up to a great adventure, perhaps the supreme adventure, for when a space shuttle becomes little more than another subway or bus ride, the growth and birth of new human life will continue to be marveled at and not yet fully understood.

—Emanuel Martin Greenberg, M.D.
New York, 1978

JOURNEY
TO MOTHERHOOD

I

THE URGE TO LOVE

We need so little room, we two—
thus on a single pillow. . . . as we move
    nearer, nearer, heaven—
until I burst inside you like a screaming rocket.

—Walter Benton, *This Is My beloved*

I could be content that we might procreate like trees, without conjunction, or that there were any way to perpetuate the world without this trivial and vulgar way of coition: it is the foolishest act a wise man commits in all his life, nor is there any thing that will more deject his cooled imagination, when he shall consider what an odd and unworthy piece of folly he hath committed. I speak not in prejudice, nor am averse from that sweet sex, but naturally amorous of all that is beautiful.

—Sir Thomas Browne, *Religio Medici*

Love is a smoke rais'd with the fume of sighs;
Being purg'd, a fire sparkling in lovers' eyes;
Being vex'd, a sea nourish'd with lovers' tears.
What is it else? A madness most discreet,
A choking all, and a preserving sweet.

—William Shakespeare, *Romeo and Juliet*

From *The Song of Solomon,* 4:1-16

Behold, thou art fair, my love; behold, thou art fair; thou hast doves' eyes within thy locks; thy hair is as a flock of goats, that appear from mount Gilead.

Thy teeth are like a flock of sheep that are even shorn, which came up from the washing; whereof every one bear twins and none is barren among them.

Thy lips are like a thread of scarlet, and thy speech is comely; thy temples are like a piece of a pomegranate within thy locks.

Thy neck is like the tower of David builded for an armoury, whereon there hang a thousand bucklers, all shields of mighty men.

Thy two breasts are like two young roes that are twins, which feed among the lilies.

Until the day break, and the shadows flee away, I will get me to the mountain of myrrh, and to the hill of frankincense.

Thou art all fair, my love; there is no spot in thee.

Come with me from Lebanon, my spouse, with me from Lebanon: look from the top of Amana, from the top of Shenir and Hermon, from the lions' dens, from the mountains of the leopards.

Thou hast ravished my heart, my sister, my spouse; thou hast ravished my heart with one of thine eyes, with one chain of thy neck.

How fair is thy love, my sister, my spouse! how much better is thy love than wine! and the smell of thine ointments than all spices!

Thy lips, O my spouse, drop as the honeycomb; honey and milk are under thy tongue; and the smell of thy garments is like the smell of Lebanon.

A garden inclosed is my sister, my spouse; a spring shut up, a fountain sealed.

Thy plants are an orchard of pomegranates, with pleasant fruits, camphire, with spikenard.

Spikenard and saffron; calamus and cinnamon, with

all trees of frankincense; myrrh and aloes, with all the chief spices:

A fountain of gardens, a well of living waters, and streams from Lebanon.

Awake, O north wind; and come, thou south; blow upon my garden, that the spices thereof may flow out. Let my beloved come into his garden, and eat his pleasant fruits.

But 'twill be wise, and prudent to remove
And banish all incentives unto Love.

—LUCRETIUS

THE URGE TO LOVE

from *Childbirth Without Fear*
by GRANTLY DICK-READ

This irresistible but nebulous urge to love is so mysterious that one girl of fifteen wrote to me from school—"I wish you could explain to me why I feel as I do this term; it has never been like it before. I am so deliriously happy. There is no reason that I know of, but I am fond of everybody. I seem to see the good in them, and want to *think* lovely things, as if I were possessed of a heavenly spirit making me so much better than my real self."

And so with every girl in varying degrees this power which will rule their lives begins to develop at an early age, until in due course they find themselves in love, and here the hotchpotch of their emotional life becomes concentrated, with all its thrills, its joys and anxieties, upon one semi-divine individual. It is the spiritual refinement of her own ideal. In the normal course of events she becomes betrothed but is unwilling to believe that there are others who are equally fortunate, and is blissfully ignorant of the fact that she is but an instrument in the design of nature. Eventually she marries, and if all goes well she conceives and prepares to bear her child.

Love may be beset by anxieties and doubts, but of itself it stimulates all the noblest and greatest qualities of which human nature is characterized at its best. It is the greatest power in the world, and without it the races of mankind would finish in but a few generations.

LIVING IN A DELIRIUM

from *Tales of the South Pacific*

by JAMES A. MICHENER

Three more times Cable made that midnight trip. He was now living in a delirium which carried into waking hours the phantasms that assailed him when he slept and sweated at noonday. He and Liat were experiencing a passion that few couples on this earth are privileged to share. Could it have been indefinitely prolonged, it is probable that their love for one another would have sustained them, regardless of their color, throughout an entire lifetime. This is not certain, however, for Cable and Liat knew of the impossibilities that surrounded them.

LOVE CAME BY FROM THE RIVERSMOKE

from *John Brown's Body*

by STEPHEN VINCENT BENET

Love came by from the riversmoke,
    When the leaves were fresh on the tree,
But I cut my heart on the blackjack oak
    Before they fell on me.

The leaves are green in the early Spring,
    They are brown as linsey now,
I did not ask for a wedding-ring
    From the wind in the bending bough.

Fall lightly, lightly, leaves of the wild,
    Fall lightly on my care,
I am not the first to go with child
    Because of the blowing air.

I am not the first nor yet the last
    To watch a goosefeather sky,
And wonder what will come of the blast
    And the name to call it by.

Snow down, snow down, you whitefeather bird,
    Snow down, you winter storm,
Where the good girls sleep with a gospel word
    To keep their honor warm.

The good girls sleep in their modesty,
    The bad girls sleep in their shame,
But I must sleep in a hollow tree
    Till my child can have a name.

I will not ask for the wheel and thread
    To spin the labor plain,
Or the scissors hidden under the bed
    To cut the bearing-pain.

I will not ask for the prayer in church
Or the preacher saying the prayer,
But I will ask the shivering birch
To hold its arms in the air.

Cold and cold and cold again,
Cold in the blackjack limb,
The winds in the sky for his sponsor-men
And a bird to christen him.

Now listen to me, you Tennessee corn,
And listen to my word,
This is the first child ever born
That was christened by a bird.

He's going to act like a hound let loose
When he comes from the blackjack tree,
And he's going to walk in proud shoes
All over Tennessee.

I'll feed him milk out of my own breast
And call him Whistling Jack.
And his dad'll bring him a partridge nest,
As soon as his dad comes back.

From *The Scandals of Clochemerle*
by GABRIEL CHEVALLIER

"Indeed I have been considering the matter, Madame la Baronne. I have been praying to God for guidance. There are so many scandals—"

The Curé Ponosse sighed deeply, and took the plunge.

"Madame la Baronne, there is more to tell you. You

know young Rose Bivaque, one of our Children of Mary, who is just eighteen?"

"Isn't she that blushing little silly—plump, my goodness—who sings less out of tune than the other little simpletons in the sisterhood?"

The Curé Ponosse, by a show of consternation, let it be understood that he would be lacking in Christian charity if he assented to such a description.

"Very well, then," the Baroness went on, "what has the child been doing? She looks as if butter wouldn't melt in her mouth."

The Curé of Clochemerle was quite overcome.

"I—I can hardly tell you, Madame la Baronne. I fear we must face a conception which will not be . . . er . . . immaculate, alas!"

"Do you mean that she is pregnant? Then say so. Say, someone has given her a child. Somebody did the same to me, and I'm still alive. (Estelle, sit up straight!) Yes, somebody did so to your respectable mother. There's nothing nasty about it."

"It is not so much what happened, Madame la Baronne, as the absence of the sacrament which grieves me."

"That *is* true. I'd quite forgotten! Well, my dear Ponosse, they're a nice lot, your Children of Mary! I can't think what you teach them in your little gatherings. . ."

"Oh, Madame la Baronne!" exclaimed the Curé of Clochemerle, whose distress and fear had now reached their crowning point.

The task of giving this information to the president of the Children of Mary had filled him with dread. He feared her reproaches, or, worse still, that she might resign. But the Baroness asked:

"And who was the bright lad who showed such clumsiness? Is it known?"

"You mean, Madame la Baronne, the . . . er—"

"Yes, Ponosse, yes. Don't look so bashful."

"It was Claudius Brodequin, Madame la Baronne."

"What is he doing, this boy?"

"He is doing his military service. He was here on leave in April."

"He will have to marry Rose. Or else he must go to prison, to penal servitude. I shall see that his colonel knows about it. Does this young soldier think he can treat the Children of Mary as though they were women in a conquered country? By the way, Ponosse, you must send Rose to see me. She will have to be looked after, to see that she doesn't do anything foolish. Send her along tomorrow. To the chateau."

There are people who blame her and call her a senseless little creature, this Rose Bivaque, this girl-mother only eighteen years old. But as I see her trudging along the road, a solitary figure with the bloom of health on her cheeks, with a faint smile reflecting the exuberance and the animality of youth, I find her a touching, an appealing figure, almost pretty, this little Bivaque who accepts her fate without protest, knowing as she does, knowing absolutely—she who knows nothing at all—that one can play no tricks with human destiny, and that a woman's lot must be fulfilled, fulfilled to the uttermost, whether she wills it or no, so soon as the time has come for her wholehearted collaboration with the world's great scheme of human birth.

Neither remorse nor uneasiness is with her as she goes her way, but her mind is troubled at the thought of finding herself in the Baroness' presence. Now here she is entering the chateau, mounting a grand flight of steps and being led to the door of a big room that is lovelier and more splendid than the interior of a church. She hardly dares venture onto the bright slippery floor. The sound of a voice with a tone of authority makes her turn her head. The Baroness addresses her:

"That is you, Rose Bivaque? Come here, my child. It's that Claudius Brodequin, so I hear, who has done this to you?"

Blushing and awkward, the young delinquent makes her confession:

'Yes, it was, Madame la Baronne."

"And what fine tales did he tell you, this young man, that he managed to seduce you? Will you please explain?"

Rose Bivaque's faculty of exposition is quite unequal to such a task. She replies:

"He didn't tell me anything, Madame la Baronne."

"He told you nothing? Better and better! Well, then?"

Driven into a corner, the girl blushes still more hotly. Then she explains, with simple sincerity, the manner of her fall.

"He didn't tell me anything. . . he. . . just. . . acted."

This reply, which reminds her of the time when she herself wasted no words, disconcerts the Baroness. But she continues, with unrelaxed severity:

"He acted! I like that! He acted because you let him, you little simpleton!"

"I couldn't stop him, Madame la Baronne," is the girl's candid reply.

"Good heavens!" the lady of the manor exlaims. "Then any young coxcomb who comes along can do what he likes with you? Look at me, Mademoiselle. Answer me."

This reproof is countered by Rose Bivaque by a display of firmness. Her consciousness that she is telling the truth emboldens her:

"Oh no, Madame la Baronne! There's lots of boys who'd like to make up to me. I'd never, never listen to them. But Claudius—he makes me feel all funny. . ."

The Baroness recognizes the language of passion. With innumerable recollections of surrenders no less inevitable, she closes her eyes. When she opens them once more, her expression is lenient and kind. With practiced eye she takes Rose in at a glance, her dumpy figure and fresh, healthy looks.

"Nice little creature!" she says, patting her cheek. "And tell me, my child, is he talking to you about marriage, this irresistible young man?"

"Claudius'd be willing enough for us to marry, but his father and mine can't stop quarreling about the Bonne-Pente vines."

Rose Bivaque had suddenly acquired an air of self-confidence; an avaricious tendency—together with a spirit of submissiveness—is one of the primitive instincts which she has inherited from the women of her breed. She is a child of the soil, and, young though she is, she knows full well the importance of a patch of vineyard that lies well in the sun. The Baroness, on the contrary, has no notion of this, being too much of the great lady to condescend to an interest in such vulgar trifles. Rose Bivaque has to explain to her the circumstances of the strife between the two families. She is now in floods of tears. As she listens to her, the Baroness notices that this deluge has no ill effect on the girl's features. A happy age, she thinks to herself. If I cried like that I should look a perfect sight! You've got to be young to have troubles. . . She ends by saying:

"Set your mind at rest, my child. I shall go and give all those skinflints a shaking-up as soon as I possibly can. You shall have your Claudius, and the vineyard into the bargain, I promise you."

Then she adds, for her own benefit:

"I must do what I can to keep all these wretched peasants in better order."

Again, for the last time, she looks thoughtfully at Rose Bivaque, such a simple creature, with all her cheerful serenity now restored, like a rose a trifle battered after rain. Deliciously stupid, but how genuine! In dismissing her, she says:

"And I will be its godmother. But in future, for heaven's sake, look after yourself better."

Then she smiles, and adds:

"In any case it won't mean much to you in future. It's only once that it means so much. And on the whole it's a good thing to get through with it as soon as possible. Women who have waited too long became incapable of taking the plunge. Women need so much unconsciousness. . ."

These words are not intended for the ears of Rose Bivaque, who is already some distance away and would not understand them. The thought of her Claudius overshadows all else. He must surely be awaiting her on the road, halfway between the chateau and the town.

"What did she say to you? Was she nice or nasty?" Claudius asks at once, as soon as he sees her.

Rose Bivaque tells him of the interview in her own way; and Claudius, with his arm around her shoulders, kisses her on the cheek.

"You'll be married before any of 'em."

They gaze at each other. Happiness is theirs. It is a splendid day, very hot. They have finished all their little secrets. They listen to the kindly concert which the birds are giving in their honor. They walk along in silence. Then Claudius says:

"Three more weeks of this weather and the wine'll be first-rate!"

From *The Book of Genesis,* 34:1-9

And Dinah, the daughter of Leah, which she bare unto Jacob, went out to see the daughters of the land.

And when Shechem, the son of Hamor the Hivite, prince of the country, saw her, he took her and lay with her, and defiled her.

And his soul clave unto Dinah, the daughter of Jacob, and he loved the damsel, and spake kindly unto the damsel.

And Shechem spake unto his father Hamor, saying, Get me this damsel to wife.

And Jacob heard that he had defiled Dinah his daughter; now his sons were with his cattle in the field; and Jacob held his peace until they were come.

And Hamor the father of Shechem went out unto Jacob to commune with him.

And the sons of Jacob came out of the field when they heard it; and the men were grieved, and they were very wroth, because he had wrought folly in Israel in lying with Jacob's daughter; which thing ought not to be done.

And Hamor communed with them, saying, The soul of my son Shechem longeth for your daughter: I pray you give her him to wife.

And make ye marriages with us, and give your daughters unto us, and take our daughters unto you.

From *The Flame of Life*
by D'ANNUNZIO

It was one of those sublime moments that have no return. Before even his soul was conscious of it, his hands went out to her in their desire, touched her body, drew it towards him, found pleasure in feeling that it was cold and sweet.

When she felt his strong hands on her bare arm, the woman threw her head back as if about to fall. Under her dying eyelids, between her dying lips, the white of her eyes and the white of her teeth glittered like things that glitter for the last time. Then quickly she raised her head and revived; her mouth sought the mouth that was seeking it. They stamped themselves on each other. No seal was ever deeper. Love, like the shrub above them, covered both those deluded ones.

They separated; they gazed at each other without seeing. They could see nothing. They were blind. They could hear a terrible roll as if the quiver of bronze bells had re-entered their very forehead. Nevertheless they heard the dull thud of a pomegranate that had fallen on the grass from a branch they had shaken in their violent clasp. They shook themselves as if to throw off a mantle that was burdening them. They saw each other and became lucid again. They heard the voices of their friends who were scattered about the garden and a distant indistinct clamour from the canals where perhaps the antique pageants were repassing.

"Well," asked the young man, eagerly, scorched to the marrow by that kiss that had been full of flesh and soul.

The woman bent down to the grass to pick up the pomegranate. It was quite ripe and broken by its fall; its blood-like juice was flowing; it moistened her parched hand and stained her light dress. With the remembrance of the laden boat, the pale island, and the meadow of asphodel, the words of the Lifegiver came back to her loving spirit. "This is my body. . . . Take and eat."

"Well?"

"Yes."

She pressed the fruit in her hand with an instinctive movement, as if to crush it. The juice trickled in a streak over her wrist. Then her whole body contracted and vibrated as if round a knot of fire, craving for subjection. Again the icy river submerged her, passing over her, chilling her from the roots of her hair to the points of her fingers without extinguishing that knot of fire.

"How? Tell me!" the young man urged, almost roughly, as he felt his madness rising again and the odor of the Orgy returning from afar.

"Leave when the others leave, then come back. I will wait for you at the gate of the Gradenigo Garden."

IMPROVEMENT OF THE BREED

from *The Republic*

by PLATO

Why, I said, the principle has been already laid down that the best of either sex should be united with the best as often, and the inferior with the inferior, as seldom as possible; and that they should rear the offspring of the one sort of union, but not of the other, if the flock is to be maintained in first-rate condition. Now these goings on must be a secret which the rulers only know, or there will be a further danger of our herd, as the guardians may be termed, breaking out into rebellion.

Had we not better appoint certain festivals at which we will bring together the brides and bridegrooms, and sacrifices will be offered and suitable hymeneal songs composed by our poets: the number of weddings is a matter which must be left to the discretion of the rulers, whose aim will be to preserve the average of population? There are many other things which they will have to consider, such as the effects of wars and diseases and any similar agencies, in order as far as this is possible to prevent the State from becoming either too large or too small.

. . . We shall have to invent some ingenious kind of lots which the less worthy may draw on each occasion of our bringing them together, and then they will accuse their own ill-luck, and not the rulers.

And I think that our braver and better youth, besides their other honours and rewards, might have greater facilities of intercourse with women given them; their bravery will be a reason, and such fathers ought to have as many sons as possible.

LOVELY LITTLE PLAYTHINGS

from *The Cloister and the Hearth*
by CHARLES READE

The couple were well to do, and would have been free from all earthly care but for nine children. When these were coming into the world, one per annum, each was hailed with rejoicings, and the saints were thanked, not expostulated with; and when parents and children were all young together, the latter were looked upon as lovely little playthings invented by Heaven for the amusement, joy, and evening solace of people in business.

But as the olive-branches shot up, and the parents grew older, and saw with their own eyes the fate of large families, misgivings and care mingled with their love. They belonged to a singularly wise and provident people; in Holland reckless parents were as rare as disobedient children. So now, when the huge loaf came in on a gigantic trencher, looking like a fortress in its moat, and, the tour of the table once made, seemed to have melted away, Elias and Catherine would look at one another and say, "Who is to find bread for them all when we are gone?"

LOVE AND BREAD

by AUGUST STRINDBERG

When young Gustaf Falk, the assistant councillor, made his ceremonial proposal for Louise's hand to her father, the old gentleman's first question was: "How much are you earning?"

"No more than a hundred kroner a month. But Louise—"

"Never mind the rest," interrupted Falk's prospective father-in-law. "You don't earn enough."

"Oh, but Louise and I love each other so dearly! We are so sure of one another."

"Very likely. However, let me ask you: is twelve hundred a year the sum total of your resources?"

"We first became acquainted at Lidingo."

"Do you make anything besides your government salary?" persisted Louise's parent.

"Well, yes, I think we shall have sufficient. And then, you see, our mutual affection—"

"Yes, exactly; but let's have a few figures."

"Oh," said the enthusiastic suitor, "I can get enough by doing extra work!"

"What sort of work? And how much?"

"I can give lessons in French, and also translate. And then I can get some proofreading."

"How much translation?" queried the elder, pencil in hand.

"I can't say exactly, but at present I am translating a French book at the rate of ten kroner per folio."

"How many folios are there altogether?"

"About a couple of dozen, I should say."

"Very well. Put this at two hundred and fifty kroner. Now, how much else?"

"Oh, I don't know. It's a little uncertain."

"What, you are not certain, and you intend to marry? You seem to have queer notions of marriage, young man! Do you realize that there will be children, and that you will have to feed and clothe them, and bring them up?"

"But," objected Falk, "the children may not come so very soon. And we love each other so dearly, that—"

"That the arrival of children may be prophesied quite safely." Then, relenting, Louise's father went on:

"I suppose you are both set on marrying, and I don't doubt but what you are really fond of each other.

So it seems as though I should have to give my consent after all. Only make good use of the time that you are engaged to Louise by trying to increase your income."

Young Falk flushed with joy at this sanction, and demonstratively kissed the old man's hand. Heavens, how happy he was—and his Louise, too! How proud they felt the first time they went out walking together arm in arm, and how everybody noticed the radiant happiness of the engaged couple!

"I was thinking," he said, "that it would be heaven to have children with you. To live somewhere together. Somewhere like Bali-ha'i."

—JAMES A. MICHENER, *Tales of the South Pacific*

II

THE SPERM, THE EGG, AND THE EMBRYO

Menstrual bleeding represents the abrupt termination of a process designed to prepare board and lodging, as it were, for a fertilized ovum; it betokens the breakdown of a bed which was not needed because the "boarder" did not materialize; its purpose then, is to clear away the old bed in order that a new and fresh one may be created the next month.

—NICHOLAS J. EASTMAN

OVULATION AND FERTILIZATION

from *Expectant Motherhood* (1940)

by NICHOLAS J. EASTMAN

Each month, with punctilious regularity, a blisterlike structure about half an inch in diameter develops on the surface of one or the other ovary. Inside this bubble, almost lost in the fluid about it, lies a tiny speck, scarcely visible to the naked eye; a thimble would hold three million of them. This little speck contains within its diminutive compass all that you are heir to; it possesses not only the potentialities of developing into a man or woman with all the complicated physical organization entailed, but embodies the mental as well as the physical traits of yourself and your forbears; perhaps your own brown eyes, or your father's tall stature, possibly your mother's love of music, or your grandfather's genius at mathematics. These, and a million other potentialities, are all wrapped up in this little speck, or ovum, so small that it is about one fourth the size of the period at the end of this sentence.

After the ovum has been discharged from the ovary it faces a perilous seven-day journey. Its goal is the cavity of the uterus, more than three inches away. The only pathway of approach is the tortuous Fallopian tube whose lining is wrinkled unevenly into countless little hills and valleys, and whose passageway at the inner end is no larger than a bristle. The ovum, moreover, has no means of locomotion itself but must depend on "hitchhiking" a ride, as it were, through this winding, bumpy tunnel.

As soon as the ovum comes near the army of spermatozoa, the latter, as if they were tiny bits of steel drawn by a powerful magnet, fly at the ovum. One penetrates, but only one. By what mechanism the countless other sperms are prevented from entering the ovum is not known, but it is well-established that as soon as one enters, the door is shut on all suitors. Now, as if electrified, all the particles which make up the ovum (now fused with the sperm) exhibit vigorous agitation, as if they were being rapidly churned about by some unseen force; this becomes more and more violent until it amounts to such an upheaval that the fertilized ovum divides into two cells. This process is repeated again and again until masses containing sixteen, thirty-two, and sixty-four cells are successively produced, and so on endlessly. Meanwhile this growing aggregation of cells is being carried down the Fallopian tube in the direction of the uterine cavity.

It is the germ cell of the father, the spermatozoon, which determines the sex of the future baby; the germ cell of the mother, the ovum, can grow into either a boy or a girl—a fact well worth mentioning to any husband who is disappointed by the sex of the child!

Meanwhile another important structure has formed, the afterbirth. This is a fleshy, disclike organ which late in pregnancy measures about eight inches in diameter and one inch in thickness. It receives its name from the fact that its birth follows that of the child; physicians refer to it as the "placenta," a term derived from the Latin word for "cake," which it resembles in shape. The placenta is connected to the fetus by means of the umbilical cord, a gelatinous, coiling structure about twenty inches long. Within it are vessels whose blood carries oxygen and food from placenta to fetus and waste products from fetus to placenta.

The Chinese count a person's age not from the day of birth but from the time of conception, a good way of reminding the expectant mother that all this time a living, human creature is being nourished, who will soon be "nine months old." During this vital, formative period the child is in greater need of proper nourishment and suitable environment than at any other time in his life.

EMBRYOLOGY

from *The Magic Mountain*
by THOMAS MANN

Our young adventurer, supporting a volume of embryology on the pit of his stomach, followed the development of the organism from the moment when the spermatozoon, first among a host of its fellows, forced itself forward by a lashing motion of its hinder part, struck with its forepart against the gelatine mantle of the egg, and bored its way into the mount of conception, which the protoplasm of the outside of the ovum arched against its approach. There was no conceivable trick or absurdity it would have not pleased nature to commit by way of variation upon this fixed procedure. In some animals, the male was a parasite in the intestine of the female. In others, the male parent reached with his arm down the gullet of the female to deposit the semen within her; after which, bitten off and spat out, it ran away by itself on its fingers, to the confusion of scientists, who for long had given it Greek and Latin names as an independent form of life. Hans Castorp lent an ear to the learned strife between ovists and animalculists: the first of whom asserted that the egg was in itself the complete little frog, dog, or human being, the male element being only the incitement to its growth; while the second saw in a spermatozoon, possessing head, arms and legs, the perfected form of life shadowed forth, to which the egg performed only the office of "nourisher in life's feast." In the end they agreed to concede equal meritoriousness to ovum and semen, both of which, after all, sprang from originally indistinguishable procreative cells.

I AM BEGOT

from *The Life and Opinions of Tristram Shandy*

by LAURENCE STERNE

I wish either my father or my mother, or indeed both of them, as they were in duty both equally bound to it, had minded what they were about when they begot me; had they duly considered how much depended upon what they were then doing;—that not only the production of a rational Being was concerned in it, but that possibly the happy formation and temperature of his body, perhaps his genius and the very cast of his mind;—and, for aught they knew to the contrary, even the fortunes of his whole house might take their turn from the humours and dispositions which were then uppermost;—Had they duly weighed and considered all this, and proceeded accordingly,—I am verily persuaded I should have made a quite different figure in the world, from that in which the reader is likely to see me.

The Homunculus, Sir, in however low and ludicrous a light he may appear, in this age of levity, to the eye of folly or prejudice;—to the eye of reason in scientific research, he stands confessed—a Being guarded and circumscribed with rights.—The minutest philosophers, who, by the bye, have the most enlarged understandings, (their souls being inversely as their enquiries) show us incontestably, that the Homunculus is created by the same hand,—engendered in the same course of nature,—endowed with the same locomotive powers and faculties with us:—That he consists as we do, of skin, hair, fat, flesh, veins, arteries, ligaments, nerves, cartilages, bones, marrow, brains, glands, genitals, humours, and articulations;—is a Being of as much activity,—and, in all senses of the word, as much and as truly our fellow creature as my Lord Chancellor of England.—He may be benefited,—he may be injured,—he may obtain redress;—in a word, he has all the claims and rights of humanity, which Tully, Puffendorf, or the best ethic writers allow to arise out of that state and relation.

Now, dear Sir, what if any accident had befallen him in his way alone!—or that, through terror of it, natural to so young a traveller, my little Gentleman has got to his journey's end miserably spent;—his muscular strength and virility worn down to a thread;—his own animal spirits ruffled beyond description,—and that in this sad disordered state of nerves, he had lain down a prey to sudden starts, or a series of melancholy dreams or fancies, for nine long, long months together.—I tremble to think what a foundation had been laid for a thousand weaknesses both of body and mind, which no skill of the physician or the philosopher could ever afterwards have set thoroughly to rights.

THE UNION OF THE SPERM AND THE EGG

from *Expectant Motherhood* (1940)
by NICHOLAS J. EASTMAN

In all Nature's wide universe of miracles there is no process more wondrous, no mechanism more incredibly fantastic, than the one by which a tiny speck of tissue, the human egg, develops into a crying, seven-pound baby. So miraculous did primitive peoples consider this phenomenon that they ascribed it all to superhuman intervention and even overlooked the fact that sexual intercourse was a necessary precursor. At this very moment certain primitive tribes in East Australia belive that female babies are created by Bahloo, the moon, while male infants are fashioned at a near-by boy factory supervised by Boomayahmayahmul the wood lizard. According to their belief, the babies, after being created in spirit by these woodland deities, suspend themselves on certain coolabah trees whence they enter—more or less promiscuously—the bodies of passing women and there become incarnated. It is not surprising to note further that the women of this tribe, when they see a whirlwind coming, cover themselves with blankets and avoid drooping coolabah trees!

Throughout unremembered ages our own primitive ancestors doubtless held similar beliefs, but now we know that pregnancy comes about in only one way: from the union of the female germ cell, the egg or ovum, with a male cell, the spermatozoon.

From *Biography of the Unborn* (1938)
by MARGARET SHEA GILBERT

Life begins for each of us at an unfelt, unknown and unhonored instant when a minute, wriggling sperm plunges headlong into a mature ovum or egg. The quiet ovum, as if electrified by the entrance of this strange creature, reacts with violent agitation, a spurt of activity, and a release of all the man-forming potencies that are inherent in the human egg cell. It is at this moment of fusion of the sperm and the ovum (a process called fertilization) that a new human being is created. From the ovum and sperm, each of which, unless it fuses with its mate, is destined shortly to die, there arises a new individual who contains the potentialities for unnumbered generations of men.

"The journey of a sperm in search of an ovum" might well be the caption for the next section of the human story. The extremely minute sperm (so small that all the sperm required to produce the next generation in North America could be contained in a pin head) must travel over a long, tortuous, and hazardous course before it can accomplish its sole purpose in life—fusion with an ovum. Millions of sperm fail for each one that succeeds. From the testes, the male sex glands in which the sperm are formed, the sperm must travel for a distance of more than twenty feet through the coiled sex ducts of the male before they can be ejaculated. Through the lashing of their thread-like tails they are able to swim forward at the rate of approximately one inch in twenty minutes, which in relation to their length compares well with the average swimming ability of a man. Rhythmic muscular contractions of the walls of the female sex ducts move the mass of sperm through these organs and toward the ovary, aiding and perhaps directing the spern in the arduous trip to its rendezvous with an ovum.

The ovum falls, or is moved in a fashion not clearly understood, into the open, full-shaped end of the uterine tube, and starts on its journey of life, which differs from that of the sperm in being shorter, slower, less hazardous, and probably requiring no activity of the ovum itself. It moves slowly down the uterine tube and into the uterus, traversing a distance of about four inches in approximately three days. If during this journey it is met and entered by an active sperm, it at once embarks on the astounding process of becoming a human being. If it misses this rendezvous for which it was created, nurtured and matured, it languishes for a short time within the uterus, dies a degenerate death and is probably soon expelled from the body.

When the fertilized egg reaches the uterus, the tissues lining the uterus are in a very active state—rich in blood, glands prepared for secretion, everything "ripe" and ready for the coming egg, much as well-plowed, fertilized field is ready for seed. This fortunate preparedness does not result from consciousness that an egg has been fertilized and will soon embed. The same process occurs each month when an egg is released from the ovary—a forehanded move on the part of the uterus to be ready if the egg should be fertilized. If fertilization does not occur, the uterus suddenly loses its excess tissue and blood in the menstrual flow, and starts on a new period of repair and growth, on the principle of better luck next time.

Oddly enough, it seems to be his heart and his brain that interest him most since it is these two structures in their simplest forms which first develop.

As we follow the embryo through succeeding months we shall see the front end of this tube expand to form the brain; the back part of the tube will become the spinal cord. In this fourth week of life none of these complex structures are present. Yet this tube represents the beginning of the nervous system—the dawn of the brain that in its maturity will serve man as his most precious possession.

Within twenty-five days after the simple egg was fertilized by the sperm, the embryo is a small creature with head and tail and a back and a belly, measuring about 2.6 mm. in length. True, he does not look much like a human being, but he has a human heart beating within him, human blood flowing through his vessels, and a human brain taking form within his head. He lacks a face or neck so his heart lies close against his brain. He has no arms or legs, and his belly-side, instead of being covered with body-wall, lies spread out flat over the large yolk-sac which hangs between the heart and tail regions. Within this unhuman exterior, however, he has started to form his lungs, which first appear as a shallow groove on the floor of the foregut; his liver is arising as a thickening in the wall of the foregut just behind the heart; and he has entered on a long and devious path which will ultimately lead to the formation of his kidneys.

So the human embryo completes the first month of life. The dawn of humanness shows in its simple organs. With the successful establishment of a constant supply of food from the placenta, a great burst of activity sweeps through the embryo; within little more than a week the foundations for almost all the organs of the human body are laid down. In thirty days the new human being has travelled the path from the mysteriously simple egg and sperm to the threshold of humanity.

At the close of the second month, the lower jaw is still small, and the chin is poorly defined; seen in profile the embryo looks almost chinless. The nose is broad and flat with the nostrils opening forward rather than downward. The eyes are far apart. The forehead is prominent and bulging, giving the embryo a very "brainy" appearance. In fact, it is interesting to note that the embryo is truly "brainy" in the sense that the brain forms by far the largest part of the head. It will take the face many years to overcome this early dominance of the brain and to reach the relative size the face has in an adult.

As the sculptor first fashions his work in plastic clay

and then, when he knows that his design is adequate, casts the statue in rigid bronze, so the developing embryo seems to plan out its skeleton in cartilage and then cast it in bone, removing the cartilage model as the bone is formed.

So the second month of life closes with the stamp of human likeness clearly imprinted on the embryo. His face, although slightly grotesque by our standards, has a distinctly human character. Bones and muscles have given his body smooth contours as well as the ability to move. Sexual differences have arisen and the sex of the embryo can be determined. The internal organs are well laid down. During the remaining seven months the chief changes will be largely growth and detailed development within each organ.

In fact, so completely is the fundamental plan of the human body shown by the two-month embryo that the biologist marks this as the end of the embryonic period of life. Within the normal span of human life occur five distinct epochs. Each man is in turn an embryo, fetus, child, adolescent and adult. At the end of the second month the first epoch, that of the embryo, is completed. Henceforth the young human being is called a fetus.

No longer is there any question whether or not the fetus is a living, individual member of mankind. Not only have several of the internal organs taken on their permanent functions, but the well-developed muscles now produce spontaneous movements (that is to say, under the normal, undisturbed condition of the uterus) of the arms, legs, and shoulders, and even of the fingers. The beat of the fetal heart is now strong enough to be heard with a stethoscope through the mother's abdominal wall. And it is quite possible that those peculiarities of structure, of general form, of intensity of bodily activities—the many characteristics that distinguish each man from his fellow man—may have already put the stamp of individuality on the three-month-old fetus.

Death throws its shadow over man before he is

born, for the stream of life flows most swiftly through the embryo and young fetus, and then inexorably slows down, even within the uterus. If time is measured for living creatures by internal events and changes, then half a lifetime is lived during our first two months.

Now the still, silent march of the fetus along the road from conception to birth becomes enlivened and quickened. The fetus stirs, stretches, and vigorously thrusts out arms and legs. The first movements perceived by the mother may seem to her like the fluttering of wings, but before long his blows against the uterine wall inform her in unmistakable terms that life is beating at the door of the womb. For this is the time of the "quickening in the womb" of folklore.

Man is an enigma; he is both one and many, indivisible and yet complex. He is composed of hundreds of separate parts that are constantly dying and being renewed, yet he retains a mysterious unity which we call individuality. A continuous stream of inanimate materials flows through the enclosed space that he calls his body, becoming momentarily alive and then passing on to the external world, yet the continuity that he calls his life remains unbroken from conception to death.

The human body may be compared to a cooperative society whose members band together for mutual support and protection, presenting a common front to the external world, and sharing equally in the privileges and responsibilities of their internal world. Division of labor, specialization, and the exchange of produce are just as important in the society of cells and organs as in the society of men. Certain organs specialize in converting the materials taken in as food into usable components of living cells; these are the digestive organs. The circulating fluids of the body form an extensive transportation system. Nerves are the cables of the communications system while the brain acts as the central exchange through which activities in widely separated regions are correlated and controlled. The potent endocrine glands might be called the supervisors since their secretions determine the speed and constancy on many activities. Overlying all these specialized systems is the skin. . . the protector, conservator, and inquirer of the society of organs.

The five-month fetus is a lean creature, with wrinkled skin, about a foot long and weighing about one pound. If born (or strictly speaking aborted) it may live for a few minutes, take a few breaths, and perhaps cry. But it soon gives up the struggle and dies. Although able to move its arms and legs actively, it seems to be unable to maintain the complex movements necessary for continued breathing. Some vital function, perhaps of the brain, of the nervous reflexes, or even of the lung itself is still too poorly developed to carry its share of the burden of life.

Now the waiting fetus crosses the unknown ground lying between dependence and independence. For although he normally spends two more months within the secure haven of the uterus, he is nonetheless capable of independent life. If circumstances require it, and the conditions of birth are favorable, the seven-month fetus is frequently able to survive premature birth.

The fetus is by no means a quiet, passive creature, saving all his activity until after birth. He thrashes out with arms and legs, and may even change his position within the somewhat crowded quarters of the uterus. He seems to show alternate periods of activity and quiescence, as if perhaps, he slept a bit and then took a little exercise. Although he may not breath in the watery surroundings of the uterus, it is quite possible that the chest muscles later to be used in breathing now undergo alternate contraction and relaxation, producing a breathing-like movement of the chest. He probably swallows some of the amniotic fluid, and there is good evidence that he silently but unmistakingly hiccoughs.

The journey through the narrow confines of the birth canal, with or without external aid, is frequently an arduous and hazardous one for the infant. He may be bruised, or even have bones broken; the thin and loosely joined bones of the skull may be pressed into distorted positions. But if he was endowed at fertilization with sufficient viability, if the course of development has been normal, and if the birth passageways are normal in size, the infant survives the journey without mishap.

"The newborn infant cries without tears. . . ."

Thus the first nine months are completed. From a minute, fertilized egg the new human being has passed through two epochs of his life—the embryonic and the fetal. He has grown enormously in size, weight and complexity during his nine months of parasitic life within his mother. The manifold changes occurring during this period form the first personal history of each member of the human race. It is the one phase of life which we all have in common; it is essentially the same for all men. But even here it cannot rightly be said that "all men are created equal," for behind every generation lies the preceding generation, and the hereditary traits of structure and perhaps of function with which each man is endowed at fertilization, makes his life individual and characteristic, even during these first nine months.

HISTORY OF FROZEN SEMEN
from *Idant Laboratories* (1975)

Preserving human semen by freezing is not a new idea. Montegazza, an Italian scientist, in 1866 was the first to propose banks for frozen semen. He reported that human sperm cells could survive freezing and suggested that a soldier killed in war might beget a legal heir by his frozen and stored semen. But at that time so few sperm survived the freezing process that it was not practical to preserve semen for later use. Only recently, in 1949, was it discovered that the addition of a small amount of glycerol (a common naturally occurring organic compound) before freezing resulted in a much improved survival of sperm cells of man and of other mammals.

This discovery led to the extensive use of frozen semen in dairy and beef cattle. Millions of calves have been born using frozen bull semen. There has been no reported increase in birth defects in over four generations of calves conceived exclusively with frozen semen.

The first conception using frozen semen in man occurred in 1953. Since then there have been over 400 children born who were conceived with frozen semen.

Since 1949 there have been many improvements in both the freezing and storage of semen. Idant's method results in a consistently high recovery of the originally motile (swimming) sperm cells.

However, even if there is good survival of the sperm cells during the freezing process there remains the problem of maintaining the sperm in the frozen state. In the early stages of development it was found that the sperm cells became less fertile during storage in the frozen state. It was soon discovered that a greater number of sperm survived over a longer period of time as the storage temperature was reduced. The death of sperm cells is caused by certain destructive chemical and physical reactions occurring in and around the cells. The lower the temperature, the slower these reactions take place. Idant stores semen under the surface of liquid nitrogen, a temperature of 321° below zero Fahrenheit.

In the field of animal husbandry, bull semen has been used successfully after as long as sixteen years of frozen storage. And human semen frozen by a process quite similar to ours has been successfully used after ten years of storage. However, it may be that because of individual variations some men's semen will not store as long as others.

Of course, the ultimate goal of the entire process of freezing and storing semen is to achieve conception when the semen is used at a later date. We apply our best efforts to preserve the fertilizing ability of the specimen. However, aside from freezing and storage there are other factors which will improve the chances of conception. These are related to the technique of insemination. To achieve conception a doctor places the semen in the birth canal at the time of ovulation (the time at which the woman is most fertile). In many cases it is difficult to tell the precise time of ovulation and it is wise therefore to have enough semen available for other attempts in case the first insemination is not successful. Fortunately, the entire specimen of semen (the ejaculate) does not have to be used for one insemination.

The ejaculate may be divided into a number of separate small portions so that enough is available for a number of inseminations without a great loss in the fertilizing capacity of any one insemination. Each ejaculate is divided into portions sufficient for about twelve inseminations. Sometimes the doctor performing the inseminations may choose to do more than one insemination during one of the woman's fertile periods in order to increase the chances of conception in that period. Even so there should still be a sufficient quantity to provide for inseminations over a number of fertile periods. On the average, it takes 2-4 monthly cycles to achieve pregnancy with frozen semen. Idant will require a minimum of three ejaculates to provide sufficient semen for many inseminations.

It must be emphasized that Idant cannot guarantee that you will be able to have a child using the semen you have preserved. Each person is unique and there are many factors in both the husband and wife which will affect the ultimate probability of success.

Common Questions about Semen Banks and Frozen Semen

Q. Why would someone want to preserve his semen in a semen bank?

A. Perhaps the most common reason is that he wants to preserve his semen before having a vasectomy (an operation where the sperm ducts are tied off). A vasectomy is one of the safest, most convenient and effective methods of birth control, particularly suited for those who do not intend to have children. However, its major drawback is that it is extremely hard to reverse. Reversal of a vasectomy involves a difficult, uncomfortable, and expensive surgical procedure. Even if the reversal surgery is successful, the sperm which is produced is often infertile. Few people want to take an irreversible step if it can be prevented. The storage of semen helps keep options open. It is a completely harmless procedure that can only serve to increase the chances of having children should some tragedy or change in circumstances reawaken the desire to do so. By preserving his semen at a semen bank a man may still retain the potential of having children while enjoying the benefits of simple and effective birth control.

Q. Are there other reasons why a man might preserve his semen?

A. Men who will suffer an involuntary loss of fertility through a prostate operation or from ailments for which they must take certain drugs which will render them sterile, might wish to preserve their fertility by storing their semen. Also, men whose occupation might accidentally subject them to high doses of radiation—nuclear-power-plant workers or radiotherapists, for example—could consider preserving their semen as insurance in the event of radiation damage which may cause mutations or birth defects.

Q. How will I know if the specimen I withdraw is actually mine?

A. Accurate identification of samples is one of the most important considerations in storing semen. Idant has gone to great lengths to see to it that a specimen will be correctly identified. Since correct identification is of such great concern, Idant has provided for the client's direct participation in the identification process. By carefully filling out a number of special purpose labels, he himself sets up a system of cross-checking codes whereby the identification is established by four independent coding criteria. Thus, the recovery of the correct sample is not dependent upon the transcribing of information by a secretary, but upon the records created by the client himself. In addition, a minimum of three independently coded ejaculates are required. For additional safety, the ejaculates are stored in separate liquid nitrogen refrigerators.

Q. What will happen to the refrigerators in case of a power failure or a city-wide blackout?

A. There is no danger from a power failure or blackout. Liquid-nitrogen refrigerators do not use electricity. They remain cold through the evaporation of the liquid nitrogen surrounding the stored semen. The refrigerators are kept constantly filled with liquid nitrogen. Under these conditions, the semen could remain preserved for an entire month without refilling the refrigerator.

Q. Is there an increased risk of birth defects using frozen semen?

A. Insofar as available data indicate, the answer is NO. Since 1953 there have been over 400 children born who were conceived with frozen semen. Up to the present time there has been no reported increase in birth defects. Thus, though there is a risk of a birth defect, this risk appears to be no greater with frozen semen than it is with fresh semen.

Q. If I intend to have children in the future, should I rely on the combination of vasectomy and frozen semen storage as a means of contraception?

A. Definitely not. If you intend to have children in the future, the combination of vasectomy and frozen semen storage is not a recommended contraceptive technique. The storage of frozen semen is to provide for the eventuality that some tragedy or change in circumstances reawakens the desire to have another child after a man has had a vasectomy. Since we cannot guarantee of the long-term fertilizing capacity of frozen semen Idant does not recommend the use of frozen semen and vasectomy as a means of contraception for those who still intend to have children.

Q. Does every man have a better than fifty-fifty chance of having a child with his frozen preserved semen?

A. No. Some men will have a better than a fifty-fifty chance. On the other hand, some men have a lower fertility than average and it may be that the ability of some men's sperm cells to withstand the freezing process is not as good as others. The semen will be evaluated for sperm cell concentration and motility before freezing, and a small sample of the semen will be checked for motility after thawing. If for some reason the results of freezing a particular client's semen are unsatisfactory he will be notified, and should he decide not to store his semen as a result of this information, his fee will be refunded.

Q. Is there then a risk of having no children?

A. Yes. As mentioned previously, there can be no guarantee that you will be able to father a child using the semen you have preserved. It is not possible to predict precisely the fertility of your semen nor can we predict the future fertility of your wife.

III

EXPECTANT MOTHERS AND FATHERS

Now, in all life's encounters there are probably few experiences which are at first more upsetting, mentally and emotionally, than the realization by a young woman that she is pregnant.

—NICHOLAS J. EASTMAN

OF MY BIRTH AND PARENTAGE

from *The Adventures of Roderick Random*

by TOBIAS SMOLLETT

During her pregnancy, a dream discomposed my mother so much that her husband, tired with her importunity, at last consulted a highland seer, whose favourable interpretation he would have secured before-hand by a bribe, but found him incorruptible. She dreamed she was delivered of a tennis-ball, which the devil (who, to her great surprise, acted the part of a mid-wife) struck so forcibly with a racket, that it disappeared in an instant; and she was for some time inconsolable for the loss of her offspring; when all of a sudden, she beheld it return with equal violence, and enter the earth, beneath her feet, whence immediately sprung up a goodly tree covered with blossoms, the scent of which operated so strongly on her nerves that she awoke. The attentive sage, after some deliberation, assured my parents, that their first-born would be a great traveller; that he would undergo many dangers and difficulties, and at last return to his native land, where he would flourish in happiness and reputation. —How truly this was foretold. . .

THE SIGNS OF PREGNANCY

from *Expectant Motherhood* (1940)

by NICHOLAS J. EASTMAN

In ancient Rome it was customary for a young woman after marriage to wear about her neck a snug-fitting band of some rigid material such as gold, silver or brass. These bandeaux were often exquisitely wrought, but their main purpose was not ornamental but diagnostic. From many an old wives' tale the young woman had learned that when pregnancy supervened the bandeau would become uncomfortably tight. Its removal, accordingly, carried an obvious implication and was the occasion of great rejoicing in the household, for it meant that the young woman had set forth on the Great Adventure—the creation of a new life.

Although many centuries have passed since the time of the Roman bandeau, human curiosity remains much the same and the first visit of the modern expectant mother to her doctor is usually prompted by the old query: Am I really pregnant? Oddly enough this is the one question which the physician may answer equivocally because even the most careful examination will rarely reveal clear-cut evidence of pregnancy until two menstrual periods have been missed, and occasionally the diagnosis may remain uncertain for a longer time. The physician bases his decision on three main types of evidence: the patient's observations; the physical examination; and, in some instances, on laboratory tests.

Although cessation of menstruation is the earliest and one of the most important symptoms of pregnancy, it should be noted that pregnancy may occur without prior menstruation and that menstruation may occasionally continue after conception. Several examples of the former circumstance will come to mind at once. For instance, in certain Oriental countries, where girls marry at a very early age, pregnancy frequently occurs before the menstrual periods set in; again, nursing mothers, who usually do not menstruate during the period of lactation, often conceive at this time; more rarely, women who think they have passed the menopause are startled to find themselves pregnant. Conversely, it is not uncommon for a woman to have one or two periods after conception, but almost without exception these are brief in duration and scant in amount. In such cases the first period ordinarily lasts two days instead of the usual five and the next only a few hours. Although there are instances in which women are said to have menstruated every month throughout pregnancy, these are of questionable authenticity and are probably ascribable to some abnormality of the reproductive organs. Indeed, *vaginal bleeding at any time during the pregnancy should be regarded as abnormal and reported to the physician at once.*

Absence of menstruation may result from a number of conditions other than pregnancy. Probably one of the most common causes of delay in the onset of the period is psychic influence, particularly fear of pregnancy. Change of climate, exposure to cold, as well as certain chronic diseases such as anemia, may likewise suppress the menstrual flow.

Quickening is usually felt toward the end of the fifth month as a tremulous fluttering low in the abdomen. The first impulses caused by the stirring of the baby may be so faint as to raise some doubt as to their cause; later on, however, they grow stronger and become often so vigorous that many mothers are inclined to wonder if the baby is not destined to become an acrobat. Although quite painless, they may occasionally disturb the mother's sleep during the later weeks.

Many babies who are alive and healthy seem to move about very little in the uterus and not infrequently a day or so may pass without a movement being felt. Inability to feel the baby move does not mean that it is dead or in any way a weakling, but in all probability that it has assumed a position in which its movements are not so readily felt by the mother.

Despite the best efforts of the dressmaker at a camouflage, pregnancy begins to "show" about the time the growing uterus reaches the navel, that is at the end of the fifth month, and thereafter it is usually impossible to conceal the condition. Attempts to do so by tight lacing are dangerous, and not a few serious accidents have resulted from this practice.

Curiously enough, these heart sounds were first encountered more or less by accident. Something over a hundred years ago it so happened that a Swiss physician thought it might be interesting to place his ear over the abdomen of a pregnant woman and try to hear the baby splashing about in the fluid surrounding it. Anticipating splashes, he was amazed to hear faint, rhythmic beats which resembled the ticking of a watch under a pillow, and shortly he realized that he was listening—for the first time in history—to the heartbeats of a baby within the uterus. The rate of the fetal heart is much faster than the usual rate of the maternal heart and ordinarily approximates 140 beats a minute. Under favorable circumstances these sounds become audible about the middle of the fifth month but often are not heard until several weeks later. By this time, accumulated evidence of other types has usually made the diagnosis so clear that this final proof is scarcely necessary. Nevertheless, these tick-tock messages from within the uterus, proclaiming in unequivocal terms the welfare of the baby, are always reassuring to mother and physician alike.

WITH CHILD

from *Travelling Standing Still*

by GENEVIEVE TAGGARD

Now I am slow and placid, fond of sun.
Like a sleek beast, or a worn one:
No slim and languid girl—not glad
With the windy trip I once had,
But velvet-footed, musing of my own,
Torpid, mellow, stupid as a stone.

You cleft me with your beauty's pulse, and now
Your pulse has taken body. Care not how
The old grace goes, how heavy I am grown,
Big with this loneliness, how you alone
Ponder our love. Touch my feet and feel
How earth tingles, teeming at my heel!
Earth's urge, not mine—my little death, not hers;
And the pure beauty yearns and stirs.

It does not heed our ecstasies, it turns
With secrets of its own, its own concerns,
Toward a windy world of its own, toward stark
And solitary places. In the dark,
Defiant even now, it tugs and moans
To be untangled from these mother's bones.

From *Biography of the Unborn* (1938)

MARGARET SHEA GILBERT

But the most prevalent belief—and it persists even to this day—has been in the effect of maternal impressions on the fetus. Too numerous to recount have been the tales of some specific event, some shock or fright, some special appetite, desire or unusual action of the pregnant mother that has caused a specific and related effect or "mark" on the fetus. No authentic medical evidence can be brought to the support of such a theory. No nervous or other direct connection exists between mother and child to serve as the agent in such marking. Yet belief in the relation of maternal impressions to fetal abnormalities is a stubbornly persistent part of our folklore.

MATERNITY DRESS HER SPECIALTY

from *The New York Times* (September 28, 1951)

Her most famous type of garment—the maternity dress—was fashioned after a request from a customer who was an expectant mother and desired something "presentable but comfortable." The basis of the historic dress was a bodice that was attached by an elastic band to an accordion-pleated skirt. With the production of this garment, Lane Bryant's enterprises were well established.

I WORKED TILL MY BABY WAS BORN

from *Today's Woman* (January 1951)
by ELLEN RAYMOND

On February 11 of last year, at 12:30 P.M. I checked out of my job as reporter on a trade journal after more than a year of unfailing attendance. The reason I remember the date so well is that my baby was born the same day.

And it was the day on which my obstetrician and I joined sighs across the delivery table to mark *finis* to an experiment that had begun with my first visit to his consulting room nearly eight months before.

When my suspicion of pregnancy was confirmed, I thought hard before timidly asking the question that working wives have probably been putting to working physicians since Eve raised Cain: "Doctor, how long can I go on with my job?"

Familiar with the experiences of other career wives, I waited unhappily to hear that my maximum work-expectancy would be about four months; five months on the outside. But I was reckoning without the open-minded attitude of my doctor.

"How long would you like to go on with your job?" he countered.

"It would be a great help if I could go all the way through—nine months," I replied, giving it the tone of a feeble joke.

"I don't see why that can't be arranged," he answered casually.

That was my first joyful intimation that the processes of pregnancy were not rigid and inflexible, fixed by the taboos and injunctions handed down by generations of nonprofessional authorities on the subject, i.e.: relatives and friends.

But when the first flow of enthusiasm receded, I found myself suddenly worried and contrite about the actual principal in the affair.

"What about the baby?" I said. "I don't want to do it if it's going to hurt the baby."

It was then that the doctor revealed that this was no case of quixotic accommodation on his part, but rather a welcome opportunity to test a deep conviction.

"It can actually benefit the baby," he said. "I have always maintained that child-bearing is one of the most natural and naturally accomplished functions of woman. And retaining a spirit of naturalness—in your case, working—can, under normal circumstances, provide one of the most helpful aids to a worry-free pregnancy and a calm and successful delivery."

He went on to list some of the traditional fears that tend to beset the young woman having her first child: fear of decreased family income; fear that comes with brooding on impending labor; and its corollary, fear generated by old wives' tales of bodily processes and anticipated pains.

"Continuing to work," he said, "will tend to ease the economic fear. It will fill your hours so that there will be less opportunity for the fear that comes from brooding. However, if mental comfort were the only benefit to be derived from working, I might still be inclined to follow my customary practice and. . ."

I interrupted, surprised. "You mean this isn't your customary practice—letting wives work straight through?"

"Unfortunately, no," he said. "Few of them seem to want to—or perhaps they don't think I'll sanction it. Mental comfort isn't the only benefit that can come from working. I believe that there is frequently actual physical good to be obtained from staying on the job.

"Now take your own case. You're twenty-seven and in perfect health," he said generously. (Actually I was almost twenty-eight with a left upper bicuspid that was far from sound.) "Your job doesn't demand any undue physical exertion like lifting or excessive bending, yet it provides enough steady action so that it can influence your circulation favorably; and it can give you muscular relaxation and toning that can be a real aid in a healthful delivery . . ."

Another dampening question suddenly rose to my mind.

"But doctor, there's one thing," I faltered. "My job. . . well, it's important that I look presentable, and I wonder. . ."

He smiled. "What you mean is you don't want to *look* pregnant—gain too much weight. I don't *want* you to gain too much weight. I don't want the child to be abnormally large. But I do want you to gain the right kind of weight—make every pound count. That means a diet. And there again, your job is an aid. Keeps your mind off food; keeps you away from the temptations of a nearby refrigerator.

"It comes down to this," he said. "I have a conviction; you have a job. Let's see if we can retain both. I'll try to keep you working successfully to the end of your term if you try to abide by all the instructions I've laid down."

We shook hands.

Besides the doctor, I could count on one other ally in my impending Battle of the Bulge: the new fashions, which seem to have been conceived with an eye to conception. Each day spent in the full-fronted concealment of my own moderately priced clothes, I knew, meant one day less in that expensive sandwich-board of pregnancy, the maternity gown. Relying then on high fashion and low calories, I set out on my intimate endeavor to control the shape of things to come.

The second month of my pregnancy was comparatively uneventful, characterized only by the expected onset of nausea. But even that my doctor alleviated somewhat with a new kind of pill. At my office they didn't even know I was sick. I enrolled in a class for expectant mothers in response to an assertion by the doctor that "when you know what's going on inside you, two-thirds of the battle against fear is won."

The next month I met a new adversary: hunger.

And contrary to tradition my wants weren't exotic; just unceasing. With the abatement of nausea, I suddenly developed a wanton urge to buy sweets and spices and starches. Instead I bought a tape measure.

My next checkup showed a weight increase of two pounds, pulse normal. No one in my organization yet knew, for no one had yet detected that I had moved the buttons of my best sailor-type outfit one notch to the starboard.

The fourth month nothing happened except that the secretaries in my office got suspicious. They resisted addressing me on the subject as long as they could, but finally their resistance collapsed, so to speak, of my own weight.

"Dearie," said their spokesman, with timing as delicately subtle as a snore in church, "there's something I've got to ask you. It's personal. I hope you won't mind."

I waited, together with the fourteen other passengers in the elevator.

"Have you taken to drinking or something?" she asked. "We were talking, us girls. It's a shame a nice figure like yours should go to pieces this way. Now I know a gymnasium that. . ."

By the sixth month they were leaving me alone, reasoning sensibly that they had done their bit and it was no longer any concern of theirs if I persisted in looking like the water-wagon I refused to get on.

My next checkup revealed an even gain and a monotonously normal pulse.

But the evenness ceased and the monotony crashed in the seventh month. My monthly visit to the doctor revealed an alarming gain in weight. And the frightening aspect of it all was that I had done nothing to precipitate it. I had adhered carefully to my diet of pills and protein; religiously I had walked my mile a day; regularly I had gone to bed owing myself at least one of the four glasses of liquid allotted me each day. What had I done wrong?

"Nothing," explained the doctor with what seemed to me a shade too much resignation. "Remember, I said I would *try* to keep you in shape. I had in mind these unpredictables. All we can do is hope it's an aberration rather than a trend."

In his tone I read the veiled suggestion that he might yet call the whole thing off. I grew panicky. I was sure that everything was out of control, that all my business contacts would soon "know" and that my value to the organization would cease with that knowledge. I discontinued my morning cup of coffee; I separated the chaff from the wheat in my diet and discarded the wheat. I edited my clothes, wore a large muff of the same material as my loose-fitting fur coat and kept the coat on whenever possible. At business luncheons I perfected a system of squirming into my chair in a sort of concealing crouch like a halfback frozen in his occupational attitude.

And whether it was a testament to my reinforced health measures or to lack of observation by the men at my office, or whether all along I had been making a mountain out of a protrusion, all these tactics seemed to work. My next checkup was heartening, strangers' glances appeared to have lost their X-ray quality and I was beginning to feel calm again when a new and deadlier peril broke.

Relatives and friends, from whom my condition couldn't be concealed, suddenly and in remarkable concert swooped down like crows in a cornfield, cawing at me in the strident monotones of outraged convention. Some almost succeeded in frightening my husband with their doom-shrieking.

Relatives took to calling the doctor, pleading, advising, and in at least one case threatening him with full responsibility "for anything that happened." One friend reported me to my head employer, three hundred miles away.

For weeks they kept it up, the pressure rising and tightening in me, like a strangled calliope, until finally something just had to give. And something did: my son.

With the delivery came calm and release and welcome justification of all that I had done. My diet turned out to have been not a convenience but a surgical necessity, for half the fifteen pounds I had gained proved to be baby. Dietary indulgence would have produced a child beyond my capacity to deliver normally.

And most gratifying, my normal delivery was due in no small measure to the suppleness I had retained by living an active existence—by working.

But actually—now that the long rest has given way to the long view—I am not so self-centered as to believe seriously that I did anything remarkable. Since my first visit, my doctor has guided several other working wives through similarly successful experiences.

There is one factor that makes my doctor's persistent faith in his somewhat unorthodox methods noteworthy. And that factor is this: I am—and he knew that I am—almost a physiological replica of my mother. And my mother died in childbirth.

TIME FOR CHILD-BEARING

from *The Republic*

by PLATO

. . . . And what is the prime of life? May it not be defined as a period of about twenty years in a woman's life, and thirty in a man's?

Which years do you mean to include?

A woman, I said, at twenty years of age may begin to bear children to the State and continue to bear them until forty; a man may begin at five-and-twenty, when he has passed the point at which the pulse of life beats quickest, and continue to beget children until he be fifty-five.

Certainly, he said, both in men and women those years are the prime of physical as well as of intellectual vigour.

Seven are my Daughters, of a Form Divine,
With seven fair Sons, an indefective Line.
Go, Fools, consider this, and ask the Cause
From which my Pride its strong Presumption draws.

—CROXAL

It was the custom of the Greeks to hand the newborn infant to the father, who acknowledged it as his own by lifting it into his arms. If he did not, the nurse placed it on the steps of the temple, to die of exposure or starvation, be eaten by buzzards or adopted by some kindly passerby. In spite of the Four Horsemen of the Apocalypse, civilization has made some progress in the past twenty-four centuries.

—WILLIAM J. CARRINGTON, *Safe Convoy*

EXPECTANT FATHERHOOD

from *One on the Aisle* (1949)

by WILLIAM A. LEONARD

It is one of the curious oversights of our civilization that so little attention has been paid to the physical and emotional care of the male animal during the most critical period—or periods—of his life. A materialistic world has been all too inclined to toss aside the very grave matter of paternity with "Oh, you're the father, huh?" Indeed, except for an assortment of limp articles purporting to guide man's behaviour during the corridor-pacing stage immediately before birth, plus a collection of tiresome quips aimed at making men feel that they are of dubious importance in the process of procreation, little or nothing has been written or said to comfort or advise the potential papa in the hours of his greatest need.

Women, in whom nature has seen fit to display a more pronounced indication of what's cooking, have made damn sure that all the attention, all the sympathy, all the laurels fall on them. I expect a tirade of abuse—from quarters as close as my own wife—when I state bluntly, as I am about to do, that the period of gestation and birth is every bit as difficult for Adam as for Eve. I feel qualified to speak out on this matter (in non-technical, lay terms at least), for I have undergone four pregnancies, three since World War II. If others would join me in what I could be convinced is a veritable crusade on behalf of the rights of man, let them qualify by proper breeding.

LARGE FAMILIES

from *The Spectator*

by ADDISON AND STEELE

Sir,

You who are so well acquainted with the Story of Socrates, must have read how, upon his making a Discourse concerning Love, he pressed his Point with so much Success, that all the Bachelors in his Audience took a Resolution to marry by the first Opportunity, and that all the married Men immediately took Horse and galloped home to their Wives. I am apt to think your Discourses, in which you have drawn so many agreeable Pictures of Marriage, have had a very good Effect this way in England. We are obliged to you, at least for having taken off that senseless Ridicule, which for many Years the Witlings of the Town have turned upon their Fathers and Mothers. For my own part, I was born in Wedlock, and I don't care who knows it: For which reason, among many others, I should look upon myself as a most insufferable Coxcomb, did I endeavor to maintain that Cuckoldom was inseparable from Marriage, or to make use of Husband and Wife as Terms of Reproach. Nay, Sir, I will go one Step further, and declare to you before the whole World, that I am a married Man, and at the same time I have so much Assurance as not to be ashamed of what I have done.

Among the several pleasures that accompany this state of Life, and which you have described in your former Papers, there are two you have not taken notice of, and which are seldom called into the Account, by those who write on this Subject. You must have observed, in your Speculations on human Nature, that nothing is more gratifying to the Mind of Man than Power or Dominion; and this I think myself amply possessed of, as I am the Father of a Family. I am perpetually taken up in giving out Orders, in prescribing Duties, in hearing Parties, in administering Justice, and in distributing Rewards and Punishments. To speak in the

Language of the Centurion, I say unto one, Go and he goeth; and to another, Come, and he cometh; and to my Servant, Do this and he doth it. In short, Sir, I look upon my Family as a Patriarchal Sovereignty, in which I am myself both King and Priest. All great Governments are nothing else but Clusters of these little private Royalties, and therefore I consider the Masters of Families as small Deputy Governors presiding over the several little Parcels and Divisions of their Fellow-Subjects. As I take great Pleasure in the Administration of my Government in particular, so I look upon myself not only as a more useful, but as a much greater and happier Man than any Bachelor in England, of my Rank and Condition.

There is another accidental Advantage in Marriage, which has likewise fallen to my Share, I mean the having of a multitude of Children. These I cannot but regard as very great Blessings. When I see my little Troop before me, I rejoice in the Additions which I have made to my Species, to my Country and to my Religion, in having produced such a number of reasonable Creatures, Citizens, and Christians. I am pleased to see myself thus perpetuated; and as there is no Production comparable to that of a human Creature, I am more proud of having been the occasion of ten such glorious productions, than if I had built a hundred Pyramids at my own Expence or published as many Volumes of the finest Wit and Learning. In what a beautiful Light has the Holy Scripture represented Abdon, one of the Judges of Israel, who had forty Sons and thirty Grandsons, that rode on threescore and ten Ass-Colts, according to the Magnificence of the Eastern Countries? How the Heart of the Old Man must have rejoiced, when he saw such a beautiful Procession of his own Descendents, such a numerous Cavalcade of his own raising? For my own part, I can sit in my Parlour with great Content, when I take a review of half a dozen of my little Boys mounting upon Hobby Horses, and of as many little Girls tutoring their Babies, each of them endeavoring to excel the rest, and to do something that may gain my Favour and Approbation. I cannot question but he who has blessed me with so many Children, will assist my Endeavors in providing for them. There is one thing I am able to give each of them, which is a virtuous Education. I think it is Sir Francis Bacon's Observation, that in a numerous Family of Children, the eldest is often spoiled by the Prospect of an Estate, and the youngest by being the Darling of the Parent; but that some one or other in the middle, who has not perhaps been regarded, has made his way in the World, and overtopped the rest. It is my business to implant in every one of my Children the same Seeds of Industry, and the same honest Principles. By this means I think I have a fair Chance, that one or other of them may grow considerable in some or other way of Life, whether it be in the Army, or in the Fleet, in Trade, or any of the three learned Professions; for you must know, Sir, that from long Experience and Observation, I am persuaded of what seems a Paradox to most of those with whom I converse, namely, That a Man who has many Children, and gives them a good Education, is more likely to raise a Family, than he who has but one, notwithstanding he leaves him his whole Estate. For this reason I cannot forbear amusing myself with finding out a General, an Admiral, or an Alderman of London, a Divine, a Physician, or a Lawyer among my little People who are now perhaps in Petticoats; and when I see the motherly Airs of my little Daughters when they are playing with their Puppets, I cannot but flatter myself that their Husbands and Children will be happy in the Possession of such Wives and Mothers.

If you are a Father, you will not perhaps think this Letter Impertinent; but if you are a single Man, you will not know the Meaning of it, and probably throw it into the Fire: Whatever you determine of it, you may assure yourself that it comes from one who is

Your most humble Servant
and Well-wisher
Philogamus.

SYMPATHETIC NAUSEA

from *Safe Convoy* (1944)

by WILLIAM J. CARRINGTON

Unusual instances have been recorded in which a loving husband suffered from sympathetic nausea. In the conservative *Lancet,* a British medical journal, a case was reported of husband and wife who began to vomit the same day and who finished in a dead heat with the score tied, if mixed metaphors are permitted. Sir Francis Bacon and S. Weir Mitchell wrote freely about this bizarre phenomenon. It is no harder to believe than a host of other silly superstitions: in fact, there is such a condition as male hysteria.

From *Disorder and Early Sorrow*

by THOMAS MANN

. . . . And once and for all his heart belongs to the little one, as it has since the day she came, since the first time he saw her. Almost always when he holds her in his arms he remembers that first time: remembers the sunny room in the Women's Hospital, where Ellie first saw the light, twelve years after Bert was born. He remembers how he drew near, the mother smiling the while, and cautiously put aside the canopy of the diminutive bed that stood beside the large one. There lay the little miracle among the pillows: so well formed, so encompassed, as it were, with the harmony of sweet proportions, with little hands that even then, though so much tinier, were beautiful as now; with wide-open eyes blue as the sky and brighter than the sunshine—and almost in that very second he felt himself captured and held fast. This was love at first sight, love everlasting: a feeling unknown, unhoped for, unexpected—in so far as it could be a matter of conscious awareness; it took entire possession of him, and he understood, with joyous amazement, that this was for life.

One of the nurses notifies father, and the glad tidings send him off in a frenzied ectasy to the cellarette where the decanter is kept and thence to the cigar store where he fills his pockets ready to counterattack the well wishes of the admiring friends.

—WILLIAM J. CARRINGTON, *Safe Convoy*

IV

THE TIME DRAWS NEAR

From *Whistler's Mother*
by ELIZABETH MUMFORD

Both sister and mother came to be with her as "her time" drew near. . . . The three women drew together in mysterious rites involving lavender and fine linen, elaborate bits of flannel, and blankets that seemed a mere whiff of warmth edged with pink scallops. As the July sun beat down outside they sat within a shaded room, needlessly fluent, tongues brightly to the point; or sewed silently to the smooth murmur of a chapter from the Reverend Mr. Shuttleworth.

If it was a cause of anything but regret to Whistler that he should be called away from this feminine idyll for a business trip of three weeks, he was far too chivalrous to admit it. His wife always relished women's companionship, especially now; but it did not keep her from a secret plea that he might return in time.

From *Tomorrow Will Be Better*
by BETTY SMITH

Margy was proud of her swelling breasts. She admired herself. But that wasn't enough. She wanted Frankie to look and admire.

She stood before him in her slip. "Look!" she said.

"At what?" he asked.

"My bust."

"What about it?"

"It's filled out."

"So what?"

"So I look better. So I won't have any trouble nursing the baby."

"That's good." He turned away as if to terminate the conversation.

"Feel!" she commanded.

"Don't be silly," he said.

"Don't you be silly."

She took his hands and placed them on her breasts. His hands started to curve instinctively over the breasts, then flew open with the fingers rigid. With a sudden laugh she released his hands with a throwing-away motion. He was relieved and angry.

"Say it," he said. "Say what you're thinking."

"What am I thinking?" she asked, puzzled.

"That if I won't, someone else will."

"I thought no such thing," she said indignantly. "Besides, I don't know anybody else." She thought of Mr. Prentiss.

She got into her bathrobe and knotted the cord firmly about her waist. He relaxed, now that nothing more was expected of him. But obscurely, he was ashamed of his relief. He tried to make amends.

"I've been noticing," he said, "that your dresses do fit better."

"That's right," she agreed, then with unashamed vanity added, "I can wear the cheapest dress now and it looks as though I'm modeling it."

Her vanity went deeper than that. She felt that she looked very feminine and desirable now and she walked the streets to the stores with her head held proudly.

She was content. She was fed, housed, clothed and fulfilling her destiny as a woman. She felt no woman should want more than that. Of course, she wanted more, but it was a dreamy want and nothing that had to be fought for at the moment. She wanted love and companionship. Well, she had Frankie's love such as it was and his companionship, such as it was. Maybe, she thought, that's all there is to marriage and I mustn't look for more. Bluntly, she felt the need of a more satisfying mating. She felt the need of security; an owned home so that there'd be no worry about being asked to move, or the rent raised. She wanted to be sure that there would always be food—that she'd never have to say to her child, "Eat that, and be lucky you got it." No, she thought, no child should be commanded to feel lucky just because he had the food and shelter and care that all children born are entitled to.

Frankie talked the situation over with his best friend and newly made brother-in-law, Marty.

"Look, Marty, we were getting along pretty good and then this had to happen."

"It's a trap of nature," explained Marty, "to keep the world populated."

"Well, what has to be, will be," sighed Frankie.

"Is that bad, after all?" Marty wanted to know. "Ask me now if I want kids and I'll say, hell, no! But if they come along, I'll get used to it, I guess. I figure this way: things is got to be kept going on."

"True enough," agreed Frankie.

"Of course, there are enough other dopes in the world to keep it going," philosophized the friend, "and maybe a couple guys like us should be allowed to step aside."

"Yeah, I'm only one guy. Who'd ever miss my addition to the world?"

"They say," offered Marty consolingly, "that a lot of guys feel that way—don't want a kid at first. But when it comes along, why they're nuts about it."

"There's something in that. Right now I don't want it," admitted Frankie. "But somehow I got the feeling that I'm going to be crazy about the little feller."

"Sure you are," agreed Marty. "That's how nature makes suckers out of all of us."

TELEGONY

from *Safe Convoy* (1944)

by WILLIAM J. CARRINGTON

Some years ago an unusually intelligent expectant mother become terribly worried. Her husband was an ideal one and home life was perfect, but she had been married before and to a "perfect rotter." Although she had not set eyes on her first husband for years, she had an inordinate fear that the child of the second husband might resemble the first. A thoughtless breeder of fine stock had told her that if a thoroughbred cow had ever been mated to an unregistered bull, there was ever afterwards the possibility of a "throwback" even when she had been served by a registered bull. A similar superstition is prevalent among those who breed dogs. Indeed telegony is hoary with antiquity. The ancient Israelites believed in it (*Deuteronomy*).

My nervous patient's fears were groundless. She gave birth to a son who was the living image of her second husband. As the sunlight of science streams in, it pushes material impressions and telegony into the shadows to gather dust and cobwebs. The supernatural of yesterday is the natural of today.

Perhaps the greatest hoax in the musty archives of obstetric history was foisted on the gullible public of the eighteenth century by Mary Toft of Sussex, England. She declared that she gave birth to a litter of rabbits and the doctor and the nurse who attended her swore to the truth of her statement! The weird tale created so much fear and furor that King George I appointed Dr. Nathaniel St. André to make an official investigation. Although St. André was in the King's good graces, for he played the violin and spoke German fluently, he knew nothing of physiology. He was duped easily but his report failed to satisfy the public. The King then appointed a regular physician who found hay and lettuce in the lower bowel of one of the rabbits which was supposed to have been stillborn. When his examination of Mary Toft showed that she never had been pregnant, she confessed and the case was closed, but for a time there was more excitement over the rape of Mary Toft than there was over the invasion of New Jersey by Orson Welles's men of Mars.

From *Moll Flanders*
by DANIEL DEFOE

I now grew big, and the people where I lodged perceived it, and began to take notice of it to me, and, as far as civility would allow, intimated that I must think of removing. This put me to extreme perplexity, and I grew very melancholy, for indeed I knew not what course to take. I had money, but no friends, and was like now to have a child upon my hands to keep, which was a difficulty I had never had upon me yet, as the particulars of my story hitherto make appear.

In the course of this affair I fell very ill, and my melancholy really increased my distemper; my illness proved at length to be only an ague, but my apprehensions were really that I should miscarry. I should not say apprehensions, for indeed I would have been glad to miscarry, but I could never be brought to entertain so much as a thought of endeavoring to miscarry, or of taking anything to make me miscarry; I abhorred, I say, so much as the thought of it.

However, speaking of it in the house, the gentlewoman who kept the house proposed to me to send for a midwife. I scrupled it at first, but after some time consented to it, but told her I had no particular acquaintance with any midwife, and so left it to her.

It seems the mistress of the house was not so great a stranger to such cases as mine was as I thought at first she had been, as will appear presently, and she sent for a midwife of the right sort—that is to say, the right sort for me.

The woman appeared to be an experienced woman in her business, I mean as a midwife; but she had another calling too, in which she was as expert as most women, if not more. My landlady had told her I was very melancholy, and that she believed had done me harm; and once, before me, said to her, "Mrs. B———" (meaning the midwife), "I believe this lady's trouble is of a kind that is pretty much in your way, and therefore if you can do anything for her, pray do, for she is a very civil gentlewoman"; and so she went out of the room.

I really did not understand her, but my Mother Midnight began very seriously to explain what she meant, as soon as she was gone. "Madam," says she, "you seem not to understand what your landlady means; and when you do understand it, you need not let her know at all that you do so.

"She means that you are under some circumstances that may render your lying in difficult to you, and that you are not willing to be exposed. I need say no more, but to tell you, that if you think fit to communicate so much of your case to me, if it be so, as is necessary, for I do not desire to pry into those things, I perhaps may be in a condition to assist you, and to make you perfectly easy, and remove all your dull thoughts upon that subject."

Every word this creature said was a cordial to me, and put new life and new spirit into my very heart; my blood began to circulate immediately, and I was quite another body; I ate my victuals again, and grew better presently after it. She said a great deal more to the same purpose, and then, having pressed me to be free with her, and promised in the solemnest manner to be secret, she stopped a little, as if waiting to see what impression it made on me, and what I would say.

I was too sensible of the want I was in of such a woman, not to accept her offer; I told her my case was partly as she guessed, and partly not, for I was really married, and had a husband, though he was in such fine circumstances, and so remote at that time, as that he could not appear publicly.

She took me short, and told me that was none of her business; all the ladies that came under her care were married women to her. "Every woman," says she, "that is with child has a father for it," and whether that father was a husband or no husband, was no business of hers; her business was to assist me in my present circumstances; whether I had a husband or no. "For, madam," says she, "to have a husband that cannot appear, is to have no husband in the sense of the case; and, therefore, whether you are a wife or a mistress is all one to me."

I found presently, that whether I was a whore or a wife, I was to pass for a whore here, so I let that go. I told her it was true, as she said, but that, however, if I must tell her my case, I must tell her as it was; so I related it to her as short as I could, and I concluded it to her thus. "I trouble you with all this, madam," said I, "not that, as you said before, it is much to the purpose in your affair, but this is to the purpose, namely, that I am not in any pain about being seen, or being public or concealed, for 'tis perfectly indifferent to me; but my difficulty is, that I have no acquaintance in this part of the nation."

"I understand you, madam," says she; "you have no security to bring to prevent the parish impertinences usual in such cases, and perhaps," says she, "do not know very well how to dispose of the child when it comes." "The last," says I, "is not so much my concern as the first." "Well, madam," answers the midwife, "dare you put yourself into my hands? I live in such a place; though I do not inquire after you, you may inquire after me. My name is B———; I live in such a street"—naming the street—"at the sign of the Cradle. My profession is a midwife and I have given many ladies that come to my house to lie in. I have given security to the parish in general terms to secure them from any charge from whatsoever shall come into the world under my roof. I have but one question to ask in the whole affair, madam," says she, "and if that be answered, you shall be entirely easy for all the rest."

I presently understood what she meant, and told her, "Madam, I believe I understand you. I thank God, though I want friends in this part of the world, I do not want money, so far as may be necessary, though I do not abound in that neither": this I added because I would not make her expect great things. "Well, madam," says she, "that is the thing indeed, without which nothing can be done in these cases; and yet," says she, "you shall see that I will not impose upon you, or offer anything that is unkind to you, and if you desire it, you shall know everything beforehand, that you may suit yourself to the occasion, and be either costly or sparing as you see fit."

I told her she seemed to be so perfectly sensible of my condition, that I had nothing to ask of her but this, that as I had told her that I had money sufficient, but not a great quantity, she would order it so that I might be at as little superfluous charge as possible.

She replied that she would bring in an account of the expenses of it in two or three shapes, and like a bill of fare, I should choose as I pleased; and I desired her to do so.

The next day she brought it, and the copy of her three bills was as follows:—

	£	s.	d.
1. For three months' lodging in her house, including my diet, at 10 s. a week	6	0	0
2. For a nurse for the month, and use of childbed linen	1	10	0

3. For a minister to christen the child, and to the godfathers and clerk	1	10	0
4. For a supper at the christening if I had five friends at it	1	0	0
For her fees as a midwife, and the taking off the trouble of the parish	3	3	0
To her maidservant attending	0	10	0
	£13	13	0

This was the first bill; the second was in the same terms:—

1. For three months' lodging and diet, etc. at 20s. per week	13	0	0
2. For a nurse for the month, and the use of linen and lace	2	10	0
3. For a minister to christen the child, etc. as above	2	0	0
4. For a supper, and for sweetmeats	3	3	0
For her fees as above	5	5	0
For a servant-maid	1	0	0
	£26	18	0

This was the second-rate bill; the third, she said, was for a degree higher, and when the father or friends appeared:—

1. For a three months' lodging and diet, having two rooms and a garret for a servant	30	0	0
2. For a nurse for the month, and the finest suit of childbed linen	4	4	0
3. For the minister to christen the child, etc.	2	10	0
4. For a supper, the gentlemen to send in the wine	6	0	0
For my fees, etc.	10	10	0
The maid, besides their own maid, only	0	10	0
	£53	14	0

I looked upon all three bills, and smiled, and told her I did not see but that she was very reasonable in her demands, all things considered, and for that I did not doubt but her accommodations were good.

Today is the day they give babies away
with ½ lb. of tea
—If there are any ladies who want any babies—
just send them around to me!

—Old Nursery Rhyme

V

LABOR AND CHILDBIRTH

From *A Tree Grows in Brooklyn*
by BETTY SMITH

In a few months, to their innocent amazement and consternation, Katie found out that she was pregnant. She told Johnny that she was "that way." Johnny was bewildered and confused at first. He didn't want her to work at the school. She told him she had been that way for quite a while without being sure and had been working and had not suffered. When she convinced him that it was good for her to work, he gave in. She continued working until she got too unwieldy to dust under the desks. Soon she could do little more than go along with him for company and lie on the gay couch no longer used for love-making. He did all the work now. At two in the morning, he made clumsy sandwiches and over-boiled coffee for her. They were still very happy although Johnny was getting more and more worried as the time wore on.

Towards the end of a frosty December night, her pains started. She lay on the couch, holding them back, not wanting to tell Johnny until the work was finished. On the way home, there was a tearing pain that she couldn't keep back. She moaned and Johnny knew that the baby was on the way. He got her home and put her to bed without undressing her, and covered her warmly. He ran down the block to Mrs. Gindler, the midwife, and begged her to hurry. That good woman drove him crazy by taking her time.

She had to take dozens of curlers out of her hair. She couldn't find her teeth and refused to officiate without them. Johnny helped her search and they found them at last in a glass of water on the ledge outside the window. The water had frozen around the teeth and they had to be thawed out before she could put them in. That done, she had to go about making a charm out of a piece of blessed palm taken from the altar on Palm Sunday. To this, she added a medal of the Blessed Mother, a small blue bird feather, a broken blade from a penknife and a sprig of some herb. These things were tied together with a bit of dirty string from the corset of a woman who had given birth to twins after only ten minutes of labor. She sprinkled the whole business with holy water that was supposed to have come from a well in Jerusalem from which it was said that Jesus had once quenched His thirst. She explained to the frantic boy that this charm would cut the pains and assure him of a fine, well-born baby. Lastly she grabbed her crocodile satchel—familiar to everyone in the neighborhood and believed by all the youngsters to be the satchel in which they had been delivered, kicking, to their mothers—and she was ready to go.

Katie was screaming in pain when they got to her. The flat was filled with neighbor women who stood around praying and reminiscing about their own child-bed experiences.

"When I had my Vincent," said one, "I . . ."

"I was even smaller than her," said another, "and when . . ."

"They didn't expect me to come through it," proudly declared a third, "but . . ."

They welcomed the midwife and shooed Johnny out of the place. He sat on the stoop and trembled each time Katie cried out. He was confused, it had happened so suddenly. It was now seven in the morning. Her screams kept coming to him even though the windows were closed. Men passed on their way to work, looked at the window from behind which the screams were coming and then looked at Johnny huddled on the stoop and a somber look came over their faces.

Katie was in labor all that day and there was nothing that Johnny could do—nothing that he could do. Towards night, he couldn't stand it any longer. He went to his mother's house for comforting. When he told her that Katie was having a baby, she nearly raised the roof with her lamentations.

"Now she's got you good," she wailed. "You'll never be able to come back to me." She would not be consoled.

Johnny hunted up his brother, Georgie, who was working a dance. He sat drinking, waiting for Georgie to finish, forgetting that he was supposed to be at the school. When Georgie was free for the night, they went to several all-night saloons, had a drink or two at each place and told everyone what Johnny was going through. The men listened sympathetically, treated Johnny to drinks and assured him that they had been through the same mill.

Towards dawn, the boys went to their mother's house where Johnny fell into a troubled sleep. At nine, he woke up with a feeling of coming trouble. He remembered Katie and, too late, he remembered the school. He washed and dressed and started home. He passed a fruit stand which displayed avocados. He bought two for Katie.

He had no way of knowing that during the night, his wife in great pain, and after nearly twenty-four hours of labor, gave bloody birth to a fragile baby girl. The only notable thing about the birth was that the infant was born with a caul which was supposed to indicate that the child was set apart to do great things in the world. The midwife surreptitiously confiscated the caul and later sold it to a sailor from the Brooklyn Navy Yard for two dollars. Whoever wore a caul would never die by drowning, it was said. The sailor wore it in a flannel bag around his neck.

While he drank and slept the night away, Johnny did not know that the night had turned cold and the school fires which he was supposed to tend had gone out and the water pipes had burst and flooded the school basement and the first floor.

When he got home, he found Katie lying in the dark bedroom. The baby was beside her on Andy's pillow. The flat was scrupulously clean; the neighbor women had attended to that. There was a faint odor of carbolic acid mixed with Mennen's talcum powder. The midwife had gone after saying, "That will be five dollars and your husband knows where I live."

She left and Katie turned her face to the wall and tried not to cry. During the night, she had assured herself that Johnny was working at the school. She had hoped that he would run home for a moment during the two o'clock eating period. Now it was late morning and he should be home. Maybe he had gone to his mother's to snatch some sleep after the night's work. She made herself believe that no matter what Johnny was doing, it was all right and that his explanation would set her mind at ease.

Soon after the midwife left, Evy came over. A neighbor's boy had been sent for her. Evy brought along some sweet butter and a package of soda crackers and made tea. It tasted so good to Katie. Evy examined the baby and thought it didn't look like much but she said nothing to Katie.

When Johnny got home, Evy started to lecture him. But when she saw how pale and frightened he looked and when she considered his age—just twenty years old, she choked up inside, kissed his cheek, told him not to worry and made fresh coffee for him.

Johnny hardly looked at the baby. Still clutching the avocados, he knelt by Katie's bed and sobbed out his fear and worry. Katie cried with him. During the night, she had wanted him with her. Now she wished she could have had that baby secretly and gone away somewhere and when it was over come back and tell him that everything was fine. She had had the pain; it had been like being boiled alive in scalding oil and not being able to die to get free of it. She had had the pain. Dear God! Wasn't that enough? Why did he have to suffer? He wasn't put together for suffering but she was. She had borne a child but two hours ago. She was so weak that she couldn't lift her head an inch from the pillow, yet it was she who comforted him and told him not to worry, that she would take care of him.

DELIVERING HOUR

from *Fantasia*

by WADE OLIVER

Into the long, warm darkness where I waited,
A voiceless atom biding birth's release,
Her dear love sent down laughter, and the bated
Breath of her heart's bright beauty; out of these
My sinews quickened, though I did not know,
And, all unheeding, bone and flesh waxed strong
For that delivering hour when I should go
Out of her body into a sun of song.

When-as my little tale of life is written,
How shall I fear the sovereignty of earth
Whose warm, long darkness like a song is litten
With beauty of her who gave my body birth?
Over her grave let no least dark leaf stir,—
I go once more to quickening life in her.

A NOTE ON THE STORK

from *The New York Times* (June 24, 1950)

The stork, international symbol of expanding family life, is being blamed for an approaching manpower shortage in the United States. During the 1930 depression years, Dr. Stork, according to the United States Selective Service System, failed to deliver the requisite number of babies for today's emergency needs.

Should the stork be called to account for his actions, the National Geographic Society says, few birds—feathered or otherwise—would be able to command a better defense. In the first place, the stork has a well-nigh spotless record as a devoted family man.

Because of his long, well-publicized association with babies, the white or common stork, *Ciconia ciconia,* has achieved a fame unequalled by other birds. His snowy plumage, black wing quills and bright red bill and legs are as familiar as breakfast cereal, yet the stork has been seen by comparatively few persons in the United States. Of his family only a distant cousin, the shy wood ibis of the southern coast, is a native of this continent.

To see the white stork at home, one must travel to Europe. There, by late spring, he is settling for the nesting season, after having winged in from winter quarters along the banks of Africa's Nile. A strictly monogamous bird, the male stork usually—and considerately—arrives at the old home nest a few days before his mate, to get things spruced up for her arrival.

The birds apparently enjoy human association because they build their nests in the hearts of villages, atop roofs, chimneys or wagon wheels suspended above ground for their use. Although the storks never consider the nest entirely completed—and are constantly making additions—four or five eggs are laid in April or May. Father and mother stork share equally the arduous task of incubating them continuously for a month.

The storklings are ready to fly when about three months old. Their parents encourage this new skill by placing food within flight-provoking nearness to the nest. Even after the youngsters are able to fly on food-foraging trips of their own, they continue—during that first summer—to return home in the evenings and sleep at the family nest.

AN UNUSUAL BIRTH

No amorous Hero ever gave thee Birth,
Nor ever tender Goddess brought thee forth:
Some rugged Rock's hard Entrails gave thee Form,
And raging Seas produc'd thee in a Storm:
A Soul well suiting thy tempestuous Kind
So rough thy Manners, so untam'd thy Mind.

—ALEXANDER POPE

(Editor's note: Minerva, the goddess of wisdom, was the daughter of Jupiter. She was said to have leaped forth from his brain, mature and in complete armour.)

THE BIRTH STOOL

from *Safe Convoy* (1944)
by WILLIAM J. CARRINGTON

According to Westcar Papyrus, one of the earliest written records of mankind (2500 B.C.), its hieroglyphics reveal that women were delivered in the sitting position on the birth stool. That custom prevailed down through the centuries. Rachel referred to the practice of the ancient Hebrew midwives of holding their patients on their laps (Genesis 30:3). However, when the Hebrews were exiled to Egypt they used obstetric stools (Exodus). Up until the eighteenth century European women were delivered in the sitting position. Midwives carted huge and sometimes elaborately carved obstetric chairs about with them from patient to patient. The seat was cut out like the seat of a crescent-shaped commode. Finally, after many centuries, Mauriceau, the leading accoucher of France, made the bold innovation of delivering women in bed, but for many years thereafter the brides of the Low Countries included delivery chairs in their trousseaux.

A SIXTEENTH-CENTURY BIRTH

from *Into This Universe*

by DR. ALAN FRANK GUTTMACHER

Marguerite de Puis moved fitfully in the huge bed, careful lest she disturb François, her husband. Eleven months before, in April 1548, she had come to it a bride—a slip of a girl, whom François had first seen and admired on the tennis court. As she lay restless in her bed, she mused on the changes the months had wrought.

Tears of self-pity wet her soft cheeks. The past few months had proved so irksome. Her grievances paraded before her mind's eye like the reflected beam of a carriage lamp which slowly traces its way across the darkness of the ceiling. There had been the sacrifice of her beautifying alum baths, soft luxurious rainwater, sweetened with leaves of rosemary and flowers of myrtle. Then, too, she missed dancing; she hadn't danced the gaillarde for months, and at seventeen death alone seemed more tragic. She hadn't even been allowed to lift her arms above her head. It was said that this loosed the ligaments which held the womb in place. The coach with its blooded, prancing, gaily caparisoned stallions was denied her, and she had to go about the streets of Paris in a stuffy, curtained litter, borne by her men-servants; so all Paris had known for months that she was enceinte. Then, too, all the other young people of her set had journeyed out beyond the wall to see the wondrous Biddenden Maids who were tented there, a marvel of nature,—two complete wenches joined at the waist. Marguerite wasn't allowed to see them, for if she did, she might give birth to such a monster. She had to be wary lest a black cat zigzag across her path and make her baby squint-eyed. No longer could she lie curled up in bed, for that would render it crook-backed. There were a thousand wearisome "Don'ts."

But on second thought these things were trivial when she remembered her lovely trousseau so carefully selected, so soon discarded—especially the beautiful purple court dress. She had to leave off her bodice stiffened with whalebone, and discontinue the tight lacing which made her waist so appealingly slim. The nursekeeper said that by enclosing the belly in so straight a mold she might hinder the infant from taking its free growth, and moreover might make it come forth horribly misshapen. And so perforce the purple dress had to be laid away in a great cedar chest with the prayerful hope of future use.

The defeat of her vanity was complete when, in order to prevent her stomach from becoming marred by knotted and broken veins or from being left wrinkled and furrowed, she had agreed to support her belly with a broad linen swath on top of a dogskin. The dogskin had to be prepared according to an exact ritual. Everyone said the belly of her Cousin Anne was so unsightly after the birth of Henri because her nursekeeper had forgetfully omitted the goose grease.

Marguerite de Puis finally wept herself to sleep. She slept soundly and was awakened by some knave who had disobeyed the city laws in not properly greasing the axle of his dung-cart. A tester of thick velvet which surrounded the bed made it difficult to separate night from day; yet it must be day, for she was alone. Hearing her stir, the nursekeeper came in with a bowl of pleasantly scented water in which a hot iron had been dipped. After washing her, the nurse rubbed her abdomen with a pomade made of the marrow of sheep's feet, well brushed and broken in pieces to the number of thirty or forty, duck's grease, spermaceti, and white wax, which had been agreeably perfumed with the oil of water lilies.

Marguerite arose and sat before the fire. With a soft hand she annointed her privities with an hysterical balsam as she had done each morning and evening for months. Then a warm decoctation of periwinkle, sage, ground-ivy, and hemlock boiled in wine and water was brought. With a sponge dipped therein she bathed her breasts for a quarter-hour, wiping and drying them afterwards with a reasonably warm cloth. After girding up her belly with the dogskin and linen swath, she put on the loose garments which her vanity so despised. While the maid combed and oiled her hair, the nurse brought breakfast: figs, new-laid eggs, and white bread toasts spread with sweet fresh butter.

Having dressed and finished her breakfast, she called for her litter and ordered the bearers to repair to Notre Dame. The litter jolted violently as the bearers avoided deep ruts, and Marguerite was seized with a sharp, sudden pain. It lasted a short time, and minutes later, just as she reached the cathedral, the pain returned; certainly it marked the onset of her travail. She offered a silent prayer to the Madonna at the entrance of Her Church—an imploring supplication. She was frightened by the experience that awaited her, an experience which she could in no way avoid. Inevitable pain was bad enough, but more terrifying the realization that death chooses many from among those who bring life. She found solace in the remembrance of her prayers and penances of the past months and felt that Our Gracious Lady would intervene with the Lord Jesus to spare her life. In His great compassion He might even grant her a living son and perhaps even a speedy delivery. She ordered the litter to return and on the way back she sobbed.

When Marguerite returned, the household seethed with excitement. Couriers were dispatched hither and thither. One went to the Hotel de Ville to notify François, who had gone to a meeting of the town council, another ran for Louise Grisson, wife of the butcher Grisson, famous throughout Paris for her great knowledge of the midwife's art and in the delivery of women; and another sought the three lesser women who were to assist. The priest too had to be informed.

When the sage-femme arrived, she led Marguerite into the room where she was to lie in. The room was bare except for a low pallet bed and several wooden stools. A small fire made it neither too warm nor too cool. The window curtains were drawn, and the only light came from flickering logs and a single candle.

Marguerite was urged to walk about and with each throe to hold her breath and bear down. Her aged Aunt Therese brought some specially potent sneeze-wort. She commanded her niece to smell of it at frequent intervals. This Marguerite did, and each time it induced a virtual bombardment of sneezes. As Marguerite paced back and forth monotonously, the midwife and her helpers sat on their gossip stools, outdoing each other with the most lurid tales of tragic obstetrical happenings. Poor Marguerite began to marvel that there were five women in Paris who had survived their accouchements. When she grew very weary, she was allowed to sit on the bed for a few moments while the women rubbed her legs with oils derived from egg and nuts.

The respite was short, and once more Marguerite was made to pace the floor. As the hours passed, the pain and fatigue unnerved her. If only there were a new invention to free her from these four gibbering old fools who poked her with their fingers and terrified her with their ghastly gossip.

The throes did not come often enough to satisfy the

midwives, and following a consultation, Madame Grisson determined to examine the patient. After paring her nails closely and annointing her hand with butter, she inserted her fingers into the birth-passage while Marguerite stood leaning on the shoulders of one of the helpers. The examination was thorough, long, and painful. A second consultation followed, the midwives huddling together like four goblins while Marguerite continued to parade back and forth. She heard herself discussed as though she were a common milch cow. The consensus seemed to be that something should be done to stimulate the pains of labor, and each of the four women had her favored method; eventually all four were tried. Though Marguerite protested, the will of the midwives was the inescapable law of the lying-in chamber.

Marguerite was so fatigued by the many unremitting hours of labor, the incessant pacing, and the strenuous medication, that she pleaded to be allowed to lie down. The midwives permitted it, and during the rest period brought her a light meal—a cup of jellied broth, and a few spoonfuls of burnt wine. Soon they made her walk again, but now a woman on each side supported her under the arms.

Night came and still there was no respite. The pains had become very bad; so bad that she was forced to cry out, imploring the aid of the Mother. At about midnight the head midwife re-examined Marguerite and pronounced her ready to lie in. She was laid upon the bed, and a long, broad, multi-layered swath was placed under her back and hinder parts. Two women, one on either side, held its ends and at each pain pulled it gently toward them, raising her off the bed in order to ease the pain in her back. As labor became more furious, two more assisting women were needed, and from the assortment of kinsfolk that waited without, Madame Grisson chose Marguerite's cousins, Anne and Renée, since they had been successfully delivered of sons within the year and so might extend good fortune to their travailing cousin. Madame Grisson cautioned the cousins not to cross their fingers nor to shut one within the other while in the labor-room, since that delays birth and makes it the more difficult. The new helpers were stationed on either side of the bed and during the course of each throe clenched Marguerite's hands in one of theirs, placing the free hand on top of her shoulder to prevent her from lifting herself up. Marguerite braced her feet against a board placed across the foot of the bed, and with each pain pushed and bore down with such force that her face became suffused with scarlet and the veins of her neck protruded like small throbbing ropes. The sweat stood forth like dew on her upper lip. With each throe Madame Grisson pressed the upper part of the belly with the palm of her hand, stroking the child downward little by little.

Still the infant was not born. François and the others became alarmed, and at each cry they pushed the door ajar and demanded a fresh bulletin. Madame Grisson continually encouraged the patient, saying that after the very next throe a handsome boy would be born. The constant repetition of this unfulfilled promise made it worthless, and poor Marguerite, exhausted, sobbed with pain and terror.

At the first break of dawn François insisted that the famous master barber-surgeon, Ambrose Paré, be sent for. This was no ordinary birth, he contended, which women could handle unassisted, and they had need for a man-midwife. When once more Marguerite's agonized screams pierced the apprehensive stillness, he sent his most trusted servant post-haste to fetch the great man.

Paré lived within a stone's throw, on the Place du Pont Saint-Michel, and it did not take him long to appear. Those in the company who had never seen him were much impressed by his youthful appearance and his assured but humble manner. He greeted the company, and knelt before the door of the sickroom, closing his eyes in a fervent prayer: "Jesus Christ Our Lord, the only Preserver and Saviour in danger! Since there appeareth difficulty in bringing forth this child, we implore Thee that Thou allowest me, Thy humble servant, to assist Thee in happily delivering this wretched woman. We ask it for Thy name's sake." The whole assemblage responded: "Amen." Paré arose and declared that with God's guidance he was confident he could bring the baby.

In the lying-in chamber he at once became master of the situation, assuring Marguerite that her pain would soon be over. He placed her athwart the bed, raising her buttocks on a hard stuffed pillow and propped her back with a bolster so that she was half lying, half sitting. He instructed her to bend her knees and to draw her heels close to her body. She was bound in this position with a broad linen bandage. To reinforce this vise in which she was held, the bystanders firmly grasped her legs and shoulders. Her privy parts and thighs were covered with a warm double cloth, that neither air nor wind might enter into the womb, and that the operation might be done with more decency. Paré noted the mask of terror which disfigured Marguerite's face and once more assured her that all would end well. They then laid her head upon a bolster and put a cloth over her eyes.

He crossed himself and without further preliminaries rolled up the sleeves of his doublet and annointed well his bare arms and hands with oil. Further, he lifted the modesty cloth and poured much oil into the birth-passage to make it slippery. He inserted his hand to determine the form and situation of the child. Immediately he encountered the intact bag of waters which he broke between two fingernails, kept especially long and sharpened for this purpose. A dark, turbid fluid gushed forth, and all who watched knew by that sign that the babe would be lost unless delivery could be speedily effected.

He pushed up the head which presented and dexterously turned the child in the womb so that it came feet foremost. Despite the imprisoning bandages Marguerite struggled and writhed in agony. She was bathed in a cold sweat. He brought forth one foot and a little above the heel tied a silk band indifferently tight. He then returned this foot into the womb, leaving the loose end of the band protruding, and maneuvered to bring down the second foot. When he accomplished this, he pulled on the band attached to the first foot and it too came forth. He grasped both feet close together and, pulling on them, delivered the bttocks and genitals of a male child. A murmur of excitement ran through the room, and Renée went out to tell the men that for some woman as yet unconceived a lover was being born. By this time all the women kin had crowded into the small room to be present at this miraculous and brand-new operation. The midwives were amazed, the relatives astonished—all seemed to enjoy the spectacle though poor Marguerite still screamed. Paré made further traction on the feet, and soon the belly and then the chest appeared. He then slipped a hand into the uterus past the baby, and placed one of its arms above its head and the other down alongside of its body. He directed the midwives to help by pressing the patient's belly downward with their hands, and at this juncture exhorted Marguerite to close her mouth and nose and to drive her breath downward with great violence, but she was too exhausted to be of much assistance. By the combination of pulling and pushing the boy was born.

His part completed, Paré withdrew to the hall, where the women crowded about him with congratulations. He was further complimented by François and the other men. With becoming humility he said that praise and thanks were due to God alone, for if He had not inclined His ear unto his petition, delivery could never have been effected. François opened his purse and counted out ten silver écus. Affected by the uncommon generosity of his host, the master barber-surgeon determined to remain in the house in case he could be of further service.

The child neither cried nor seemed to breathe, but he could be given no succor until the womb was freed of its after-burden; and all efforts were centered upon this.

Marguerite was made to swallow a four-scruple dose of Gesner's remedy. She was also given two small bags of warm salt to clench in either hand and directed to blow into them. Meanwhile, Madame Grisson took hold of the navel string, wagging, shaking, and gently dragging it, while another woman pressed the top of the belly, and stroked it lightly downward. But nothing availed until a few grains of a powder made from old shoes, burnt feathers, castoreum, pepper, and asafetida were put into each nostril. The acrid, stinking mixture made Marguerite sneeze and vomit—this, combined with the stroking of the belly and the pulling on the navel cord, fairly catapulted the afterbirth from the birth-passage.

Madame Grisson gathered in a warm blanket both the child and the afterbirth to which it was still attached by the navel string. The babe was as blue as the velvet of her robe, and from the difficult labor its head was curiously molded into a peak. It lay limp, neither moving or breathing. The priest hastily sprinkled the infant with holy water, pronouncing in a rich, mellow voice: "I baptize thee, in the name of the Father, the Son, and the Holy Ghost." All present said "Amen." In the meantime Renée removed the afterbirth from the child's belly and tossed it into the fire, milking the vessels of the navel string toward the babe to communicate the strength and warmth of the blaze. Master de Puis now began to take a few feeble breaths. At first they came very seldom, merely an occasional sucking in of the belly. Soon they became more frequent, the chest too taking part. Madame Grisson applied linen dipped in warm wine to the child's breast and belly. His face was uncovered and his mouth held open a little, that he might draw his breath more easily. She cleansed his nostrils with small tents dipped in white wine, and chafed every part of his body with warm cloths to awaken his spirit. Little by little he gained strength, stirring one limb after another; he cried, weakly at first, then with a vigor that was pleasant to hear. Led by the priest, the whole assemblage within the room and without sank on their knees in a silent prayer of thanksgiving.

Madame Grisson went back to Marguerite while Angeline, one of the midwife's assistants, tended the child. She called Anne and Renée to witness the navel string before she cut it, for from it they could learn whether Marguerite would have any more children. Fortunately there was not knottiness nor curliness where the cord joined the infant, for that would portend further barrenness; instead there were eleven knots higher up on the cord indicating that she would be the mother of twelve. The knots were very close together, foretelling that the births would be separated by only the necessary months. Furthermore, the first knot was red and not white, which showed that the next child would also be a boy.

Angeline then proceeded to perform the most ancient operation in the realm of surgery; omphalotomy, or the cutting of the navel string; even Adam and Eve practiced it on their first-born.

As she was about to begin, someone called: "Make him good measure," at which all the others laughed merrily. Everyone knew that in the case of a boy the cord must be left longer, because this extra length makes both his tongue and privy member the longer, whereby he might speak the plainer, and be more serviceable to the ladies. Moreover, tying it short in a female and close to her belly makes her tongue less free and her nautral part more straight and agreeable.

Angeline dug deep into her reticule and drew forth a stout brown string which had been doubled several times and knotted on the ends. She tied a double knot about the navel string and cut it above the knot with a sharp scissors. The cut end was wrapped in a small rag dipped in oil of roses, and the whole firmly compressed by a linen swath four fingers broad. The son of Marguerite and François was then wrapped in a blanket and taken to another room, where he was to receive a warm bath in red wine and water, in which the petals of red roses and the leaves of myrtle had been boiled. And after the bath he would receive his first swaddling. As the child was carried through the hall, François tried to lift the blanket that covered its face, but desisted when roundly abused by the midwife for daring to expose a baby's eyes so soon to the light.

Marguerite appeared strong and alert immediately after the birth, due perhaps to the vast relief she felt. When unleashed from the bonds which imprisoned her, she folded her hands in prayer. A little later her face, and her hands and feet, became cold and clammy, her speech almost inaudible, her strength dangerously enfeebled, and her pulse critically weak. Madame Grisson wrapped Marguerite's hands and feet in warm woolens and covered her with blankets. She cupped her hand over the ill women's lips so that she could rebreathe her own vital spirits and her breath, reverberating, would also warm her face. Hot cloths were put to her forehead, and the warm face of another woman was applied to her cold cheeks. Several stone bottles filled with hot water and wrapped around with napkins were placed in the bed with her. These things renewed the heat in her, and forthwith she revived.

Marguerite's large bed in her own room was prepared with hot bricks, and several strong bodies carried her to it, for it was preferable that she should not walk. The curtains, windows, and doors were sealed shut and the tester about the bed drawn closed, since it was very prejudicial for a newly lain-in woman to be exposed in any way to cold air.

Marguerite was cautioned to lie flat on her back, and to turn neither to one side nor the other, and she was encouraged to cross one leg over its fellow, the better to exclude the cold air. She was told to talk as little as possible and then only in a subdued voice. A cradle containing her properly swaddled son was brought in and placed next to her bed. Marguerite had not seen him, and since she was not allowed to turn, she could only steal a sidelong glance. She saw by the dim candlelight that the top of the cradle was completely covered and that every now and then the cover jumped, as though a kitten was under it. She was weary and yearned to sleep, but Madame Grisson would not allow her; she said that it was harmful for a mother to go to sleep until her child was at least four hours old.

At long last she was permitted to sleep, and just as she was dozing off, she heard the street-crier shout:

"Good tidings. Be it known that this very morning a man child was born to François de Puis, our Town Councillor, and his spouse Marguerite. Praise ye the Lord." The cry was repeated before each house. It became soft and distant and much confused with her dreams of a midwife with the face of a gargoyle, who was devouring her very, very slowly.

EYES LIKE JOHN'S

from *Forever Amber*

by KATHLEEN WINSOR

As was customary for a lying-in chamber, the room had been largely cleared of its furniture. Now there remained only the bed with its tall head and footboards and linen side curtains, half a dozen low stools, and the midwife's birth-stool, which had arm rests and a slanting back and cut-out seat. Beside the fireplace was a table with a pewter water-basin on it, brown cord and a knife, bottles and ointment-jars, and a pile of soft white cloths. Near the head of the bed was a very old hooded cradle, still empty.

The village women, all perfectly silent, stood close

about the bed, watching what was happening there with tense, anxious faces. Sympathetic anguish, pity, apprehension, were the expressions they showed as their eyes shifted from the tiny red baby lying beside the woman who had just given it birth to the sweating midwife bending down and working with her hands beneath the spread blankets. One of the women, pregnant herself, leant over the child, her eyes frightened and troubled—and then all at once the baby gasped, gave a sneeze, and opening its mouth began to yell. The women sighed, relieved.

"Sarah—" the midwife said softly.

The pregnant woman looked up. They exchanged some words in low murmuring voices and then—as the midwife went to the fireplace and sat down to bathe the child from a basin-full of warm red wine—the other slid her hands beneath the blankets and with firm gentle movements began to knead the mother's abdomen. There was a look of strained anxiety on her face that amounted almost to horror, but it vanished swiftly as the woman on the bed slowly opened her eyes and looked at her.

"Sarah-Sarah, is that my baby crying?"

Sarah did not stop working but nodded her head, forcing a quick bright smile. "Yes, Judith. That's your baby—your daughter." The baby's angry-sounding squalls filled the room.

"My daughter?" Even exhausted as she was, her disappointment was unmistakable. "A girl—," she said again, in a resentful tired little whisper. "But I wanted a boy. John would have wanted a boy." Tears filled her eyes and ran from the corners, streaking across her temples; her head turned away, wearily, as if to escape the sound of the baby's cries.

But she was too exhausted to care very much. A kind of dreamy relaxation was beginning to steal over her. It was something almost pleasant and as it took hold of her more and more insistently, dragging at her mind and body, she surrendered herself willingly, for it seemed to offer release from the agony of the past two days. She could feel the quick light beating of her heart. Now she was being sucked down into a whirlpool, then swirled up and up at an ever-increasing speed, and as she spun she seemed lifted out of herself and out of the room—swept along in time and space . . .

Of course John won't care if it's a girl. He'll love her just as much—and there will be boys later—boys, and more girls, too. For now the first baby had been born it would be easier next time. That was what her mother had often said, and her mother had had nine children.

She saw John's face, the shock of surprise when she told him that he was a father, and then the sudden breaking of happiness and pride. His smile was broad and his white teeth glistened in his tanned face and his eyes looked down at her with adoration, just as they had looked the last time she had seen him. It was always his eyes she remembered best, for they were amber-colored, like a glass of ale with the sun coming through it, and about the black centers were flecks of green and brown. They were strangely compelling eyes, as though all his being had come to focus in them.

Throughout her pregnancy she had hoped that this baby would have eyes like John's, hoped with such passionate intensity she never doubted her wish would come true.

HOW GARGANTUA WAS BORN IN A STRANGE MANNER

from *The First Book of Rabelais, Treating of the Inestimable Life of the Great Gargantua*

by FRANÇOIS RABELAIS

Whilst they were on this discourse, and pleasant tattle of drinking, Gargamelle began to be a little unwell in her lower parts, whereupon Grangousier arose from off the grass, and fell to comfort her very honestly and kindly, suspecting that she was in travail, and told her that it was best for her to sit down upon the grass, under the willows, because she was like very shortly to see young feet; and that, therefore, it was convenient she should pluck up her spirits, and take a good heart at the new coming of her baby; saying to her withal, that although the pain was somewhat grievous to her, it would be but of short continuance; and that the succeeding joy would quickly remove that sorrow, in such sort that she should not so much as remember it. "On with a sheep's courage," quoth he; "dispatch this boy, and we will speedily fall to work for the making of another."

From *A Farewell to Arms*

by ERNEST HEMINGWAY

One morning I awoke about three o'clock hearing Catherine stirring in the bed.

"Are you all right, Cat?"

"I've been having some pains, darling."

"Regularly?"

"No, not very."

"If you have them at all regularly we'll go to the hospital."

I was very sleepy and went back to sleep. A little while later I woke again.

"Maybe you'd better call up the doctor," Catherine said. "I think maybe this is it."

I went to the phone and called the doctor. "How often are the pains coming?" he asked.

"How often are they coming, Cat?"

"I should think every quarter of an hour."

"You should go to the hospital then," the doctor said. "I will dress and go there right away myself."

I hung up and called the garage near the station to send up a taxi. No one answered the phone for a long time. Then I finally got a man who promised to send up a taxi at once. Catherine was dressing. Her bag was all packed with the things she would need at the hospital and the baby things. Outside in the hall I rang for the elevator. There was no answer. I went downstairs. There was no one downstairs except the night-watchman. I brought the elevator up myself, put Catherine's bag in it, she stepped in and we went down. The night-watchman opened the door for us and we sat outside on the stone slabs beside the stairs down to the driveway and waited for the taxi. The night was clear and the stars were out. Catherine was very excited.

"I'm so glad it's started," she said. "Now in a little while it will be all over."

"You're a good brave girl."

"I'm not afraid. I wish the taxi would come, though."

We heard it coming up the street and saw its headlights. It turned into the driveway and I helped Catherine in and the driver put the bag up in front.

"Drive to the hospital," I said.

We went out of the driveway and started up the hill.

At the hospital we went in and I carried the bag. There was a woman at the desk who wrote down Catherine's name, age, address, relatives and religion, in a book. She said she had no religion and the woman drew a line in the space after the word. She gave her name as Catherine Henry.

"I will take you up to your room," she said. We went up in an elevator. The woman stopped it and we stepped out and followed her down a hall. Catherine held tight to my arm.

"This is the room," the woman said. "Will you please undress and get into bed? Here is a nightgown for you to wear."

"I have a nightgown," Catherine said.

"It is better for you to wear this nightgown," the woman said.

I went outside and sat on a chair in the hallway.

"You can come in now," the woman said from the doorway. Catherine was lying in the narrow bed wearing a plain, square-cut nightgown that looked as though it were made of rough sheeting. She smiled at me.

"I'm having fine pains now," she said. The woman was holding her wrist and timing the pains with a watch.

"That was a big one," Catherine said. I saw it on her face.

"Where's the doctor?" I asked the woman.

"He's lying down sleeping. He will be here when he is needed."

"I must do something for Madame, now," the nurse said. "Would you please step out again?"

I went out into the hall. It was a bare hall with two windows and closed doors all down the corridor. It smelled of hospital. I sat on the chair and looked at the floor and prayed for Catherine.

"You can come in," the nurse said. I went in.

"Hello, darling," Catherine said.

"How is it?"

"They are coming quite often now." Her face drew up. Then she smiled.

"That was a real one. Do you want to put your hand on my back again, nurse?"

"If it helps you," the nurse said.

"You go away, darling," Catherine said. "Go out and get something to eat. I may do this for a long time the nurse says."

"The first labour is usually protracted," the nurse said.

"Please go out and get something to eat," Catherine said. "I'm fine, really."

"I'll stay awhile," I said.

The pains came quite regularly, then slackened off. Catherine was very excited. When the pains were bad she called them good ones. When they started to fall off she was disappointed and ashamed.

"You go out, darling," she said. "I think you are just making me self-conscious." Her face tied up. "There. That was better. I so want to be a good wife and have this child without any foolishness. Please go and get some breakfast, darling, and then come back. I won't miss you. Nurse is splendid to me."

"You have plenty of time for breakfast," the nurse said.

"I'll go then. Good-bye, sweet."

"Good-bye," Catherine said, "and have a fine breakfast for me too."

"Where can I get breakfast?" I asked the nurse.

"There's a cafe down the street at the square," she said. "It should be open now."

Outside it was getting light. I walked down the empty street to the cafe. There was a light in the window. I went in and stood at the zinc bar and an old man served me a glass of white wine and a brioche. The brioche was yesterday's. I dipped it in the wine and then drank a glass of coffee.

"What do you do at this hour?" the old man asked.

"My wife is in labour at the hospital."

"So. I wish you good luck."

"Give me another glass of wine."

He poured it from the bottle slopping it over a little so some ran down on the zinc. I drank this glass, paid and went out. Outside along the street were the refuse cans from the houses waiting for the collector. A dog was nosing at one of the cans.

"What do you want?" I asked and looked in the can to see if there was anything I could pull out for him; there was nothing on top but coffee-grounds, dust and some dead flowers.

"There isn't anything, dog," I said. The dog crossed the street. I went up the stairs in the hospital to the floor Catherine was on and down the hall to her room. I knocked on the door. There was no answer. I opened the door; the room was empty, except for Catherine's bag on a chair and her dressing-gown hanging on a hook on the wall. I went out and down the hall, looking for somebody. I found a nurse.

"Where is Madame Henry?"

"A lady has just gone to the delivery room."

"Where is it?"

"I will show you."

She took me down to the end of the hall. The door of the room was partly open. I could see Catherine lying on a table, covered by a sheet. The nurse was on one side and the doctor stood on the other side of the table beside some cylinders. The doctor held a rubber mask attached to a tube in one hand.

"I will give you a gown and you can go in," the nurse said. "Come in here, please."

She put a white gown on me and pinned it at the neck in back with a safety-pin.

"Now you can go in," she said. I went into the room.

"Hello, darling," Catherine said in a strained voice. "I'm not doing much."

"You are Mr. Henry?" the doctor asked.

"Yes. How is everything going, doctor?"

"Things are going very well," the doctor said. "We came in here where it is easy to give gas for the pains."

"I want it now," Catherine said. The doctor placed the rubber mask over her face and turned a dial and I watched Catherine breathing deeply and rapidly. Then she pushed the mask away. The doctor shut off the pet-cock.

"That wasn't a very big one. I had a very big one a while ago. The doctor made me go clear out, didn't you, doctor?" Her voice was strange. It rose on the word doctor.

The doctor smiled.

"I want it again," Catherine said. She held the rubber tight to her face and breathed fast. I heard her moaning a little. Then she pulled the mask away and smiled.

"That was a big one," she said. "That was a very big one. Don't you worry, darling. You go away. Go have another breakfast.

"I'll stay," I said.

We had gone to the hospital about three o'clock in the morning. At noon Catherine was still in the delivery room. The pains had slackened again. She looked very tired and worn now but she was still cheerful.

"I'm not any good, darling," she said. "I'm so sorry. I thought I would do it very easily. Now—there's one—" she reached out her hand for the mask and held it over her face. The doctor moved the dial and watched her. In a little while it was over.

"It wasn't much," Catherine said. She smiled. "I'm a fool about the gas. It's wonderful."

"We'll get some for the home," I said.

"There one comes," Catherine said quickly. The doctor turned the dial and looked at his watch.

"What is the interval now?" I asked.

"About a minute."

"Don't you want lunch?"

"I will have something pretty soon," he said.

"You must have something to eat, doctor," Catherine said. "I'm so sorry I go on so long. Couldn't my husband give me the gas?"

"If you wish," the doctor said. "You turn it to the numeral two."

"I see." I said. There was a marker on a dial that turned with a handle.

"I want it, now," Catherine said. She held the mask tight to her face. I turned the dial to number two and when Catherine put down the mask I turned it off. It was very good of the doctor to let me do something.

"Did you do it, darling?" Catherine asked. She stroked my wrist.

"Sure."

"You're so lovely." She was a little drunk from the gas.

"I will eat from a tray in the next room," the doctor said. "You can call me any moment." While the time passed I watched him eat, then, after a while, I saw that he was lying down and smoking a cigarette. Catherine was getting very tired.

"Do you think I'll ever have this baby?" she asked.

"Yes, of course you will."

"I try as hard as I can. I push down but it goes away. There it comes. Give it to me."

At two o'clock I went out and had lunch. There were a few men in the cafe sitting with coffee and glasses of Kirsch or marc on the table. I sat down at a table. "Can I eat?" I asked the waiter.

"It is past time for lunch."

"Isn't there anything for all hours?"

"You can have choucroute."

"Give me choucroute and beer."

"A demi or a bock?"

"A light demi."

The waiter brought a dish of sauerkraut with a slice of ham over the top and a sausage buried in the hot wine-soaked cabbage. I ate it and drank the beer. I was very hungry. I watched the people at the tables in the cafe. At one table they were playing cards. Two men at the table next to me were talking and smoking. The cafe was full of smoke. The zinc bar, where I had breakfasted, had three people behind it now; the old man, a plump woman in a black dress who sat behind a counter and kept track of everything served to the tables, and a boy in an apron. I wondered how many children the woman had and what it had been like.

When I was through with the choucroute I went back to the hospital. The street was all clean now. There were no refuse cans out. The day was cloudy but the sun was trying to come through. I rode upstairs in the elevator, stepped out and went down the hall to Catherine's room, where I had left my white gown. I put it on and pinned it in back at the neck. I looked in the glass and saw myself looking like a fake doctor with a beard. I went down the hall to the delivery room. The door was closed and I knocked. No one answered so I turned the handle and went in. The doctor sat by Catherine. The nurse was doing something at the other end of the room.

"Here is your husband," the doctor said.

"Oh darling, I have the most wonderful doctor," Catherine said in a very strange voice. "He's been telling me the most wonderful story and when the pain came too badly he put me all the way out. He's wonderful. You're wonderful, doctor."

"You're drunk," I said.

"I know it," Catherine said. "But you shouldn't say it." Then "Give it to me. Give it to me." She clutched hold of the mask and breathed short and deep, pantingly, making the respirator click. Then she gave a long sigh and the doctor reached with his left hand and lifted away the mask.

"That was a very big one," Catherine said. Her voice was very strange. "I'm not going to die now, darling. I'm past where I was going to die. Aren't you glad?"

"Don't you get in that place again."

"I won't. I'm not afraid of it though. I won't die, darling."

"You will not do any such foolishness," the doctor said. "You would not die and leave your husband."

"Oh, no. I won't die. I wouldn't die. It's silly to die. There it comes. Give it to me."

After a while the doctor said, "You will go out, Mr. Henry, for a few moments and I will make an examination."

"He wants to see how I am doing," Catherine said. "You can come back afterward, darling, can't he, doctor?"

"Yes," said the doctor. "I will send word when he can come back."

I went out the door and down the hall to the room where Catherine was to be after the baby came. I sat in a chair there and looked at the room. I had the paper in my coat that I had bought when I went out for lunch and I read it. It was beginning to be dark outside and I turned the light on to read. After a while I stopped reading and turned off the light and watched it get dark outside. I wondered why the doctor did not send for me. Maybe it was better I was away. He probably wanted me away for a while. I looked at my watch. If he did not send for me in ten minutes I would go down anyway.

Poor, poor dear Cat. And this was the price you paid for sleeping together. This was the end of the trap. This was what people got for loving each other.

BIRTH
from *The Citadel*
by A. J. CRONIN

An hour elapsed. It was a long, harsh struggle. Then, as the first streaks of dawn strayed past the broken edges of the blind, the child was born, lifeless.

As he gazed at the still form a shiver of horror passed over Andrew. After all that he had promised! His face, heated with his own exertions, chilled suddenly. He hesitated, torn between his desire to attempt to resuscitate the child, and his obligation towards the mother, who was herself in a desperate state. The dilemma was so urgent he did not solve it consciously. Blindly, instinctively, he gave the child to the nurse and turned his attention to Susan Morgan who now lay collapsed, almost pulseless, and not yet out of the ether, upon her side. His haste was desperate, a frantic race against her ebbing strength. It took him only an instant to smash a glass ampule and inject Pituitrin. Then he flung down the hypodermic syringe and worked unsparingly to restore the flaccid woman. After a few minutes of feverish effort, her heart strengthened; he saw that he might safely leave her. He swung around, in his shirt sleeves, his hair sticking to his damp brown.

"Where's the child?"

The midwife made a frightened gesture. She had placed it beneath the bed.

In a flash Andrew knelt down. Fishing amongst the sodden newspapers below the bed, he pulled out the child. A boy, perfectly formed. The limp warm body was white and soft as tallow. The cord, hastily slashed, lay like a broken stem. The skin was of a lovely texture, smooth and tender. The head lolled on the thin neck. The limbs seemed boneless.

Still kneeling, Andrew stared at the child with a haggard frown. The whiteness meant only one thing, asphyxia pallida, and his mind, unnaturally tense, raced back to a case he once had seen in the Samaritan, to the treatment that had been used. Instantly he was on his feet.

"Get me hot water and cold water," he threw out to the nurse. "And basins too. Quick! Quick!"

"But—Doctor—" she faltered, her eyes on the pallid body of the child.

"Quick!" he shouted.

Snatching a blanket he laid the child upon it and began the special method of respiration. The basins arrived, the ewer, the big iron kettle. Frantically he splashed cold water into one basin; into the other he mixed water as hot as his hand could bear. Then, like some crazy juggler, he hurried the child between the two, now plunging it into the icy, now into the steaming bath.

Fifteen minutes passed. Sweat was now running into Andrew's eyes, blinding him. One of his sleeves hung down, dripping. His breath came pantingly. But no breath came from the lax body of the child.

A desperate sense of defeat pressed on him, a raging hopelessness. He felt the midwife watching him in stark consternation, while there, pressed back against the wall where she had all the time remained,—her hand pressed to her throat, uttering no sound, her eyes burning upon him,—was the old woman. He remembered her longings for a grandchild, as great as had been her daughter's longing for this child. All dashed away now; futile, beyond remedy . . .

The floor was now a draggled mess. Stumbling over a sopping towel, Andrew almost dropped the child, which was now wet and slippery in his hands, like a strange white fish.

"For mercy's sake, Doctor," whimpered the midwife, "It's still-born."

Andrew did not heed her. Beaten, despairing, having laboured in vain for half an hour, he still persisted in one last effort, rubbing the child with a rough towel, crushing and releasing the little chest with both his hands, trying to get breath into that limp body.

And then, as by a miracle, the pigmy chest, which his hands enclosed, gave a short convulsive heave. Another . . . And another . . . Andrew turned giddy. The sense of life, springing beneath his fingers after all that unavailing striving, was so exquisite it almost made him faint. He redoubled his efforts feverishly. The child was gasping now, deeper and deeper. A bubble of mucus came from one tiny nostril, a joyful iridescent bubble. The limbs were no longer boneless. The head no longer lay back spinelessly. The blanched skin was slowly turning pink. Then, exquisitely, came the child's cry.

"Dear Father in Heaven," the nurse sobbed hysterically, "it's come—it's come alive."

Andrew handed her the child. He felt weak and dazed. About him the room lay in a shuddering litter; blankets, towels, basins, soiled instruments, the hypodermic syringe impaled by its point in the linoleum, the ewer knocked over, the kettle on its side in a puddle of water. Upon the huddled bed the mother still dreamed her way quietly through the anaesthesia. The old woman still stood against the wall. But her hands were together, her lips moved without sound. She was praying.

Mechanically Andrew wrung out his sleeve, pulled on his jacket.

"I'll fetch my bag later, Nurse."

He went downstairs, through the kitchen into the scullery. His lips were dry. At the scullery he took a long drink of water. He reached for his hat and coat.

Outside he found Joe standing on the pavement with a tense, expectant face.

"All right, Joe," he said thickly. "Both all right."

It was quite light. Nearly five o'clock. A few miners were already in the streets: the first of the night shift moving out. As Andrew walked with them, spent and slow, his footfalls echoing with the others under the morning sky, he kept thinking blindly, oblivious to all other work he had done in Blaenelly: "I've done something; oh, God! I've done something real at last."

THE AFTERBIRTH

from *Safe Convoy* (1944)

by WILLIAM J. CARRINGTON

While the ancient Chinese regarded the placenta as a pillow for the fetus, we now know that it is an intermediary or liaison sponge-like organ. The moment it separates from the uterus, the baby is on his own. He must breathe for himself and perform all other necessary functions. During the third stage of labor, there is some loss of blood, an average of eight fluid ounces. To prevent excessive bleeding a hypodermic injection is given or medicine is adminstered by mouth, and the physician or a nurse keeps a hand on the abdomen over the womb to make sure that it remains firmly contracted into a hard mass about the size of a grapefruit. Some ten minutes or so after the birth of the infant, the blood vessels in the umbilical cord cease pulsating. The cord is then tied, cut, painted with tincture of iodine and covered with a sterile dressing.

Many ingenious devices were used to stop the flow of blood after the umbilical cord was cut before someone thought of tying a string around it. The ancient Chinese sprinkled horse-radish over it. In Latin America it was the almost universal custom for centuries to dress the stump with cobwebs. Notwithstanding the frequent occurrence of lockjaw which resulted from this practice the method is used today in the lower walks of South American life. But they did better on the Yucatan peninsula. Long before white men came they cut the cord with a sliver of bamboo and seared the stump with a flame. There was no lockjaw among the newborn infants of Yucatan.

Assistance in the expulsion of the placenta is practiced almost universally in some form or another, such as pressure over the abdomen or traction on the umbilical cord. Premature pressure is a mistake, and it is pernicious ever to pull or haul on the cord. This statement is neither original or recent. Soramus of Ephesus practiced medicine in Rome during the time of Trajan and wrote a treatise on the diseases of women in which he described the inversion of the uterus, or the turning of it inside out by forcible traction of the cord. Primitive people fastened a wide belt around the abdomen, a good example of which was the "squaw belt" of the North American Indians. The belt was drawn as tight as the strength of the attendant and the endurance of the patient allowed. The ancient Chinese treated retained placenta by trampling on the abdomen; the natives of the islands of the Coral Sea tickled the woman's nose to make her sneeze and thus expel the afterbirth, and the natives of the Papaya Indians tied one end of a buckskin thong to the cord and the other end to the foot of the woman who then kicked it out herself. In the Greece of the days of Homer the removal of the placenta was less precipitate. The woman took her seat in the chair with a hole in it, which was used for vaginal fumigations at other times. The infant with the cord still attached was placed on a large leather water bag filled with air on the floor. The bag was pricked so that the air slowly escaped as from an automobile tire with a slow leak. The infant sank slowly and pulled out the placenta by its own weight.

Modern methods are mild and gentle. After the placenta separates, the patient herself expels it with a few grunts by contracting the abdominal muscles and bearing down. External pressure is used by the obstetrician only for some good reason.

THE SILVER CORD

from *The Golden Bough* (1890)
by SIR JAMES G. FRAZER

Other parts which are commonly believed to remain in a sympathetic union with the body, after the physical connexion has been severed, are the navel-string and the afterbirth, including the placenta. So intimate, indeed, is the union conceived to be, that the fortunes of the individual for good or evil throughout life are often supposed to be bound up with one or other of these portions of his person, so that if his navel-string or afterbirth is preserved and properly treated, he will be prosperous; whereas if it be injured or lost, he will suffer accordingly. Thus certain tribes of Western Australia believe that a man swims well or ill, according as his mother at his birth threw the navel-string into water or not. Among the natives on the Pennefather River in Queensland it is believed that a part of the child's spirit (*cho-i*) stays in the afterbirth. Hence the grandmother takes the afterbirth away and buries it in the sand. She marks the spot by a number of twigs which she sticks in the ground in a circle, tying their tops together so that the structure resembles a cone. When Anjea, the being who causes conception in women by putting mud babies into their wombs, comes along and sees the place, he takes out the spirit and carries it away to one of his haunts, such as a tree, a hole in a rock, or a lagoon where it may remain for years. But sometime or other he will put the spirit again into a baby, and it will be born once more into the world. In Ponape, one of the Caroline Islands, the navel-string is placed in a shell and then disposed of in such a way as shall best adapt the child for the career which the parents have chosen for him; for example, if they wish to make him a good climber, they will hang the navel-string on a tree. The Kei islanders regard the navel-string as the brother or sister of the child, according to the sex of the infant. They put it in a pot with ashes, and set it in the branches of a tree, that it may keep a watchful eye on the fortunes of its comrade. Among the Bataks of Sumatra, as among many other peoples of the Indian Archipelago, the placenta passes for the child's younger brother or sister, the sex being determined by the sex of the child, and it is buried under the house. According to the Bataks it is bound up with the child's welfare, and seems, in fact, to be the seat of the transferable soul, of which we shall hear something later on. The Karo Bataks even affirm that of a man's two souls it is the true soul that lives with the placenta under the house; that is the soul, they say, which begets children.

Thus in many parts of the world the navel-string, or more commonly the afterbirth, is regarded as a living being, the brother or sister of the infant, or as the material object in which the guardian spirit of the child or part of its soul resides. Further, the sympathetic connexion supposed to exist between a person and his afterbirth or navel-string comes out very clearly in the widespread custom of treating the afterbirth or navel-string in ways which are supposed to influence for life the character and career of the person, making him, if it is a man, a nimble climber, a strong swimmer, a skilful hunter, or a brave soldier, and making her, if it is a woman, a cunning sempstress, a good baker, and so forth. Thus the beliefs and usages concerned with the afterbirth or placenta, and to a less extent with the navel-string, present a remarkable parallel to the widespread doctrine of the transferable or external soul and the customs founded on it. Hence it is hardly rash to conjecture that the resemblance is no mere chance coincidence, but that in the afterbirth or placenta we have a physical basis (not necessarily the only one) for the theory and practice of the external soul.

At last your abdomen is flat—to most women an almost unbelievable achievement!

—Nicholas J. Eastman

VI

THE CONQUEST OF PAIN AND FEAR IN CHILDBIRTH

Going with a Child is as it were a rough Sea, on which a big-bellied Woman and her Infant floats the Space of nine Months: And Labour, which is the only Port, is so full of dangerous Rocks, that very often both the one and the other, after they are arrived and disembarked, have yet need of much help to defend them against divers Inconveniences which usually follow the Pains and Travail they have undertook in it.

—Mauriceau

I began to realize that there was no law in nature and no design that could justify the pain of childbirth.

—Grantly Dick-Read

The primary duty of the physician is to relieve the processes of pain. The second duty . . . . is to allay the processes of fear. Pain can be brought to a frightful nearness through the telescope of fear. Fear can be greatly accentuated and magnified through the microsope of pain. These two processes are . . . psychic gemini, which when present in an uncontrolled force may periscope into the sensorium an irreversible psychic trauma.

—Clifford B. Lull and Robert A. Hingson,
American pioneers in painless childbirth

But if in a normal and healthy life of girlhood and womanhood before and after childbirth we find these outstanding qualities of beauty and greatness, what justification, what reason, or what presumption of truth can there be in the acceptance of an agonizing ordeal at the very time of fulfillment of life's most essential purpose? What manner of thing is this love that leads its most natural and perfect children through the green pastures of all that is beautiful in life, and urges them on by a series of ever-increasing delights until their ultimate goal is in sight, and then suddenly and without mercy chastises them and terrifies them before hurling them unconscious, injured and resentful into the new world of motherhood? I strongly suggest that there is only one answer: This is not the course of the Power of Love. This is not the purposeful design of creation. Somewhere, for some reason, an interloper has crept in, and must be eradicated. Something stands in the way which, through blindness and ignorance in the development of our civilization, has been allowed to grow and impede the natural course of events.

—Grantly Dick-Read

ANAESTHESIA IN OBSTETRICS

from *Expectant Motherhood* (1940)

by NICHOLAS J. EASTMAN

Simpson faced a stubborn, uphill fight, for no sooner had he announced that the pains of childbirth could be relieved by chloroform than a storm of invective befell him, from the clergy and the public, as well as many members of the medical profession. "It is unnatural thus to interfere with the pains of childbirth which are a *natural* function," they cried. "But, is not walking also a natural function?" replied Simpson. "And who would think of never setting aside or superseding this natural function? If you were traveling from Philadelphia to Baltimore, would you insist on walking the distance on foot simply because walking is man's natural method of locomotion?" Exclaimed an Irish lady to him one day, "How unnatural it is for you doctors in Edinburgh to take away the pains of your patients when in labor." "How unnatural," he replied, "it is for you to have swum from Ireland to Scotland against wind and tide in a steamboat." To the clergy's objection that such anaesthesia was contrary to the Bible, and the birthpang curse of "Paradise Lost," he cited the "first surgical operation" and the "first anaesthesia": "And the Lord God caused a deep sleep to fall upon Adam; and he slept; and He took one of his ribs, and closed up the flesh instead thereof." Countless other objections were hurled at him but to each he had an answer; he pointed out, moreover, that all things new are likely to arouse censure, particularly censure of a religious nature. Thus, he recalled, when vaccination against smallpox was introduced, various clergymen attacked the practice as irreligious, referring to a tempting of God's providence and therefore a heinous crime. He cited further the introduction of table forks. At first this innovation was regarded as a very sad and uncalled-for intrusion upon the old and established natural functions of the human fingers and a number of preachers denounced it "as an insult to Providence not to touch our meat with our fingers!"

"IT WASN'T MEANT TO HURT— WAS IT DOCTOR?"

from *Childbirth Without Fear* (1944)
by GRANTLY DICK-READ

I had plowed through the mud and rain down Whitechapel Road on my bicycle between two and three in the morning, turned right and left, and innumerable rights and lefts, before I came to a low hovel by the railway arches. Having groped and stumbled my way up a dark staircase, I opened the door of a room about ten feet square. There was a pool of water lying on the floor; the window was broken; rain was pouring in; the bed had no proper covering and was kept up at one end by a sugar box. My patient lay covered only with sacks and an old black skirt. The room was lit by one candle stuck in the top of a beer bottle on the mantleshelf. A neighbor had brought in a jug of water and a basin; I had to provide my own soap and towel. In spite of this setting—which even thirty years ago was a disgrace to any civilized country—I soon became conscious of a quiet kindliness in the atmosphere.

In due course, the baby was born. There was no fuss or noise. Everything seemed to have been carried out according to an ordered plan. There was only one slight note of dissension: I had tried to persuade my patient to let me put the mask over her face and give her some chloroform when the head appeared and the dilatation of the passages was obvious, but she had refused the help, kindly yet firmly. It was the first time in my short experience that I had met opposition when offering chloroform. As I was about to leave sometime later, I asked why it was that she would not use the mask. She did not answer at once, but looked at the old woman who had been assisting to the window through which was bursting the first light of dawn; then shyly she turned to me and said, "It didn't hurt. It wasn't meant to, was it, doctor?"

PAINLESS CHILDBIRTH

from the *Journal of the American Medical Association* (1955)

In 1951, Dr. Lamaze of Paris reported on the Soviet method of psychoprophylaxis in childbirth and applied it on a large scale in the Belleville Metal Workers' Clinic of Paris. His results were so good that they were soon disseminated throughout France and abroad. Some distrust persisted, however, because of the political propaganda surrounding the method. At a recent meeting of the Geneva Medical Society, Prof. H. de Watteville, of the International Federation of Gynecology and Obstetrics, reported on his experiences with obstetric analgesia. He did not try Read's method because of its unsatisfactory results. This method requires complete relaxation, which is difficult to obtain. If it is obtained, the parturient simply undergoes childbirth in a purely passive sense; she does not collaborate. Dr. Geisendorf then reported what he had seen in Dr. Lamaze's clinic. It is hard to see how childbirth could be painless, after the medical profession has been trying for so long to combat this supposedly physiological pain by means of more and more ingenious anesthetics. According to Pavlov, the cerebral cortex conditions the final form of pain perception, while the environment, through its influence on the cortex, modifies cortical function; thus women are conditioned to pain by the tradition that teaches them that childbirth is necessarily accomplished by pain. Uterine pains, like those in other parts of the body, are capable of being conditioned. Between the cortex and the subcortical centers there is reciprocal induction, and it is necessary to reinforce cortical activity by positive conditioning, which is supplied by the preparatory lessons, in order to intercept the interoceptors. The conclusion is that physiological delivery can take place without pain if the parturient, through her prior conditioning, directs the process through active participation. Many psychological factors explain the success of this new method. The slogan "childbirth without pain" has a great psychological effect on the masses. Group psychology also has an effect, in that there is emulation between the six women who are prepared simultaneously.

Instruction of Future Mothers

The instruction of future mothers begins in the seventh month of pregnancy. These lessons do not take the place of regular medical services. The instructor is a physician, and his assistant is a psychologist with special training in this type of preparation. The classes are conducted in a simple, clear language, and the word "pain" is never mentioned but is replaced by "contraction." There are six women in each class, and each lesson lasts 45 to 60 minutes. The first lesson, conducted by the obstetrician, consists in his getting to know the patients and putting them at ease; then follows a simple lecture on fertilization and anatomy and physiology of normal pregnancy. The second is given by the psychologist and deals with the value of respiration adapted to different phases of the birth process. The psychologist also gives the third lesson, which is about education of the muscles and nerves so that they can be contracted or relaxed at will. The women are told how the exercises prescribed achieve the positively conditioned reflexes that permit painless childbirth. After the second lesson the pupils are expected to repeat the exercises at home. In the fourth lesson, the physician explains the various stages of the birth process and the behavior required of the laboring woman in each of them. In the fifth lesson, the psychologist speaks on the phase of dilatation and the attitude to adopt during it. In the sixth, he explains the effort to be made during the expulsive phase. Of the 108 women who have followed this program since November 1954, 50 have been delivered to date, and 37 of them have benefited greatly; 12 had no pain at all, and 25 had some pain but declared that their delivery had been easy. Of the rest who obtained poor results, all gained some benefit from their preparation, and there was not a single case of complete failure. Dr. Geisendorf stated that the expulsion was something extraordinary to see for an obstetrician used to the usual form of birth; there was complete relaxation of the perineum and the women were able to raise themselves without effort to see their babies appear. All women are prepared in the same manner, but, if complications occur, traditional methods must be resorted to.

Dr. Geisendorf, who comes from an old Geneva family that could hardly be suspected of having pro-Communist sympathies, has declared his enthusiasm for this method in view of the advantages to both mother and child. He also thinks that the profession of midwifery will stage a comeback, because it will have a much greater psychological influence than formerly. In Lausanne, the government has given official sanction to the psychoprophylactic method in childbirth. On Sept. 5, a credit of 2 million Swiss francs was obtained from the legislature for the creation of a special department in the maternity ward of the Cantonal Hospital of Lausanne, a department for directed delivery according to Pavlov's method. Thus, after a long period of distrust, Swiss obstetricians have indicated that they want to adopt this new method of delivery.

From *Painless Childbirth* (1959)

by DR. FERNAND LAMAZE

Having instituted this favorable climate, I decided that from the sixth month of pregnancy onwards (regardless of the presentation of the child) all women under our care at our maternity hospital would be prepared for painless childbirth. Hence I made a clean break with the practice in the U.S.S.R., where the psychoprophylactic method was offered solely to those with a normal presentation. This was undoubtedly a great risk to take, but I felt that discrimination could lead women to entertain misgivings about the method, and, for those who were not being prepared, a still greater dread of childbirth. Furthermore, this gave us the advantage offered by mass discipline.

After a short clinical trial we decided to modify slightly the respiratory method adapted once the uterus went into labor. We have kept slow breathing during the first stage of labor, but taught rapid breathing during the second stage, and finally prescribed a panting type of breathing as the child's head presents itself at the vulvar orifice.

These were the basic foundations of the psychoprophylactic method for painless childbirth, as practiced in France. . . .

One cannot say too often to women that painless childbirth by psychoprophylaxis is not synonymous with laziness.

André Bourrel in his lectures rightly keeps on repeating that childbirth without pain is not childbirth without effort. . . .

A woman must be imbued with the thought that she is essentially responsible for the success or failure of her own childbirth.

There is not the slightest doubt that Read's theories, at that time, marked an advance on the views then held on analgesia and constituted the initial effort towards a psychotherapeutic approach. Needless to say, his theories met with strong opposition both from the British medical world and the Anglican Church and resulted in Read being shunned, if not abused.

Normal respiration works by an inborn reflex. By modifying the rhythm of breathing, a conditioned reflex is initiated as a sort of "branch" of the normal reflex. The repeated teaching of this new respiratory style leads to the formation of a new conditioned reflex, which we may call the contraction respiration reflex.

To question the legitimacy of pain in childbirth, and to solve that problem effectively, required a completely new outlook on the physiology of pain. This new attitude came from Pavlov.

In fact, with the accession of the psychoprophylactic method, obstetrical analgesia becomes invested with a totally new quality. The problem no longer concerns the choice of which method to use to dull the senses, or to abolish the sensory perception of an inevitable and unpleasant symptom. The problem is now to elucidate the physiological processes whereby uterine contractions become painful: and once this is elucidated, to recondition these processes so that the contractions become painless. Hand in hand with this must go the idea that uterine contractions are quite separate from uterine pain, an attitude contrary to the classical one which looked upon contraction and pain as synonymous.

We are therefore dealing with two quite distinct phenomena: uterine contraction and pain. These two phenomena, however, can, as the result of some particular upbringing, be linked together to give rise to painful uterine contraction. It is most important for the reader to grasp the physiological processes at the root of this association, as well as those concerned with its development.

Once more, let it be recalled that the essential features of the various methods of obstetrical analgesia before the days of psychoprophylaxis were:

(*a*) That they looked upon pain as a symptom.
(*b*) That pain was an inescapable accompaniment of delivery.
(*c*) That the means used to diminish the perception of pain was that of numbing sensation. This was specially the case when drugs were used.

No one had questioned the origin of pain in

childbirth; or, if the question had been asked, it had been badly worded. The way in which pain was caused was thought to be strictly physical; that pain should be legitimately present was never disputed. It was simply a useful symptom of childbirth, and all that needed to be done was to attenuate its unpleasantness.

THE NATURAL CHILDBIRTH ILLUSION

from *Southern Medical Journal* (June 1951)

by ARTHUR J. MANDY, ROBERT FARKAS, ERNEST SCHER, and THEODORE E. MANDY

Natural childbirth differs from other good obstetrical routines today only in that the patient is prepared to participate consciously in her delivery. Whether this is really important remains to be proved. Like psychoanalysis, natural childbirth is as much a personal philosophy as it is a system of medical practice. But unlike Freud, who was quick to recognize the limitations of analytic psychology, Grantly Dick-Read has consistently exaggerated the usefulness of his own procedure. As a result natural childbirth has been oversold.

Read's original concept of the fear-tension-pain syndrome in labor is broad enough for general acceptance. It is not difficult to understand how a moderate degree of discomfort in certain women can be magnified by fright and fear of the unknown to almost intolerable proportions.

After concluding that fear of childbirth was a culturally induced hazard, Read formulated a program which would more favorably prepare his patient for her labor. Eventually this procedure crystallized itself into an elaborate system of education, diet, exercises, and relaxation technics. Whether or not one agrees with these theoretical concepts, there can be little doubt that the program answers a purpose for many women to whom this added attention is important. But whether or not this program can, by strict definition, be called natural childbirth is debatable.

While Read has referred frequently to the ease with which primitive women give birth and compared it to the hardships which the modern women endure, he did not imply a return to primitive obstetrics with all of its attendant morbidity and mortality. No preliminary care, no drugs, no interference, frequently no child, and occasionally no mother: that was truly natural childbirth, a procedure little resembling the modern programs which now masquerade under the same title.

We submit that the term natural childbirth, as it is loosely applied in this country today, is a misnomer. Careful observation of the programs employed throughout this country has left us with the following impression. Natural childbirth is conceived in the belief that maximum participation from an alert patient is essential to the development of a healthy emotional relationship between the mother and her offspring.

Originally the proponents believed that this program of indoctrination would abolish pain in labor by removing fear of childbirth. Today every honest investigator knows that analgesia is indispensable to a broader application of any natural childbirth program. Without analgesia the procedure becomes what Galloway has facetiously called "pain without fear."

Education has little value other than superficial reassurance and desensitization of the common superstitions which surround the subject of pregnancy. Certainly if one ventures too deeply with the patient into the anatomy and physiology of childbirth, that experience can be more anxiety provoking than anxiety alleviating.

Thus far we have had very little more faith in the role of exercises, since they are not only a nuisance but are seldom adhered to except by obsessive women. These feelings are supported by Rodway's careful study which included 340 exercise participating patients and a similar group of controls. She could find no appreciable difference in the length and type of labor, hemorrhage, lacerations, relief of pain, or infant mortality between the two groups.

In contrast to these other factors, however, relaxation technics constitute the cornerstone of every natural childbirth program. Read, Thoms, and others have long recognized that a patient who fails in this one phase of her indoctrination, cannot successfully cooperate in their program without the assistance of adequate analgesic drugs. What they seem unable to recognize is the significance of this observation. Despite their protests to the contrary, relaxation and suggestion (subtly used throughout the program) are sufficiently related to the phenomenon of hypnosis to explain any of the physical success that can be achieved through natural childbirth. This does not add mystery to their method; quite the reverse, it makes order out of chaos. Those familiar with the medical applications of hypnosis accept it willingly as a valuable therapeutic adjunct.

At great length Read expresses the fear that the stigma of hypnosis would bring discredit to him and eventually undermine public confidence in his work. It is difficult to understand why he labors so over the distinction. He writes, for example:

> Those who have learned relaxation not infrequently lay as if in a trance throughout the first stage, and throughout the second stage their receptivity to stimuli was lowered to such an extent that many were unconscious of incidents that occurred and words that were spoken during that time.

Could anyone but Read distinguish this from the usual light trance state of hypnosis?

The program of training for relaxation is essentially the same as for hypnosis. In both hypnosis and relaxation the candidate must not only have an abiding faith in the program, in the therapist, or in the institution concerned, but she must also have a personal need for that particular procedure. And it is more than simple coincidence that the relative success which can be achieved through natural childbirth is statistically not different from the relative hypnotizability of the public at large.

For physiologic as well as psychologic clarification, one must recognize that anxiety in pregnancy is not the result of a single emotion of fear of childbirth upon an otherwise normal psyche. It is rather the reflection of the patient's entire personality in relation to that specific event. Long before the actual labor a woman's emotions have been influenced decisively by the level of her psycho-sexual maturity and the kind of adjustment she has previously made to mother, father, siblings, husband and colleagues. She may fear many things besides labor, such as increased responsbility, loss of freedom and companionship, economic deprivation, or inadequate housing. For any or all of these reasons, she may be overwhelmed with hostility and guilt toward both her husband and her offspring.

Perhaps the most objectionable feature of these programs is in their emphasis that any normal woman can be delivered by natural childbirth. It is a condemnable act that attempts to stigmatize all those who fail to participate, particularly when the benefits of full participation are far from established.

Nothing has been said in the current literature of what happens to the natural childbirth mother after the glamor and attention of the hospital has been withdrawn, leaving her like a disillusioned Cinderella. To believe that all mothers who have successfully experienced natural childbirth are more emotionally mature is an illusion. It is entirely conceivable that natural childbirth may act not so much to develop a more mature expectant mother but rather to encourage her dependence upon an important, authoritative figure, supported by formal, complex, ritualistic routines.

Since analgesia and anesthesia have been accepted as an integral part of the natural childbirth program, it is difficult to understand in what way it is superior to the caudal technic. When successfully administered, "caudal patients" appear equally euphoric and enthused about having had their babies in this manner, conscious during the delivery but unconscious of the discomforts which natural childbirth patients experience.

SOVIET SYSTEM OF PSYCHO-PROPHYLAXIS OF LABOUR IN PAIN ABROAD AND THE METHOD OF "NATURAL CHILDBIRTH"

From *Painless Childbirth Through Psychoprophylaxis*
(Foreign Languages Publishing House, Moscow, 1960)
by I. VELVOVSKY, K. PLATONOV, V. PLOTICHER, and E. SHUGOM

In the People's Democracies the system of psychoprophylaxis of labour pain became known about the end of 1951.

The first People's Democracies to carry the system of psychoprophylaxis of labour pain into life were Bulgaria and Czechoslovakia.

In Poland the development of psychoprophylaxis of labour pain is associated with the name of Jan Lesinsky. The psychoprophylactic method of preventing labour pain began to be used in Warsaw, Szczecin, Poznan, Lodz, Bialystok, Stalinográd and other cities.

In Hungary the initiative of introducing the method proposed by us arose in Budapest.

The first cities to use psychoprophylaxis of labour pain in the German Democratic Republic were Leipzig and Berlin.

In Rumania the system of psychoprophylactic management of labour was put into practice in Bucharest, Craiova, Oradea, Câmpulung, Moldovenese, Piatra Meamt, Galatz, Sibiu and other cities.

The system of psychoprophylaxis of labour pain has also gained ground in Albania, the Korean People's Democratic Republic and the Democratic Republic of Viet-Nam.

The experience of the Chinese People's Republic, where the psychoprophylactic method of managing labour began to be used at the end of 1951 in Shanghai, then in Peking, Tientsin and other cities and was soon put into extensive practice, is important.

In China the system of psychoprophylaxis of labour pain has served as the basis for the struggle against the past lack of culture and for the propaganda of Pavlov's teachings. The Chinese have found their own organizational forms for putting the methods of psychoprophylactic prevention of labour pain into practice on so wide a scale that they reported 200,000 painless childbirths by this method as early as 1952 and 700,000 in 1955.

In other countries the system of psychoprophylaxis of labour pain has become widespread owing to the vigorous and enthusiastic activities of Fernand Lamaze. He organized psychoprophylaxis of labour pain in France after his visit to the U.S.S.R. where he had studied this work at the Institute of Obstetrics of the U.S.S.R. Ministry of Public Health in Moscow and, especially, at the Institute of Obstetrics and Gynaecology of the U.S.S.R. Academy of Medical Sciences in Leningrad.

Lamaze endeavoured to elaborate the theoretical

principles of the system in the light of Pavlov's teachings on higher nervous activity and to find organizational and methodological ways applicable to the specific conditions of public health prevailing in different countries.

By unifying the activities of neuropsychiatrists, obstetricians and gynaecologists in the scientific elaboration of the psychoprophylactic method and in putting it into practice Lamaze had undoubtedly taken the right road.

The enormous propaganda of psychoprophylaxis of labour pain conducted by Lamaze and his pupils in France and all over the world deserves special mention.

Suffice it to point out that, having organized a school of psychoprophylaxis of labour pain at the Polyclinique du Métallurgiste, Lamaze trained obstetricians and midwives for every country in the world. He published a geographic map showing the introduction of the Soviet system of psychoprophylaxis of labour pain through his pupils. The map shows that the system had spread, even before his death, through 42 countries in Europe, Asia, Africa and South America and, to a lesser extent, North America and Australia. Lamaze attracted extensive attention of the scientific and general press, especially the press of women's public organizations, to the Soviet system of psychoprophylaxis of labour pain. He found particularly ardent followers in Italy. Of these we can name Delle Piane and Malcovati and their associates Daviti, Bacialli, and others. In Italy the question of psychoprophylaxis of labour pain attracted the attention of the church and elicited a special address of its head Pope Pius XII who proclaimed that Catholics were allowed to make use of the psychoprophylactic system.

The enormous achievements of Lamaze and his followers in France and Italy include the fact that they were able to raise the question of preventing labour pain by the method of psychoprophylaxis in parliaments and municipalities, depict it in films and elicit a wide response in the general press, etc.

It is but necessary to point out that, in addition to the response the system of psychoprophylaxis of labour pain elicited and its spread abroad as a result of the vigorous activity of F. Lamaze, its success has also activated the interest of foreign obstetricians in the method of Grantly Dick-Read. This method deserves a more detailed analysis.

Read's method, designated as the method of "natural childbirth" or "childbirth without fear," is essentially hypnosuggestive. However, Read stands out among the foreign authors of hypnosuggestive pain relief by firmly maintaining that labour pain is not inborn and humanity can be rid of it. He also differs from the other foreign representatives of the method of hypnosuggestive pain relief by the fact, that, as far as we know, he is the only author to have proposed his own conception of labour pain. He elaborated an original technique of hypnotization by means of special "relaxation exercises" borrowed from Edmund Jacobson, author of the general idea of using relaxation as a therapeutic method. Besides, Read is the only foreign author who introduced into his prenatal preparation elements of insistent mediation of some obstetrical events and accessorics and certain forms of spontaneous behaviour on the part of parturient women. His method also reflects more than any other foreign methods of hypnotic suggestion the ideas of Dubois, Déjerine and Marcinowski.

However, Read himself groundlessly denies the hypnosuggestive nature of his method and considers it a discovery of fundamental and decisive importance.

Besides, Read establishes no historical connections between the ideas advanced by him and those of the above-mentioned authors whose influence on his postulates and methods is obvious. He also assumed a peculiar position as regards the Soviet system.

According to Lamaze, Vellay, Vermorel and others, Read at first opposed the method of psychoprophylaxis of labour pain proposed in the Soviet Union. But later he and some of his followers strove to identify the Soviet system with Read's method and to insist on the priority of the latter.

According to Read, labour pain is rooted in the tension of the muscles caused by uterine contractions. This tension occurs simultaneously in the longitudinal and circular muscle fibres and disturbs the "neuromuscular harmony."

These uterine contractions are wrongly interpreted by the women in our society as the cause of pain. At this moment (according to Read) there is no pain as yet, but the "error" of the brain leads to "defence" and women develop fear. The latter in its turn causes uterine contractions with a simultaneous tension of the longitudinal and circular muscle fibres, which again disturbs the "neuromuscular harmony." According to Read, real pain arises at this point as a result of such incompatible activity. The tension and spasm of the vascular wall condition the pale ischemia and become chronic. Failure to relax completely creates vascular and lymphatic congestion, disturbance of metabolism, etc. The muscular and vascular spasms assume tetanic forms which Read considers similar to the cramps in the gastrocnemius muscles with their characteristic pain. Thus, according to Read, the only factor causing pain is the peripheral stimulation in the uterus in which the circular and longitudinal muscles experience simultaneous tension caused by fear. . . .

> This complicated branch of human physiology [says Read], may be adequately explained by using the analogy of the telephone exchange. The nerves represent wires leading from all parts of the body to the central exchange which we term the thalamus. Here messages are received and replies relayed. . . . If the thalamic exchange is well organized it will not misinterpret the importance of the message it receives; but if it is in a state of excitability and anticipation arising from the imminence of disaster, it may well call upon reserves and retaliate in no way commensurate with the severity of the assumed assault.

The foregoing shows that Read now emphasizes local factors of the uterine muscular apparatus and proclaims their primacy (cramp-like pain), and now speaks of erroneous central interpretation, ascribing this "interpretation" to the thalamus rather than the cortex.

Read speaks of the participation of the cortex only from the point of view of adding certain "influences" to pain as a local and thalamic function.

The aforesaid postulates show that between our conception of pain based on the corticovisceral relations, as they are understood by Pavlov's school, and Read's conception interpreting pain in labour as of peripheral origin and its central component as thalamic, there is not only nothing in common but that they are exact opposites.

Interpreting pain in labour in the above manner Read at the same time asserts that childbirth does not necessarily have an inborn stigma of pain and fear. This postulate, not taken in the general plan of Read's conception, falls in with our convictions. But we cannot accept Read's ideas of "natural childbirth" since he refers to childbirth as natural only before it is influenced by civilization, i.e., essentially childbirth under primitive conditions. This idea of "natural childbirth" gives rise to Read's next formulation: "Civilization is the main cause of pain."

Read says that civilization has destroyed the "edifice of primitive defence," which manifests itself "in the original instinct of escape," and has engendered the emotion of fear. "The joy of new life must be the vision of motherhood, instead of the fear of death that has clouded it since civilization developed."

We agree with Vermorel who says that "this erroneous conception of the negative role of civilization" may lead to the idea that it would be expedient to return to primitive obstetrics. . . .

Read's views . . . [are] opposed to ours. His general gnoseological position concerning the possibility of cognizing labour is also at variance with our views. Thus he writes:

> The mysteries of childbirth and the problems of reproduction will not be solved by innovations and interventions. The secrets of this fundamental process of life will gradually dawn upon us as we patiently and humbly strive to discover the genius of God.

Read believes, however, that civilization has not directly caused pain. It brought tension as a protective phenomenon against fear which had arisen owing to civilization.

The pain and suffering experienced by modern woman are, according to Read, a result of "psychic exaggeration" or the "psychic climate" created around the woman. Hence the "Fear-Tension-Pain Syndrome" formulated by Read.

Moreover, fear in Read's conception is not only one of the aggravating factors—something we do not deny—but is also essentially the foremost and determining factor in labour. It is no mere accident that Read's system of "natural childbirth" was named "childbirth without fear" rather than "childbirth without pain."

Fear, according to Read, is a subjective psychological category engendered by the loss of the naturalness of childbirth and brought about by the effect of civilization.

The leading idea in Read's conception of fear is that such fear is an acquired phenomenon, although we can also find the following statement in his writings:

"This series of events is frequently the origin, not only of an inherent fear of childbirth, but of the physical manifestation of that fear."

He writes about his attitude to Pavlov as follows:

> The first of my books came out in 1933. Neither Pavlov's name nor his works were mentioned in our articles, or, to tell the truth, they were never accorded any place in them. Only in 1942 did I mention for the first time the works of the Russian scientist on conditionality and the influence it exerts on fear, tension and pain.

Read's methods are also opposed to the Soviet methods in their main and decisive aspects.

Read says that to change childbirth from unnatural to "natural" he "had to find a way of *overcoming the main* weapon of the enemies, i.e., *tension*" (emphasis by authors).

We make it our main aim to struggle against the passivity of the woman in labour and ask her to be reasonably active, and by learning the laws governing labour to regulate skilfully her own behaviour in labour.

On the other hand, Read's method is based on an appeal to the parturient woman to be as passive as possible. This is clear from the foregoing quotations, as well as from the following words addressed by Read to the women:

"How often have I said, 'You can do nothing to help yet; allow your uterus to get on with its work undisturbed by your inquisitive interest. If you interfere it will resent it, and hurt you.' "

Even Thoms and Goodrich, Read's followers, say that neither Read nor any of his followers assert that they can achieve effective pain relief. In view of this we can understand why the French scientists report that Read's method is much less effective than the Soviet psychoprophylactic method.

The foregoing quite suffices to show the differences and in some respects contrasts between our system of psychoprophylaxis and Read's method. We believe that this is not contradicted even by the fact that Read uses some undoubtedly rational techniques which may even appear identical to ours.

This "identity" lies in the series of useful measures used by Read and us in the obstetrical management of the parturient woman and apparently noted similarly by the observant clinician Read and us in the spontaneous behaviour of the parturient woman.

But even if we take those of Read's techniques that resemble ours we cannot fail to note they have different purposes and are of a different import in the total system.

It will also be observed that the most rational things in Read's conceptions—struggle against fear and other negative emotions, control of iatrogenias in obstetrical institutions, the idea that pain in labour is not inevitable for its safe course, etc.—all formed the fundamental principles of the works of Platonov, Nikolayev, Zdravomyslov and others, which appeared earlier than Read's work. For example, Vigdorovich, a Leningrad obstetrician, used essentially the same "relaxation" long before Read, only he used it without gymnastic exercises and not in groups of 8 but of 20, 40 and even 100 women whom he seated in armchairs or put on couches. He also delivered to his sleepy audience emotional lectures based on ideas of the social sanctity of motherhood, demonstration of the material concern of Soviet society for mother and child, and the honour of motherhood. Thus, besides the gymnastics, which may be considered Read's original contribution, many of the valuable things found in his writings were formerly voiced and practised by Soviet authors who relieved labour of pain by hypnosuggestive methods.

Although we are fully aware of the great differences between us and Read, we should not want our scientific discussion of his views to be regarded as reluctance to recognize his contributions.

Read's contribution to the problem of relieving labour pain by psychic influence is incontestable and we consider him a real innovator among his foreign colleagues.

We agree with him on the idea that women do not have to suffer in labour, that we can and must rid them of their suffering *en masse* and that mankind must be free of it. Like he, we consider it a boon to the childbearing women and to the offspring they bear.

We find that today it is no longer doubted that it is possible to combat the suffering of women in labour and strive for greater well-being of mother and foetus by methods of psychic influence.

This should be the main incentive in determining the unity of organizational aspirations of the adherents of the Soviet system of psychoprophylaxis of labour pain and those of Read's methods in their practical activities aimed at introducing "psychological" or "psychophysical" methods into the mass obstetrical practice throughout the world.

Our theoretical and methodological differences should not hinder us from co-operating in this field even if the advocates of the different views continue to adhere to the methods and conceptions which satisfy them more.

VII

IS IT A BOY? IS IT A GIRL?

From *Cheaper by the Dozen*
by FRANK B. GILBRETH, JR.
AND ERNESTINE GILBRETH CAREY

It was an off year that didn't bring a new Gilbreth baby. Both Dad and Mother wanted a large family. And if it was Dad who set the actual target of an even dozen, Mother as readily agreed.

Dad mentioned the dozen figure for the first time on their wedding day. . . .

"We're going to have a wonderful life, Lillie. A wonderful life and a wonderful family. A great big family."

"We'll have children all over the house," Mother smiled. "From the basement to the attic."

"From the floorboards to the chandelier."

"When we go for our Sunday walk we'll look like Mr. and Mrs. Pied Piper."

"Mr. Piper, shake hands with Mrs. Piper. Mrs. Piper, meet Mr. Piper."

Mother put the magazine on the seat beneath her and Dad, and they held hands beneath it.

"How many would you say we should have, just an estimate?" Mother asked.

"Just as an estimate, many."

"Lots and lots."

"We'll sell out for an even dozen," said Dad. "No less. What do you say to that?"

"I say," said Mother, "a dozen would be just right. No less."

"That's the minimum."

"Boys or girls?"

"Well, boys would be fine," Dad whispered. "A dozen boys would be just right. But . . . well, girls would be all right too. Sure. I guess."

"I'd like to have half boys and half girls. Do you think it would be all right to have half girls?"

"If that's what you want," Dad said, "we'll plan it that way. Excuse me a minute while I make a note of it."

He took out his memorandum book and solemnly wrote; "Don't forget to have six boys and six girls."

SPECULATIONS ON SEX OF THE UNBORN

from *Safe Convoy* (1944)
by WILLIAM J. CARRINGTON

The sex of the unborn child has always been a matter of interesting speculation. A medical papyrus, written in hieroglyphics about 1500 B.C., devotes a passage to the predetermination of sex. Musty records reveal that the ancient Greeks and Romans were concerned by the same conjectures. Medieval Germans soaked wheat and barley in the urine of the prospective mother and then planted them. If the wheat grew first a son was to be expected; if the barley, a girl! French women tossed coins over their shoulders: heads meant a boy!! Another method, equally fallible, consisted of squeezing a drop of fluid from the nipple into a glass of water. The sex could be foretold by whether the drop floated or sank. Today many grandmothers believe that they can predict sex by the manner in which the baby is carried, whether it bulges far forward over the pubic bone like a ballooned awning or whether it is carried deep in the pelvis inconspicuously between the hips.

Scientific observation on thousands of cases has shown that the fetal heart sounds are more rapid in girls than in boys (55 percent), but the difficulty lies in the upsetting fact that the fetal heart rate varies from time to time. Yet, withal this method is somewhat more accurate than the incredible belief that was prevalent over the western plains a few short years ago. If the groom went to bed on his wedding night with his boots and spurs on, the baby was sure to be a boy!

There is a belief prevalent today that women menstruate from one ovary on alternate months; and that the sex depends on whether impregnation occurred on an odd or an even month. I have delivered both boys and girls from several women who, following operations, had but one ovary. Another belief obtains that the sex is determined at the time of coitus. If the husband is more desirous of offspring there will be a girl, and if the mother's personality predominates at the moment, she will beget a boy. It is this belief that prompts the Brahmins to snip the hood of the clitoris to overcome a stubborn perversity in bearing nothing but girls.

About 280 A.D. Wan Sho Ho wrote a ten-volume treatise on the pulse with elaborate directions on how to distinguish pregnancy, twins, and sex by no other methods than feeling the pulse. But this is merely Oriental hocus-pocus.

Out of a heterogeny of fanciful theories two practical facts have emerged: (1) Those parents are happier who do not set their hearts on either a boy or a girl, but who accept either with a smile. (2) Following bloody wars, for some reason He has not revealed, the Lord replaces the losses of young men by increasing the birth rate of male infants.

Dear God, I need you awful bad,
I don't know what to do,
My pop's cross, my mama's sick,
I ain't got no friend but you.
Them keerless angels went and brung,
'Stid of the boy I ast,
A weenchy, teenchy baby girl,

I don't see how they dast.
Say, God, I wisht you'd take her back,
She's just as good as new;
Won't no one know she's second-hand,
But 'ceptin me and you.
And pick a boy, dear God, yourself,
The nicest in the fold;
But please don't choose him quite so young,
I'd like him five years old.

—*Little Boy's Prayer* (AUTHOR UNKNOWN)

From *Tomorrow Will Be Better*
by BETTY SMITH

Always she thought of the child as a girl. She knew that most women wanted sons. She didn't blame them. In some ways girls were a drug on the market and certainly they never got the breaks a boy got. A boy could be president or make a million dollars. What else could a girl do except marry? Well, she could work of course. In a factory? Never. An office? Maybe. Schoolteaching's about the best work for a woman. . . .

Maybe my daughter won't want to be a schoolteacher. Maybe she'll want to go on the stage. Oh, I hope so! I'll buy her ballet slippers and manage to get dancing lessons for her as soon as she's old enough to walk. She might turn out to be another Marilyn Miller.

I'm in love with you, Sunny, she hummed happily.

Oh, the baby *must* be a girl! If I have a son I might get to be like Mrs. Malone or Mrs. Prentiss. I can well see how that could happen. Frankie's not affectionate. So I'd look for affection in my son. Without meaning to, I'd bring him up to believe that I was the only perfect woman in the world. I'd be jealous of his girls and I'd think he was too good for his wife. Maybe I'd really believe that he was trapped into marriage. I don't want to be like that. So it's got to be a girl.

"I WANT A SON"
from *Anne of the Thousand Days*
by MAXWELL ANDERSON

HENRY

If you loved me you'd find me free.

ANNE

From your marriage?

HENRY

Here is my marriage, Nan. My older brother Arthur was heir to the kingdom. To make an alliance with Spain he married Katherine of Aragon. Then Arthur died—and I was heir to the throne of England. To continue the alliance with Spain I was advised to marry Arthur's widow, six years my senior. And I did. At seventeen I married her. I never loved her. I should never have married my brother's widow. There's a curse on the marriage. We cannot have sons. Our sons are all born dead. There is no heir male to the English crown because of this accursed union. The kingdom faces anarchy when I die, and I face anarchy in my own life, because I have no male heir—yet because of the church and our friendship with Spain, I remain Katherine's husband. More than anything in this world I want a son, and she can't give me one—yet I must not publicly put her aside. Do you understand now? This marriage is a form—important only in statecraft and churchcraft, not to you or me.

ANNE

Important or not, you can't break it. It's stronger than you are—and so you offer me nothing.

HENRY

It's not nothing, Nan. It's my whole life. I know because I tried to erase you and fill my life with other things. It won't work. I can think of nothing but you.

(She has been looking straight into his eyes. She drops her head.)

It's not only this pain, this stitch in the side, this poetry I can't keep from writing, this music that I hear when I think of you and must write down . . . I'm a man, too, Nan. I want you—and only you. I find myself—when I'm talking to an ambassador, perhaps—I find myself thinking of you. And what am I thinking? Of you and me playing at dog and bitch. Of you and me playing at horse and mare. Of you and me every way there is. I want to fill you up—night after night. I want to fill you with sons.

ANNE

Bastards? For they would be bastards, you know.

(There is a long pause. The music stops. The lights come up on the whole scene, revealing Henry and Anne in the middle of the stage, the others watching.)

HENRY

If you say one more word I shall strike you. One word more.

ANNE

(In his teeth.) But it's quite obvious that if you and I had children they would be bastards.

(There is another long pause, then Henry strikes Anne heavily across the face. She goes down to one knee. Wolsey and Boleyn step forward, but do not interfere.)

WOLSEY

(Low.) Your Majesty.

(Anne gets slowly to her feet, a little dazed, then faces the king.)

ANNE

You have not yet understood what I mean, I think. What I am trying to tell you is that you not only offer me nothing—you offer yourself nothing. You say you want a son, an heir to the throne. You need such an heir, and the kingdom needs him. But an heir must be legitimate—not baseborn—and while you are married to Katherine you can have only bastards. Fill me with as many sons as you like, you would still have no heir, and I would have—nothing. As for your music and your poetry and your love for me—you know I don't love you. You've given me good reason not to love you.

HENRY

Would you marry me if I were free of Katherine?

ANNE

You can't get free of Katherine. You know that. And I know it.

HENRY

But if I were free of her, and free to marry you, and would make you Queen of England, would you marry me?

(There is a long pause.)

ANNE

None of these things could be. Yes. If you'll make me Queen of England I will marry you.

HENRY

Wolsey!

WOLSEY

We can do many things, as you know, my sovereign. We can shake the thrones of the Emperor and of the King of France. We can sometimes get our way in Rome. But this we could not do. Try to divorce Katherine and you'll have the whole world against you. You'll be at war with all Europe.

ANNE

Very well.

HENRY

You knew you'd get this answer.

ANNE

Yes. I knew it.

WOLSEY

The King asks very little of you, Anne. Any other woman would give it readily.

ANNE

Out of fear.

WOLSEY

No.

ANNE

Out of gratitude, then. But I'm not flattered, and I'm not afraid. If he will marry me and make me Queen of England I will give him boys in plenty. But I will take nothing else.

HENRY

It's true that I go through life dragging a sick woman—cold and sick—blotched and middle-aged—and fanatic—who can give neither pleasure nor a living son. I have worked at that long enough, I think. I know what can come from that bed. There never was much need for the hair shirt she wears next her skin. And none now.

WOLSEY

Any son of the King could be made legitimate—could be made the heir.

HENRY

Yes. It's true.

ANNE

Your Majesty already has a natural son. Have you made him the heir? Is he legitimate?

WOLSEY

He's made Duke of Richmond.

ANNE

Could the Duke of Richmond inherit the throne?

WOLSEY

He may. It could be. The lad's not well. Not like to live.

ANNE

But he would come first, shall we say? And then, Mary's child. It happens that any baseborn son I might have would be younger than Mary's. Her child would come before mine. My entry would be third. Now we are affectionate sisters, Mary and I. We forgive each other the little things that sisters must forgive. Yet she would rather her son sat on the throne than mine. I'd rather mine than hers. I'd rather have no son than a son baseborn.

HENRY

I shall rid myself of Katherine. I shall make this girl Queen. I shall settle the question of the succession once for all!

WOLSEY

Oh, my lord, I beg you, as your faithful servant, I beg you, don't promise this now. It may mean your death—or the loss of your kingdom—Or her death. You are not yourself. This is not a small error. It—

HENRY

I shall make this girl Queen.

WOLSEY

She's never said she loved you!

HENRY

I shall make her Queen. If it breaks the earth in two like an apple and flings the halves into the void, I shall make her Queen.

(The lights go out.)

"A MAN CHILD!"

from *The Good Earth*
by PEARL S. BUCK

When the sun had set he straightened his back slowly and looked at the woman. Her face was wet and streaked with the earth. She was as brown as the very soil itself. Her wet, dark garments clung to her square body. She smoothed a last furrow slowly. Then in her usual plain way she said, straight out, her voice flat and more than usually plain in the silent evening air,

"I am with child."

Wang Lung stood still. What was there to say to this thing, then! She stooped to pick up a bit of broken brick and threw it out of the furrow. It was as though she had said, "I have brought you tea," or as though she had said, "We can eat." It seemed an ordinary as that to her! But to him—he could not say what it was to him. His heart swelled and stopped as though it met sudden confines. Well, it was their turn at this earth!

He took the hoe suddenly from her hand and he said, his voice thick in his throat, "Let be for now. It is a day's end. We will tell the old man."

They walked home, then, she half a dozen paces behind him as befitted a woman. The old man stood at the door, hungry for his evening's food, which, now that the woman was in the house, he would never prepare for himself. He was impatient and he called out,

"I am too old to wait for my food like this!"

But Wang Lung, passing him into the room, said,

"She is with child already."

He tried to say it easily as one might say, "I have planted the seeds in the western field today," but he could not. Although he spoke in a low voice it was to him as though he had shouted the words out louder than he would.

The old man blinked for a moment and then comprehended, and cackled with laughter.

"Heh-heh-heh-" he called out to his daughter-in-law as she came, "so the harvest is in sight."

Her face he could not see in the dusk, but she answered evenly,

"I shall prepare food now."

"Yes—yes—food—" said the old man eagerly, following her into the kitchen like a child. Just as the thought of a grandson had made him forget his meal, so now the thought of food freshly before him made him forget the child.

But Wang Lung sat upon a bench by the table in the darkness and put his head upon his folded arms. Out of this body of his, out of his own loins, life!

When the hour for birth drew near he said to the woman,

"We must have someone to help at the time—some woman."

But she shook her head. She was clearing away the bowls after the evening food. The old man had gone to his bed and the two of them were alone in the night, with only the light that fell upon them from the flickering flame of a small tin lamp filled with bean oil, in which a twist of cotton floated for a wick.

"No woman?" he asked in consternation. He was beginning now to be accustomed to these conversations with her in which her part was little more than a movement of head or hand, or at most an occasional word dropped unwillingly from her wide mouth. He had even come to feel no lack in such conversing. "But it will be odd with only two men in the house!" he continued. "My mother had a woman from the village. I know nothing of these affairs. Is there none in the great house, no old slave with whom you were friends, who could come?"

It was the first time he had mentioned the house from which she came. She turned on him as he had never seen her, her narrow eyes widened, her face stirred with dull anger.

"None in that house!" she cried out at him.

He dropped his pipe which he was filling and stared at her. But her face was suddenly as usual and she was collecting the chopsticks as though she had not spoken.

"Well, here is a thing!" he cried in astonishment. But she said nothing. Then he continued in argument, "We two men, we have no ability in childbirth. For my father it is not fitting to enter your room—for myself, I have never even seen a cow give birth. My clumsy hands might mar the child. Someone from the great house, now, where the slaves are always giving birth . . ."

She had placed the chopsticks carefully down in an orderly heap upon the table and she looked at him, and after a moment's looking she said,

"When I return to that house it will be with my son in my arms. I shall have a red coat on him and red-flowered trousers and on his head a hat with a small gilded Buddha sewn on the front and on his feet tiger-faced shoes. And I will wear new shoes and a new coat of black sateen and I will go into the kitchen where I spent my days and I will go into the great hall where the Old One sits with her opium, and I will show myself and my son to all of them."

He had never heard so many words from her before. They came forth steadily and without break, albeit slowly, and he realized that she had planned this whole thing out for herself. When she had been working in the fields beside him she had been planning all this out! How astonishing she was! He would have said that she had scarcely thought of the child, so stilly and she gone about her work, day in and day out. And instead she saw this child, born and fully clothed, and herself as his mother, in a new coat! He was for once without words himself, and he pressed the tobacco diligently into a ball between his thumb and forefinger, and picking up his pipe he fitted the tobacco into the bowl.

"I suppose you will need some money," he said at last with apparent gruffness.

"If you will give me three silver pieces . . ." she said

fearfully. "It is a great deal, but I have counted carefully and I will waste no penny of it. I shall make the cloth dealer give me the last inch to the foot."

Wang Lung fumbled in his girdle. The day before he had sold a load and a half of reeds from the pond in the western field to the town market and he had in his girdle a little more than she wished. He put the three silver dollars upon the table. Then, after a little hesitation, he added a fourth piece which he had long kept by him on the chance of his wanting to gamble a little some morning at the tea house. But he never did more than linger about the tables and look at the dice as they clattered upon the table, fearful lest he lose if he played. He usually ended by spending his spare hours in the town at the storyteller's booth, where one may listen to an old tale and pay no more than a penny into his bowl when it was passed about.

"You had better take the other piece," he said, lighting his pipe between the words, blowing quickly at the paper spill to set it aflame. "You may as well make his coat of a small remnant of silk. After all, he is the first."

She did not at once take the money, but she stood looking at it, her face motionless. Then she said in a half-whisper,

"It is the first time I have had silver money in my hand."

Suddenly she took it and clenched it in her hand and hurried into the bedroom.

Wang Lung sat smoking, thinking of the silver as it had lain upon the table. It had come out of the earth, this silver, out of his earth that he had ploughed and turned and spent himself upon. He took his life from this earth; drop by drop by his sweat he wrung food from it and from the food, silver. Each time before this that he had taken the silver out to give to anyone, it had been like taking a piece of his life and giving it to someone carelessly. But now for the first time such giving was not pain. He saw, not the silver in the alien hand of a merchant in the town; he saw the silver transmuted into something worth even more than itself—clothes upon the body of his son. And this strange woman of his, who worked about, saying nothing, seeming to see nothing, she had first seen the child thus clothed!

She would have no one with her when the hour came. It came one night, early, when the sun was scarcely set. She was working beside him in the harvest field. The wheat had borne and been cut and the field flooded and the young rice set, and now the rice bore harvest, and the ears were ripe and full after the summer rains and the warm ripening sun of early autumn. Together they cut the sheaves all day, bending and cutting with short-handled scythes. She had stooped stiffly, because of the burden she bore, and she moved more slowly than he, so that they cut unevenly, his row ahead, and hers behind. She began to cut more and more slowly as noon wore on to afternoon and evening, and he turned to look at her with impatience. She stopped and stood up then, her scythe dropped. On her face was a new sweat, the sweat of a new agony.

"It is come," she said. "I will go into the house. Do not come into the room until I call. Only bring me a newly peeled reed, and slit it, that I may cut the child's life from mine."

She went across the fields toward the house as though there were nothing to come, and after he had watched her he went to the edge of the pond in the outer field and chose a slim green reed and peeled it carefully and slit it on the edge of his scythe. The quick autumn darkness was falling then and he shouldered his scythe and went home.

When he reached the house he found his supper hot on the table and the old man eating. She had stopped in her labor to prepare them food! He said to himself that she was a woman such as is not commonly found. Then he went to the door of their room and he called out,

"Here is the reed!"

He waited, expecting that she would call out to him to bring it in to her. But she did not. She came to the door and through the crack her hand reached out and took the reed. She said no word, but he heard her panting as an animal pants which has run for a long way.

The old man looked up from his bowl to say,

"Eat, or all will be cold." And then he said, "Do not trouble yourself yet—it will be a long time. I remember well when the first was born to me it was dawn before it was over. Ah me, to think that out of all the children I begot and your mother bore, one after the other—a score or so—I forget—only you have lived! You see why a woman must bear and bear." And then he said again, as though he had just thought of it newly, "By this time tomorrow I may be grandfather to a man child!" He began to laugh suddenly and he stopped his eating and sat chuckling for a long time in the dusk of the room.

But Wang Lung stood listening at the door to those heavy animal pants. A smell of hot blood came through the crack, a sickening smell that frightened him. The panting of the woman within became quick and loud, like whispered screams, but she made no sound aloud. When he could bear no more and was about to break into the room, a thin, fierce cry came out and he forgot everything.

"Is it a man?" he cried importunately, forgetting the woman. The thin cry burst out again, wiry, insistent. "Is it a man?" he cried again, "tell me at least this—is it a man?"

And the voice of the woman answered as faintly as an echo, "A man!"

He went and sat down at the table then. How quick it had all been! The food was long cold and the old man was asleep on his bench, but how quick it had all been! He shook the old man's shoulder.

"It is a man child!" he called triumphantly. "You are grandfather and I am father!"

The old man woke suddenly and began to laugh as he had been laughing when he fell asleep.

"Yes—yes—of course," he cackled, "a grandfather —a grandfather—" and he rose and went to his bed, still laughing.

Wang Lung took up the bowl of cold rice and began to eat. He was very hungry all at once and he could not get the food into his mouth quickly enough. In the room he could hear the woman dragging herself about and the cry of the child was incessant and piercing.

"I suppose we shall have no more peace in this house now," he said to himself proudly.

When he had eaten all he wished he went to the door again and she called to him to come in and he went in. The odor of spilt blood still hung hot upon the air, but there was no trace of it except in the wooden tub. But into this she had poured water and had pushed it under the bed so that he could hardly see it. The red candle was lit and she was lying neatly covered upon the bed. Beside her, wrapped in a pair of his old trousers, as the custom was in this part, lay his son.

He went up and for the moment there were no words in his mouth. His heart crowded up into his breast and he leaned over the child to look at it. It had a round wrinkled face that looked very dark and upon its head the hair was long and damp and black. It had ceased crying and lay with its eyes tightly shut.

He looked at his wife and she looked back at him. Her hair was still wet with her agony and her narrow eyes were sunken. Beyond this, she was as she always was. But to him she was touching, lying there. His heart rushed out to these two and he said, not knowing what else there was that could be said,

"Tomorrow I will go into the city and buy a pound of red sugar and stir it into boiling water for you to drink."

And then looking at the child again, this burst forth from him suddenly as though he had just thought of it, "We shall have to buy a good basketful of eggs and dye them all red for the village. Thus will everyone know I have a son!"

The next day after the child was born the woman rose as usual and prepared food for them but she did not go into the harvest fields with Wang Lung, and so he worked alone until after the noon hour. Then he dressed himself in his blue gown and went into the town. He went to the market and bought fifty eggs, not new laid, but still well enough and costing a penny for one, and he bought red paper to boil in the water with them to make them red. Then with the eggs in his basket he went to the sweet shop, and there he bought a pound and a little more of red sugar and saw it wrapped carefully into its brown paper, and under the straw string which held it the sugar dealer slipped a strip of red paper, smiling as he did so.

"It is for the mother of a new-born child, perhaps?"

"A first-born son," said Wang Lung proudly.

"Ah, good fortune," answered the man carelessly, his eye on a well-dressed customer who had just come in.

This he had said many times to others, even every day to someone, but to Wang Lung it seemed special and he was pleased with the man's courtesy and he bowed and bowed again as he went from the shop. It seemed to him as he walked into the sharp sunshine of the dusty street that there was never a man so filled with good fortune as he.

FIRST CHILD PROBABLY BOY, U.S. BIRTH STUDY INDICATES

from *The New York Times* (August 25, 1951)

Athens, Georgia, Aug. 24—The first-born child is more likely to be a boy than children born later. This is probably the reason for any increase found in the ratio of boys to girls born during World War II rather than as a result of the greater proportion of births to young mothers.

These are the conclusions of Dr. C. A. McMahan, sociology professor at the University of Georgia here, from a study of the birth registrations in the United States during the period 1915 to 1948.

The widespread belief that the ratio rises in wartime or immediately thereafter because "nature" compensates for war casualties from battle, starvation and other factors, evidently is not so, Dr. McMahan said.

"I'M SORRY, HENRY"

from *Anne of the Thousand Days*
by MAXWELL ANDERSON

A bedroom in York Palace. Anne Boleyn lies in bed with an infant beside her. Elizabeth Boleyn, Madge Shelton, and Norfolk are in the room. Madge and Elizabeth bend over the child.

ELIZABETH

What beautiful little hands! What a beautiful face!

ANNE

I think I shall call her after you, mother.

ELIZABETH

Hush!

ANNE

Well, he must know sooner or later. It may as well be soon.

NORFOLK

The king's at the door now, in case you wish to know.

ANNE

Not yet—not yet! Make some excuse. Not quite yet.

ELIZABETH

My dear, it's her father—the king.

ANNE

She is beautiful.

ELIZABETH

Yes, she is.

NORFOLK

(At the door.) It seems all's ready, Your Majesty.
(Henry enters and stands at the door, looking at the bed.)

HENRY

Nan, sweet—

ANNE

Yes, Henry?

HENRY

Do I come too soon? Will it tire you to speak?

ANNE

No, Henry. I'm glad to see you.

(Henry comes into the room, staring at the child.)

HENRY

I won't say much. Nor stay long. I just want to look at you two—the most precious freight ever a bed carried. My queen—and my prince—my son.

ANNE

My lord—

HENRY

Hush. Rest, my dear, and get strong. I shall call him

Edward. It's been a lucky name for English kings. A lucky name and a great name. Oh, little lad, may you better them all for fortune and fair renown.

ANNE

My lord, we—

HENRY

All my life as a king I have asked only one thing of heaven—that it grant me a son to carry on what I leave. And now heaven has given me more than I asked, for this is a handsome, bold boy's face, and already there's wit behind those eyes—

ANNE

Her name's to be Elizabeth.

HENRY

Whose—name?

ANNE

We have a little daughter . . . and her name's Elizabeth.

HENRY

A daughter! Why did no one tell me?

NORFOLK

They're all afraid of you, my lord. I offered to go. What can he do to an old man, I said, beyond the usual disemboweling? But they said no, wait.

HENRY

They were wrong. Whatever happens we must look our hap in the face. Why, girl, don't look so down. If we can have a healthy girl together we can have a healthy boy together. We shall get one yet.

ANNE

I'm sorry, Henry. As if it were my fault.

HENRY

It's no fault of anyone. There must be girls as well as boys.

"IT'S A BOY!"
from *David Copperfield*
by CHARLES DICKENS

"Well, ma'am, I am happy to congratulate you."

"What upon?" said my aunt sharply.

Mr. Chillip was fluttered again, by the extreme severity of my aunt's manner; so he made her a little bow, and gave her a little smile, to mollify her.

"Mercy on the man, what's he doing!" cried my aunt, impatiently. "Can't he speak?"

"Be calm, my dear ma'am," said Mr. Chillip, in his softest accents. "There is no longer any occasion for uneasiness, ma'am. Be calm."

It has since been considered almost a miracle that my aunt didn't shake him, and shake what he had to say out of him. She only shook her own head at him, but in a way that made him quail.

"Well, ma'am," resumed Mr. Chillip, as soon as he had courage, "I am happy to congratulate you. All is now over, ma'am, and well over."

During the five minutes or so that Mr. Chillip devoted to the delivery of his oration, my aunt eyed him narrowly.

"How is she?" said my aunt, folding her arms with her bonnet still tied on one of them.

"Well, ma'am, she will soon be quite comfortable, I hope," returned Mr. Chillip. "Quite as comfortable as we can expect a young mother to be, under these melancholy domestic circumstances. There cannot be any objection to your seeing her presently, ma'am. It may do her good."

"And she. How is she?" said my aunt, sharply.

Mr. Chillip laid his head a little more on one side, and looked at my aunt like an amiable bird.

"The baby," said my aunt. "How is she?"

"Ma'am," returned Mr. Chillip, "I apprehended you had known. It's a boy."

My aunt said never a word, but took her bonnet by the strings, in the manner of a sling, aimed a blow at Mr. Chillip's head with it, put it on bent, walked out, and never came back. She vanished like a discontented fairy; or like one of those supernatural beings whom it was popularly supposed I was entitled to see; and never came back any more.

"IT'S A GIRL!"

from *Madame Bovary*

by GUSTAVE FLAUBERT

But a pleasanter care came to occupy his mind. His wife was in the family way. The closer her time grew near, the greater the fuss he made of her. It was another fleshly link between them, a sort of perpetual reminder of a more complex union. When, from a distance, he surveyed her languid walk and her figure without stays turning limply on her hips, when he had her opposite to him, he could look at her at his ease, while she assumed all kinds of tired poses in her easy-chair. He could contain himself no longer. He would get up, kiss her, stroke her face, call her "little mamma," try to make her dance and, half laughing, half in tears, deliver himself of all the tender, loving baby-talk that came into his mind. The idea of being a father pleased him immensely. There was nothing lacking now. He knew human existence all along the line, and he settled down to it with a contented mind.

At first Emma felt a great astonishment; then she was anxious to get the confinement over, so that she might know how it felt to be a mother. But not being able to spend as much as she wanted to and to have a swing cradle with pink silk curtains, and baby-caps with embroidery on them, she gave it up in a fit of temper and ordered the whole thing from a local sewing-woman without choosing or discussing anything. Thus she took no interest in all those preparations which stimulate a mother's tenderness, and so perhaps from the very beginning there was something lacking in her affection.

However, as Charles kept harping on the brat at every meal, she soon began to dwell on the matter more continuously.

She hoped it would be a boy. He should be strong and dark, and they would call him George. And the thought of having a boy seemed somehow to compensate her for all her unrequited longings in the past. A man, in all events, is free. The realms of passion and the realms of travel are his to range at will. He can override obstacles, and no sort of happiness is necessarily beyond his reach. But a woman is checkmated at every turn. Flexible, yet powerless to move, she has at once her physical disabilities and her economic dependence, in the scales against her. Her will, like the veil of her bonnet, is tied to a string and flutters in every wind. Whenever a desire impels, there is always a convention that restrains.

She was confined one Sunday morning about six, just as the sun was getting up.

"It's a girl," said Charles.

She turned away her head and fainted.

THE POOR MALES

from *The New You and Heredity* (1950)

by AMRAM SCHEINFELD

"It's a man's world!" Women have been saying this, and flattered men have believed it, no doubt from the beginning of time.

But in one important respect it's all wrong. In health and physical well-being—not only as applied to the major conditions we've discussed, but also to the great majority of other afflictions—the human female, from *before* birth and throughout life, is favored far above the male.

The reasons for much of this discrimination are now clear. First, there are the general sex differences in the makeup and functioning of the body, which endow the female with many advantages in resisting or overcoming most diseases. Second, the male is much more vulnerable to many directly hereditary diseases and defects, as we'll presently explain. Third, there are environmental factors, such as differences in occupations, habits and behavior, which expose the male to greater hazards. But these differences in the paths taken by the two sexes are in themselves, to a considerable extent, outgrowths of inherent sex differences. In short, the margin of advantage which women have over men with regard to physical defectiveness or mortality is much less due to environmental factors than is generally supposed.

Long before anyone can talk of males leading "rougher and faster" lives the discrimination is apparent. Even in prenatal life, as we've seen, the male is more vulnerable to almost every adversity, a much higher proportion of males than females being carried off before birth. Further, more males die a-borning, more come into the world with congenital abnormalities, and in the first year of life, the average death rate among boy infants is 30 percent higher than among girls. Even if a boy baby and a girl baby should both tumble down the steps—or have any other accident of exactly the same kind—the chances of fatality are markedly greater for the boy.

As childhood proceeds, and as the chief hazards are reduced for a while, the differences between the sexes in mortality diminish considerably, but with male casualties still always in the lead. Then with maturity the curve goes sharply up again, becoming more marked in the middle and older ages, where in almost every major affliction, except in diabetes, cancers peculiar to women (breast, womb and ovary) and goiter, the male death rate is much higher. (By an excess of 40 percent for males in diseases of the heart, 130 percent in diseases of the arteries and angina pectoris, 100 percent in cirrhosis of the liver, 400 percent in ulcers, etc.) Further, the more that environmental factors for the two sexes have been improved and equalized, the proportionately greater has been the advantage to women, and *the more apparent it has become that females are genetically better constructed, have a more efficient internal chemical system, and in various other ways are biologically better adapted to resist most of the modern human afflictions.*

But in addition to all their general disadvantages, males from the beginning have one special handicap in the fact that Nature has *short-changed* them in some of their genes. At conception the female is started off with *two* X chromosomes (one from each parent), while the male gets only the single X from his mother, plus the very small Y from his father. And if any "black" genes are in the male's X chromosome, it's usually far more dangerous for him than it would be for his sister even if she got the very same X. This is always so when the defective gene is recessive, as it most often is. Here's why:

Where a female gets a recessive "black" gene in one of her X chromosomes, the chances are there will be a normal gene for the job in her other X. (Like a motorist with a spare tire when there's a blow-out.)

But if a male gets such a black gene in his single X, he's in a bad spot, because most often there is no corresponding gene in his very small Y chromosome to do the job. (So he's like a motorist who hasn't any spare tire.) Inasmuch, then, as there are a great many recessive genes in the X chromosome which every so often are defective, males, by and large, are directly exposed at conception to many more special defects and afflictions than are females. At the same time, in the fact that the male's X can come only from his mother, we have the explanation for a long-standing mystery as to why certain diseases are transmitted *only by way of mothers to their sons.*

Hemophilia

Most famous of the "sex-linked" conditions is this bleeding disease, which results when the "blood-coagulating" gene, located on the X chromosome, is defective. Usually it means death in early life, but if the afflicted male survives to manhood (never much beyond) he often becomes crippled by bleeding into the joints. While hemophilia is comparatively rare, it has been given much prominence in recent decades by this dramatic fact:

A single gene for hemophilia, passed on through Queen Victoria to one of her great-grandsons, the last little Czarevitch, may well have been a motivating factor in bringing on the Russian Revolution and in changing the course of the world's history.

As the world knows, it was because of their son's affliction that the credulous Czar and Czarina became victims of the designing Rasputin, who held out hopes of a cure through supernatural powers. From Rasputin, as from a spider, spread a web of intrigue, cruelty, debauchery, demoralization and mass indignation which helped to bring on the collapse of the empire and all the subsequent political developments. *If* the Czarevitch hadn't had hemophilia, *if* his parents hadn't become the prey of Rasputin, *if* Rasputin hadn't demoralized the court. . . . Thus a momentous structure of "ifs" can be built up, like an inverted pyramid, resting on that infinitesimal bit of substance, constituting a single gene, which found its way to one sad little boy.

In all, ten of Victoria's male descendants have suffered from hemophilia, and seven of her female descendants were carriers of the gene. Prince Leopold, one of Victoria's four sons, was definitely hemophiliac, and another son, who died young, also may have been. Of Victoria's five daughters, three—Victoria, Alice and Beatrice—were carriers, as were two granddaughters, the last Czarina, who bore one hemophiliac son, and the last Queen of Spain, who bore two. (Of the latter, one died from bleeding as a child, the other died following an automobile accident in Florida in 1938).

What of the present British royal family? Prior to the birth of a son in 1948 to Princess Elizabeth and her husband, *both* descendants of Queen Victoria, many were concerned about the possibility of its being a hemophiliac. Happily, geneticists were able to give assurance that there was no fear whatsoever of this occurring. Inasmuch as the great-grandfather of Princess Elizabeth and Rose, King Edward VII, definitely did not receive the dread gene, there is no possibility that they could be carrying it; and the fact that Princess Elizabeth's husband, Philip Mountbatten, is not a hemophiliac, is proof that he is also free of the gene.

Of special interest to geneticists is the fact that the particular hemophilia gene passed on by Queen Victoria appears to have arisen through a *mutation* (a sudden change), either in her or her mother. It is precisely in this way that many other cases of hemophilia are known to arise. (Professor J. B. S. Haldane estimates that about one gene in a hundred thousand for normal blood-clotting undergoes such a change.) If it were not for this constant production of new hemophilia genes, the disease might long ago have been eliminated through the deaths of afflicted males before they reached the reproductive ages.

As for hemophilia in a *female,* this could happen only if she received *two* defective genes (by way of each

X chromosome), one from her mother and one from a hemophiliac father. There have been such instances, with exceeding rarity, but no case of a woman with true hemophilia is known, because there is reason to believe that *any double dose of hemophilia genes would usually prove fatal before birth* or soon thereafter. (What may have been a case of female hemophilia was that of a little girl who, in 1947, bled to death at the age of 3.) Recent reports indicate, however, that even where a woman has only one hemophilia gene, a mild form of bleeding may sometimes show itself in maturity, or there may be chemical symptoms in the blood. If this latter fact is established, it may prove of inestimable value in detecting the women carriers of hemophilia genes and in providing warning against their having children. For the time being there is not much hope of curing hemophiliacs, although new treatments may make it possible to prolong their lives.

Color Blindness

This is by far the more prevalent of the hereditary sex-linked conditions afflicting chiefly males. As most everyone knows, color blindness in its common form is the inability to distinguish between red and green as *colors.* This does not mean—to answer a frequent question—that color-blind persons can't tell the difference between a red traffic light and a green one, because the one appears to them different in intensity from the other. Nevertheless, the flat colors of red and green may not be so distinguished, and it is for this reason that so many color-blind men during World War II were barred from the Air Force and certain other branches of service where good color vision was essential.

About 4 percent of the American males are definitely red-green color blind, and another 4 percent are partially deficient with regard to red-green or some other type of color vision. This is at least eight times the incidence in women. (American Indians are reported as having only a fourth as much color blindness as Whites, and Negroes only half as much.)

Explaining the sex difference in color blindness is the same hereditary mechanism found in hemophilia. The "color-blindness" gene is also carried in the X chromosome, and if the one X that a male receives has that gene, he will be color blind. The man's X chromosome, remember, can come only from his mother, so, as with hemophilia, it is only through mothers that color blindness is transmitted to sons.

Where a woman carries one X with a defective color-vision gene, and her second X has a normal gene, there is a fifty-fifty chance that any son will be color blind. But if the mother herself is color blind, because she carries two defective genes—which happens to about one woman in 200—every one of her sons is almost certain to be color blind.

What about the daughters? Only if the father is color blind and the mother is a carrier of the gene, or is herself color blind, will a daughter be color blind. But there is a possibility that even with one defective gene a woman may be slightly red-green color blind, recent studies showing that in some cases the "normal" gene does not quite overcome the influence of the defective one. This has significance because in these cases the women who are carriers of the "color-blindness" gene may be identified.

Many other eye defects which strike particularly at males have been tracked down to "sex-linked" genes. Included are certain, but not all forms of extreme nearsightedness, oscillating eyes *(nystagmus),* eye-muscle paralysis, enlarged cornea, defective iris, optic atrophy, and *retinitis pigmentosa* (in which the retina fills with pigment).

Altogether, eye defectiveness, *including blindness,* is far more prevalent among males than females. While only a few of the known sex-linked conditions directly produce blindness, some hereditary influences certainly contribute considerably to the much higher incidence of blindness among males. Making full allowances for the more frequent loss of eyesight among men through injuries and accidents, it is significant that the blind population in the United States starts off with about one-third more blind boys than girls, *three-fourths of these childhood cases originating before the fifth year, and more than half being of prenatal origin.* When we remember that the male in early life is inherently more vulnerable to almost every disease and defect, there is no reason to doubt that this applies also to blindness, even where there is no inheritance, as in congenital blindness due to syphilis or some other infectious disease.

Other Sex-Linked Conditions

Speech disorders provide another category in which males are overwhelmingly in the majority, but in this case there is as yet no clear proof that heredity is involved. We know only that stuttering is from five to ten times more common in little boys than in girls, the ratio increasing with age. *Reading difficulties* in school are also much more common among boys. While psychologists are inclined to attribute many cases of both speech and reading defects to early emotional disturbances or personality disorders, it is open to question whether environmental factors alone can explain away all the cases and the whole big difference between boys and girls in the incidence of these defects. Some inherent male weakness may well be involved.

We haven't by any means presented all of the hereditary conditions which afflict chiefly or exclusively males. For instance, the peculiar sweat-gland defect which makes the victim pant as dogs do, and a form of muscular atrophy where the man can't stand properly and appears to have a drunken gait. Many other known sex-linked conditions are too rare to warrant listing here, and there is every certainty that further research will lengthen the list of anti-male discriminators.

When we look for conditions that discriminate against women, we find very few, indeed, other than those related to the specifically female organs and functions. In all organic breakdowns (circulatory, respiratory, digestive, nervous system, etc.) male casualties are in the lead. . . .

But coming back to "sex-linked" genes, there are several of these which strike *particularly at women* for a very interesting reason:

In most of the other sex-linked conditions—hemophilia, color blindness, etc., the defective gene is recessive to the "normal" one. It is only because a male getting such a gene has *no "normal" one* to counteract it, as a woman usually has, that it asserts itself. But there are a few conditions which are caused by a *dominant* "black" gene in the X chromosome to which the "normal" gene is recessive. In such cases, women, therefore, would be particularly vulnerable because their *two* Xs open them to a double chance of getting the gene: If a father is affected, every daughter (but no son) will receive his single X with the defective gene, although if the mother is affected, there is the same fifty-fifty chance for either a son or a daughter to get the X with the gene. This explains the much higher incidence in women of one type of hereditary nosebleed, *thrombasthenia* and another sex-linked condition which produces defective enamel in the teeth. Apart from these, no clearly established dominant X-gene condition of importance in human beings is now on record.

Finally, there is a special type of gene which offers one more genetic disadvantage to the male. The condition is not too serious—no man gets sick or dies of it—but it nonetheless causes much worry, leads to the wasted spending of millions of dollars annually, and otherwise is sufficiently important to many men to warrant considerable discussion. We refer to:

Baldness

Comes a time when the hair on the head of the rugged male begins to loose its hold like the seeds of an autumn dandelion, presently to be gone with the wind.

Geneticists have found that there is a special kind of "black" gene called a *"sex-limited"* gene, and that ordinary "pattern" baldness is inherited through one of this type. Unlike the "sex-linked" genes, a "sex-limited" gene is carried not in the X chromosome, but in one of the general chromosomes common to both sexes. Thus, the "baldness" gene can be inherited equally by a man or a woman. But it doesn't *act* the same way in both. It behaves like a *dominant* in a man, only *one* gene being required to produce baldness. In a woman, however, the gene acts as a *limited recessive:*

She must receive *two* "baldness" genes before she will be affected, and even then, only partial baldness or merely a thinning of the hair may result. Again, why?

The best theory is that the glandular makeup of the two sexes governs the way in which the gene expresses itself or doesn't. Apparently, in a woman the lack of an excess of "male" hormones *(androgens)* and the absence of their effects keep the hair from falling out even where the baldness tendency is present, while, in a man, the excess of "male" hormones makes the hair follicles particularly vulnerable to the action of the "baldness" genes.

All of this should prompt us to give decent burial to the age-old fallacy that men are hardier than women, and, particularly, that little boys are "sturdier" and require less attention than their (presumably) "more delicate" little sisters. Where this fallacy may have arisen is in the notion that bigger bones and heavier muscles must necessarily mean greater resistance to disease and death. But as the author has pointed out elsewhere, people might do well to recall the parable of the sturdy oak and the frail reed, and what happened to each in the thunderstorm.

SEX PRESELECTION: AN EARLY METHOD

April, 1904

Gentlemen:

If you have no son to perpetuate your name, inherit your estates and fortune, why not consult with Mrs. F. M. Foie, a world wide experienced Trained Nurse: she is middle aged, has two handsome sons (gentlemen now). It does not take her twenty minutes to convince her listener of the surety of having his hopes realized . . . and as it [sex predetermination] rests entirely with him, she objects to consulting with any mother.

Prior to the birth of Mr. Grover Cleveland's third daughter (whom he named after me, Marion, during his last presidency at the White House) I assured Mr. Grover Cleveland that the expected new arrival would be a girl and to his annoyance and great vexation, it was; but since he graciously and so willingly accepted my wonderful never failing experience, two sons have since been born to his great delight and he has ceased further reproach to his amiable wife.

A gardener does not plant an onion and expect a potato to grow from it. I would stake my life if the heir did not appear after my instructions were fully acted upon.

Respectfully,
Mrs. F. Marion Foie
1810 Amsterdam Avenue
New York, New York

FACTORS INFLUENCING SEX RATIOS

by LANDRUM B. SHETTLES, M.D., D.SC., PH.D., F.A.C.S., F.A.C.O.G.

from *International Journal of Gynaecology and Obstetrics* (September 1970)

More human males than females are conceived and born. Conception rates as high as 160 males to 100 females have been found, and the average birth rate in the United States is about 105:100. The preponderance of males born also holds true among many animal species.

Since the simple model of sex determination—in which the X or Y chromosome of the sperm is joined with the X chromosome of the egg, with the XX combination producing a female offspring and the XY producing a male offspring—would indicate an equal birth rate for males and females, there must be other influences.

Observations of human sperm have distinguished two morphologic types. One type is larger with an oval head, the other, smaller with a rounded head. Observations of spermatogenesis have shown that the Y is much smaller than the X chromosome. For this reason, and for others to be discussed, it is probable that the small roundheaded sperm carry the Y chromosome (which produces a male offspring) and the large ovalheaded sperm carry the X chromosome (which produces a female offspring). Moreover, the incidences of the two types of sperm differ.

The differences in shape and size, as well as the noncorrespondence of the overall ratio of sperm type with the conception rate by sex, suggest that factors other than pure numbers are also operating. Speed is one such factor and would seem to favor the smaller Y-bearing sperm. Since these sperm are of less mass than the larger X-bearing sperm, they should be able to migrate through the reproductive secretions at the time of ovulation at a greater speed with the same amount of energy, thus making one of them more likely to effect fertilization. When tested in a capillary tube filled with ovulation cervical mucus over a distance of 1 foot, the smallheaded sperm invariably wins the race.

Continence, or lack thereof, is another factor which could favor one or the other type, depending on the circumstances. As has been mentioned above, continence is associated with an increased frequency of roundheads. Oligospermia (low sperm count) is associated with female offspring. In men with sperm counts of 20 million cc. and under, the likelihood of female offspring varies inversely with the count. With a sperm count of 1 million or less, only female offspring resulted; with a count of 10 million or under, 80 females to 20 males were born. The last condition indicates that the X chromosome-bearing (female-producing) sperm represents the survival of the fittest.

A third factor is longevity, which seems to favor the X-bearing sperm. When the egg is ready for fertilization, this factor may be unimportant, but it is possible for fertilization to occur by a robust sperm which has survived within the tube over a period of days until the egg is released at ovulation.

Interrelated with the above factors is differential environment within the cervix before and at ovulation. At the time of ovulation, the cervical mucus is, among other things, most abundant, most alkaline, of lowest viscosity, and most conducive to sperm penetration and survival. In contrast, the more acid environment within the cervix until a day or so before ovulation is unfavorable for sperm. During this time, only the more fit sperm have a chance for survival. The potential to have male and female offspring obviously varies greatly among men. Utilization of each lot of reproductive talents, so to speak, is governed greatly by the timing of coitus in relation to ovulation. In other words, the cyclic variation in physical and chemical characteristics of the reproductive fluids greatly influences the behavior and longevity of a given emission of X and Y sperm and, consequently, the likelihood of a male or female offspring.

While the interrelationships of the factors mentioned above in determining the sex of the offspring are not precisely known, they still permit the formulation of certain principles useful in influencing the sex at fertilization. *Those considered to favor female offspring are:* (1) intercourse, ceasing 2–3 days before ovulation, preceded by an acid douche of water and vinegar, (2) intercourse without female orgasm, (3) shallow penetration by the male at the time of orgasm, and (4) face-to-face position. *Those considered to favor male offspring are:* (1) intercourse at the time of ovulation, with prior abstinence during a given cycle, preceded by an alkaline douche of water and baking soda, (2) intercourse with female orgasm, (3) deep penetration at the time of male orgasm, and (4) vaginal penetration from the rear. The alkaline endocervical and orgasmal secretions, with position favoring deposition of the sperm in the cervical mucus at the external cervical os, make for the optimal physiologic racetrack for the Y sperm to outdistance in greater numbers the X sperm and, consequently, with the booster effect of the alkaline douche, an increased likelihood of male offspring. On the other hand, the lack of female orgasm, the deposition of semen in the acid vaginal secretions by shallow penetration at orgasm, the added slowing effect of the acid douche on sperm migration and longevity, and the more hostile and lengthy migratory pathway through the acid vaginal and cervical secretions 2–3 days before ovulation make more difficult the conditions for conception, and yet, when it occurs, an increased likelihood of female offspring. In other words, the easier the conditions for conception, the greater the chances for males; the more difficult the circumstances, the greater the incidence of females. Fresh egg and fresh sperm enhance the possibilities for males while fresh egg and older sperm, i.e. after emission, females.

In animals, certain of these principles have been

used with success which, in some cases, has been astonishing. The underlying factors in animals may be similar. Bhattacharya reports two types of sperm in bulls and rabbits, although there seems to be only one type in cocks. Lindahl discusses successful attempts to control sex of offspring by centrifuging bull semen with counterflow before artificial insemination. In humans, the above principles have been applied with success, both in influencing and also in predicting before birth the sex of offspring. On the basis of clinical results from experience in this field, it has been found that insemination or coitus at ovulation time or perhaps a few hours preovulation results in a male child in at least 80 percent of trials, while insemination or coitus 2–3 days prior to the time of ovulation results equally as often in a female offspring.

In a clinical study over a period of 35 years, related entirely to the ability to time ovulation from both subjective symptoms and objective findings, Kleegman cites results based on 150 births following a single exposure in the cycle of conception to husband and donor insemination. She observed a predominance of boy babies (80 percent) when insemination is done as close to ovulation as calculable, and a like incidence of girl babies when insemination is 48 hr. or more before estimated ovulation. Over the past 12 years, following the steps outlined previously, in 22 attempts for a male offspring, 19 were successful, and in 19 attempts for a female child, 16 were correct.

ANOTHER SEX SELECTION TECHNIQUE

from *Boy or Girl?* (1977)

by DR. ELIZABETH M. WHELAN, SC.D., M.P.H.

Unlike my predecessors, I will not *guarantee* that you will have a child of the sex of your choice, nor will I even say, as others have, that the method I'll describe is 80 to 90 percent effective. The best I can offer you is a 36 percent greater chance than you would otherwise have of having a boy (that is, increase your odds from fifty-five to about 68 percent) and a more modest 16 percent greater chance of having a girl (from fifty-five to 58 percent). . . .

Shettles and Rorvik stated that: ". . . with exposure to pregnancy two to twenty-four hours before ovulation, the babies were predominantly male (78 percent); with exposure to pregnancy thirty-six or more hours before ovulation, the babies were predominantly female."

Their advice, then, was that couples wanting a boy engage in coitus just before the moment of ovulation, when the egg is high in the Fallopian tube, and that those wanting a daughter do so in the early part of the cycle, avoiding the day or days just prior to ovulation.

These recommendations were interesting, and in the absence of any other more established advice, couples eagerly tried the "Shettles method."

For example, one respected gynecologist in Texas began advising his patients to follow the procedure for having boys. When I talked with him he was so upset over the results that he had given up recommending it. The first thirty couples who had followed the Shettles advice and had sexual intercourse as close to ovulation as possible had had girls! One of his patients, an artist, had taken the formula so seriously that she put it into graphic form, showing how Y spermatozoa were leap-frogging the X ones.

From the time this method was first introduced to the public, scientists had several reservations about it.

First, the advice contradicted both those early German studies and all animal studies, which showed that it was *early,* not late, insemination that favored a male birth. Second, Rorvik and Shettles had generally relied on Dr. Kleegman's cases, which were based almost exclusively on artificial insemination. In the majority of cases Dr. Shettles had not tested his methods on couples who conceived as a result of sexual intercourse.

Third, and potentially more serious, concentrating intercourse relatively late in the cycle—that is, on the day of or the day after ovulation—may carry with it some undesirable side effects. There is reason to believe that an egg begins to deteriorate soon after it is released from the ovary. If a couple is avoiding intercourse until they feel ovulation has occurred, they may be increasing the probability of fertilizing an "old egg" and assuming an increased probability of miscarriage and possibly other problems. For that reason, it is generally a good idea to avoid sexual intercourse on the day or two immediately following ovulation or, if you prefer, to use a mechanical form of contraception.

There are three methods of identifying boy and girl days:

The Basal Body Temperature Curve

A woman using this method takes her temperature every day upon awakening (orally is fine), starting just after the end of the menstrual flow. If you are in the middle of breakfast when you remember that the thermometer is still on the night table, it's too late to use it. Just leave that day's reading blank. Record a dot for each day on the menstrual calendar. After a few months, unless you have a very irregular cycle, you'll have a good idea of how many days elapse between the beginning of a cycle and the rise in temperature which indicates that ovulation has occurred. If you want a boy, have sexual relations on the sixth, fifth, and fourth days before the expected day of the temperature rise, and avoid sex, or if you prefer use a mechanical form of contraception, until three days after the temperature rise. If you do not conceive in the first three cycles of trying, move the schedule to the "right" one day—have coitus on the fifth, fourth, and third days before the expected rise in temperature.

If you want a girl, do just the opposite: avoid sex until two or three days before the expected rise in temperature. To avoid the problems that may accompany the fertilization of an "old" egg, *do not* have sexual intercourse without contraception on the day or two immediately following ovulation. Once the temperature has risen to its postovulatory level, there is no need for further precautions. Ovulation has already taken place and there is almost no risk of pregnancy.

"Wet Days" and "Dry Days"

Over the course of a few months, take note of the changes in vaginal secretions. These will give you a clue to the onset of ovulation. As I mentioned, the observation of mucus as a means of predicting ovulation is now widely used by couples practicing natural methods of birth control, and because this method may have some practical application to your sex predetermination efforts, I'll present some of the details on its use.

In the days following the end of the menstrual flow (possibly some six or more days before ovulation), the *infertile* mucus appears. It is sticky, cloudy and gluelike. Some two or three days before ovulation, you will notice the *fertile* mucus, the clear, slippery, wet discharge that stretches without breaking. Record these changes on your temperature chart.

There is significant variation from woman to woman in the timing and quantity of mucorrhea, so take the time to learn for yourself how many days elapse between the first vaginal secretions and the rise in body temperature. Generally speaking, sexual intercourse during the so-called infertile mucus days (if that is the same as six, five or four days before the shift in body temperature) will increase the chance of conceiving a male child. Intercourse during the fertile mucus days (one or two days before the shift) will increase the chance of conception of a female child.

Calendar Predictions

If the temperature and secretion-analysis methods sound too complicated to you, a calendar may be of some help in predicting boy and girls days, particularly if you have a regular menstrual cycle. But keep in mind that calendar methods are only a crude means of predicting ovulation. They generally give just a rough idea of when the most "pregnancy prone" days will occur. Remembering that ovulation takes place approximately fourteen days before the menstrual flow begins, you might make . . . calculations on a twenty-eight-day cycle.

All the scientific evidence gathered up to now points to the conclusion that you will significantly raise your odds on having a child of the sex of your choice by following one of these insemination timing patterns. Again, we are talking of an increase from the normal 50 percent odds on a boy birth to up to 68 percent with early-cycle insemination, and for a girl to about 56 or 57 percent when insemination takes place near ovulation.

VIII

FIRST DAY BIOGRAPHIES

From *The Prince and the Pauper*
by MARK TWAIN

In the ancient city of London, on a certain autumn day in the second quarter of the sixteenth century, a boy was born to a poor family of the name of Canty, who did not want him. On the same day another English child was born to a rich family of the name of Tudor, who did want him. All England wanted him too. England had so longed for him, and hoped for him, and prayed God for him, that, now that he was really come, the people went nearly mad for joy. Mere acquaintances hugged and kissed each other and cried. Everybody took a holiday, and high and low, rich and poor, feasted and danced and sang, and got very mellow; and they kept this up for days and nights together. By day, London was a sight to see, with gay banners waving from every balcony and housetop, and splendid pageants marching along. By night, it was again a sight to see, with its great bonfires at every corner, and its troops of revelers making merry around them. There was no talk in all England but of the new baby, Edward Tudor, Prince of Wales, who lay lapped in silks and satins, unconscious of all this fuss, and not knowing that great lords and ladies were tending him and watching over him—and not caring, either. But there was no talk about the other baby, Tom Canty, lapped in his poor rags, except among the family of paupers whom he had just come to trouble with his presence.

We are born in innocence. In blood and water and pain we are born, but in an unstained purity of heart. Wizened, crushed, our fogged eyes blinded by new light, our outraged skins shocked by a thirty degree drop in the envelope about us—still we are born a good vessel, innocent of corruption.

—LAURA Z. HOBSON, *Gentleman's Agreement*

IN HER DARK WOMB

from *Look Homeward, Angel*

by THOMAS WOLFE

. . . . a stone, a leaf, an unfound door; of a stone, a leaf, a door. And of all the forgotten faces.

Naked and alone we came into exile. In her dark womb we did not know our mother's face; from the prison of her flesh have we come into the unspeakable and incommunicable prison of this earth.

Which of us has known his brother? Which of us has looked into his father's heart? Which of us has not remained forever prison-pent? Which of us is not forever a stranger and alone?

O waste of loss, in the hot mazes, lost, among bright stars on this most weary unbright cinder, lost! Remembering speechlessly we seek the great forgotten language, the lost lane-end into heaven, a stone, a leaf, an unfound door. Where? When?

O lost, and by the wind grieved, ghost, come back again.

THE CAUL

from *David Copperfield*

by CHARLES DICKENS

Whether I shall turn out to be the hero of my own life, or whether that station will be held by anybody else, these pages must show. To begin my life with the beginning of my life, I record that I was born (as I have been informed and believe) on a Friday, at twelve o'clock at night. It was remarked that the clock began to strike, and I began to cry, simultaneously.

In consideration of the day and hour of my birth, it was declared by the nurse, and by some sage women in the neighborhood who had taken a lively interest in me several months before there was any possibility of our becoming personally acquainted, first, that I was destined to be unlucky in life; and secondly, that I was privileged to see ghosts and spirits; both these gifts inevitably attaching, as they believed, to all unlucky infants of either gender, born towards the small hours on a Friday night.

I need say nothing here on the first head, because nothing can show better than my history whether that prediction was verified or falsified by the result. On the second branch of the question, I will only remark, that unless I ran through that part of my inheritance while I was still a baby, I have not come into it yet. But I do not at all complain of having been kept out of this property; and if anybody else should be in the present enjoyment of it, he is heartily welcome to keep it.

I was born with a caul, which was advertised for sale, in the newspapers, at the low price of fifteen guineas. Whether sea-going people were short of money about that time, or were short of faith and preferred cork jackets, I don't know; all I know is, that there was but one solitary bidding, and that was from an attorney connected with the bill-broking business, who offered two pounds in cash, and the balance in sherry, but declined to be guaranteed from drowning on any higher bargain. Consequently the advertisement was withdrawn at a dead loss—for as to sherry, my poor dear mother's own sherry was in the market then—and ten years afterward the caul was put up in a raffle down in our part of the country, to fifty members at half a crown a head, the winner to spend five shillings. I was present myself, and I remember to have felt quite uncomfortable and confused, at a part of myself being disposed of in that way. The caul was won, I recollect, by an old lady with a hand-basket, who, very reluctantly, produced from it the stipulated five shillings, all in halfpence, and twopence halfpenny short—as it took an immense time and a great waste of arithmetic, to endeavor without any effect to prove it to her. It is a fact which will be long remembered as remarkable down there, that she was never drowned, but died triumphantly in bed, at ninety-two.

I WISH I HAD BEEN BORN IN THE MOON

from *The Life and Opinions of Tristram Shandy*

by LAURENCE STERNE

On the fifth day of November, 1718, which to the era fixed on, was as near nine calendar months as any husband could in reason have expected,—was I Tristram Shandy, Gentleman, brought forth into this scurvy and disastrous world of ours.—I wish I had been born in the Moon, or in any of the planets, (except Jupiter or Saturn, because I never could bear cold weather) for it could not well have fared worse with me in any of them (though I will not answer for Venus) than it has been in this vile, dirty planet of ours,—which, o' my conscience, with reverence be it spoken, I take to be made up of the shreds and clippings of the rest;—nor but the planet is well enough, provided a man could be born in it to a great title or to a great estate; or could any how contrive to be called up to public charges, and employments of dignity or power;—but that is not my case,—and therefore every man will speak of the fair as his own market has gone in it;—for which cause I affirm it over again to be one of the vilest worlds that ever was made;—for I can truly say, that from the first hour I drew my breath in it, to this, that I can now scarce draw it at all, for an asthma I got in skating against the wind in Flanders;—I have been the continual sport of what the world calls Fortune; and though I will not wrong her by saying, She has ever made me feel the weight of any great or signal evil;—yet with all the good temper in the world, I affirm it of her, that in every stage of my life, and at every turn and corner where she could get fairly at me, the ungracious duchess has pelted me with a set of as pitiful misadventures and cross accidents as ever small Hero sustained.

From *The Spectator*
by ADDISON AND STEELE

I was born to a small Hereditary Estate, which according to the Tradition of the Village where it lies, was bounded by the same Hedges and Ditches in William the Conqueror's Time that is at present, and has been delivered down from Father to Son whole and entire without the Loss or Acquisition of a single Field or Meadow, during the space of six hundred Years. There runs a story in the Family, that when my Mother was gone with Child of me about three Months, she dreamt that she was brought to bed of a Judge: Whether this might proceed from a Law-Suit which was then depending in the Family, or my Father's being a Justice of the Peace, I cannot determine; for I am not so vain as to think it presaged any Dignity that I should arrive at in my future Life; though that was the Interpretation which the

Neighborhood put upon it. The Gravity of my Behaviour at my very First Appearance in the World, and all the time that I sucked, seemed to favor my Mother's Dream: For, as she has often told me, I threw away my Rattle before I was two Months old, and would not make use of my Coral 'till they had taken away the Bells from it.

A BIRTH AT THE BARRYMORES'

from *Good Night, Sweet Prince*

by GENE FOWLER

A glassed-in carriage with an Irish coachman drew up at the entrance of the old Chestnut Street wharf. It was St. Valentine's day, 1882. A smallish woman sat upright in the brougham. Even the dullest beer-guzzler among the passing river men could sense that she was a personage.

She was Louisa Lane Drew, Mrs. John Drew, manager of the Arch Street Theatre, and, of late, Joseph Jefferson's famous Mrs. Malaprop in *The Rivals.* Mrs. Drew's black brougham was awaiting the arrival of the Steamboat *John A. Warner,* expected up from Wilmington to renew its yearly traffic. On this first voyage of the season, it would be carrying among other passengers a hard-working Philadelphian. He had been summoned home by Mrs. Drew, as if by royal command, from emergency labors in Delaware.

This passenger was Dr. J. Nicholas Mitchell, eminent homeopath and cousin of the distinguished Dr. S. Weir Mitchell, neurologist and man of letters. The fact that Dr. J. Nicholas Mitchell's illustrious cousin was an allopath had not marred their devotion to each other. In fact, both practitioners had been fighting cholera in Delaware for the past two weeks, each applying his own distinctive system of medicine, when Mrs. Drew's telegram had reached the homeopathic member of the Mitchell family.

Her younger daughter Georgianna, wife of actor Maurice Barrymore, was expecting a third child on this St. Valentine's Day in 1882. This confinement may have been uppermost in the mind of Mrs. Drew as she awaited the coming of the good homeopath. Her presence at the waterfront on a muddy, rainy afternoon would support such conjecture. Still, the Drew family were a capricious, wander-thought folk, and it may have been that she did not focus exclusively on the anticipated valentine.

A whistle sounded offshore. Mrs. Drew stirred from her reflections. The coachman opened the door to announce, "She's a-dockin'! The *John A. Warner's* a-nosin' in."

When the craft had been made fast, Dr. Mitchell came ashore and went at once to the carriage. The coachman untied the now sleepy horses, climbed wetly onto the box, and drove the expectant grandmother and the learned homeopath through the rain to Number 2008 Columbia Avenue.

As Mrs. Drew entered the hallway, Polly the maid helped her remove the dolman. "Mr. Sol Smith Russell is in the parlor, waitin'. He's excited."

Mrs. Drew removed her plumed turban. "Never mind Sol Smith Russell. How's Georgie?"

"She's havin' pains."

Mrs. Drew turned to the doctor who, having wrestled off his galoshes, was eying the clinical satchel. She gestured with a long hatpin. "I think you know the way, Doctor."

The big homeopath began to climb, Mrs. Drew following after him.

Sidney Drew appeared in the hallway carrying three-year-old Ethel, kicking and squealing, and followed by four-year-old Lionel, grinning and burbling happily.

Sidney had set Ethel on her feet and was trying to mollify her with a piece of sugar from a pocket supply he kept for horses.

"Uncle Googan won four dollars," Lionel confided to Mr. Russell. "Hooray!"

"Sh! Sh!" warned Sidney, glancing at the stairs. "Mustn't tell Mum Mum."

But Mrs. Drew, now in the bedroom of her daughter Georgie, was holding in her arms a new baby boy.

THE BIRTH OF ABRAHAM LINCOLN

from *Abraham Lincoln: The Prairie Years* (1926)

by CARL SANDBURG

In May and the blossomtime of the year 1808, Tom and Nancy with little Sarah moved out from Elizabethtown to the farm of George Brownfield, where Tom did carpenter work and helped farm.

The Lincolns had a cabin of their own to live in. It stood among wild crab apple trees.

And the smell of wild crab apple blossoms, and the low crying of all wild things, came keen that summer to the nostrils of Nancy Hanks.

The summer stars that year shook out pain and warning, strange laughters, for Nancy Hanks.

The same year saw the Lincolns moved to a place on the Big South Fork of Nolin's Creek, about two and a half miles from Hedgenville. They were trying to farm a little piece of ground and make a home. The house they lived in was a cabin of logs cut from the timber near by.

The floor was packed-down dirt. One door, swung on leather hinges, let them in and out. One small window gave a lookout on the weather, the rain or snow, sun and trees, and the play of the rolling prairie and low hills. A stick-clay chimney carried the fire smoke up and away.

One morning in February of this year, 1809, Tom Lincoln came out of his cabin to the road, stopped a neighbor and asked him to tell "the granny woman," Aunt Peggy Walters, that Nancy would need help soon.

On the morning of February 12, a Sunday, the granny woman was there at the cabin. And she and Tom Lincoln and the moaning Nancy Hanks welcomed into a world of battle and blood, of whispering dreams and wistful dust, a new child, a boy.

A little later that morning Tom Lincoln threw some extra wood on the fire, and an extra bearskin over the mother, went out of the cabin, and walked two miles up the road to where the Sparrows, Tom and Betsy lived. Dennis Hanks, the nine-year-old boy adopted by the Sparrows, met Tom at the door.

In his slow way of talking—he was a slow and a quiet man—Tom Lincoln told them, "Nancy's got a boy baby." A half sheepish look was in his eyes, as though maybe more babies were not wanted in Kentucky just then.

The boy, Dennis Hanks, took to his feet, down the road to the Lincoln cabin. There he saw Nancy Hanks on a bed of poles cleated to a corner of the cabin, under warm bearskins.

She turned her dark head from looking at the baby to look at Dennis and threw him a tired, white smile from her mouth and gray eyes. He stood by the bed, his eyes wide open, watching the even, quiet breaths of this fresh, soft red baby.

"What are you goin' to name him, Nancy?" the boy asked.

"Abraham," was the answer, "after his grandfather."

Soon came Betsy Sparrow. She washed the baby, put a yellow petticoat and a linsey shirt on him, cooked dried berries with wild honey for Nancy, put the one-room cabin in better order, kissed Nancy and comforted her, and went home.

Little Dennis rolled up in a bearskin and slept by the fireplace that night. He listened for the crying of the newborn child once in the night and the feet of the father moving on the dirt floor to help the mother and the little one. In the morning he took a long look at the baby and said to himself, "Its skin looks just like red cherry pulp squeezed dry, in wrinkles."

He asked if he could hold the baby. Nancy, as she passed the little one into Dennis's arms, said, "Be keerful, Dennis, fur you air the fust boy he's ever seen."

And Dennis swung the baby back and forth, keeping up a chatter about how tickled he was to have a new cousin to play with. The baby screwed up the muscles of its face and began crying with no let-up.

Dennis turned to Betsy Sparrow, handed her the baby, and said to her, "Aunt, take him! He'll never come to much."

IT WAS JUST A HABIT

from *The Autobiography of Will Rogers* (1949)
edited by DONALD DAY

In all the Autobiographys I ever read the first line was I was born at So-and-so on Such-and-such a Date. That is the accustomed first line of any Autobiography. Now the thing that struck me was if a fellow could give a reason why he was born you'd be a novelty. Now that is what has been holding me up on this Autobiography, I was born, but why? Now I've got it.

I was born because it was a habit in those days, people dident know anything else. In those days they dident put a Bounty on you for being born. Nowadays, the income Tax allows you 200 dollars for each child. Just removing his adanoids cost more than that, to say nothing about his food, Tonsils and Fraternoty pins. In those days a Doctor would bring you into the World for two Dollars a visit and make good money at it. Everything you was born with was supposed to be buried with you, but nowadays when you die about all you have left at the funeral is Scars and stitches.

If you had the stomack Ache the Doctor cured it; if you have it nowadays they remove it.

Ether has replaced pills as our national commodity.

So I figured out I was born as a Martyr to the ignorance of old time Drs. It was the law of averages that put me here. I beat Race Suicide by just one year, I arrived when childbirth was not grounds for divorce. If a family dident have at least 8 children in those days the Father was either in jail or deceased.

Mother and Baby doing well was our National yell.

It falls to the lot of a few to be born on National Holidays. A Child born on the Fourth of July, as my good friend George Cohan was, has to spend the rest of his life waving a flag. A child born on Christmas uses the Chimney for an entrance even after he is married. The New Years child arrived with wonderful resolutions and passed out by electrocution.

I am the only child in History who claims Nov. 4th as my Birthday, that is election day. Women couldent vote in those days so My Mother thought she would do something, so she stayed home and gave birth to me. The men were all away. I decided to get even with the Government. Thats why I have always had it in for the politicians.

I was the only child born on our beat that day. The news had to cross the Country by Pony Express, so it was two years later that it reached Washington, so Garfield was shot.

I was born on the Verdigris river, one mile below where Spencer Creek enters the river. Rutherford B. Hayes was President at the time of my birth.

I was the youngest and last of 7 Children. My folks looked me over and instead of the usual drowning procedure, they said, "This thing has gone far enough, if they are going to look like this, we will stop."

I was born at our old Ranch 12 miles north of Claremore, Okla (the home of the best Radium Water in the World). It was a big two story Log House, but on the back we had three rooms made of frame. Just before my birth, my mother, being in one of these frame rooms, had them remove her into the Log part of the House. She wanted me to be born in a Log House. She had just read the life of Lincoln. So I got the Log house end of it OK. All I need now is the other qualifications.

IX

THE BABY

From *Birth Without Violence* (1975)
by FREDERICK LEBOYER

What makes being born so frightful is the intensity, the boundless scope and variety of the experience, its suffocating richness.

People say—and believe—that a newborn baby feels nothing. He feels *everything*.

Everything—utterly, without choice or filter or discrimination.

Birth is a tidal wave of sensation, surpassing anything we can imagine. A sensory experience so vast we can barely conceive of it. We must behave with the most enormous respect toward this instant of birth, this fragile moment.

> The baby is between two worlds. On a threshold. Hesitating.
>
> Do not hurry. Do not press. Allow this child to enter.
>
> What an extraordinary thing—this little creature, no longer a fetus, not yet a newborn baby.
>
> This little creature is no longer inside his mother, yet she's still breathing for them both.

An elusive, ephemeral moment. Leave this child. Alone. Because this child is free—and frightened. Don't intrude; stay back. Let time pass. Grant this moment its slowness, and its gravity.

From *Songs for Patricia*
by NORMAN ROSTEN

Now that you're born
And I spell the word out

To be alive
Is much more than your weight

Or the balance of blood
So new in your veins

To be born is
Mostly musical

Like a hymnody
After the utter dark

From a sleep is seen
The growing light

And I sit and wait
Listening to clocks

While a shadow is thrown
Beyond my death

A BABY ANNOUNCEMENT CARD

Wednesday, October 3, 1951
VARIETY OF LIFE
Legitimate

"One Night of Love"
Or
"Nine Months of Regret"
A New Melodrama
Produced by Jean Carson
by Arrangement with Stanley Parlan
Staged by Dr. Emanuel M. Greenberg
Written by Ova & Sperm Atazoa

Last evening the curtain went up at the Madison Avenue Theatre on a new melodrama by those prolific authors, Ova & Sperm Atazoa.

Show might have fared better with an out-of-town tryout, as opening night ran too long. Certain scenes could well have been eliminated. Originally set opening date was based upon premature optimism on the part of the producers, who explained the delay in the opening night was due to circumstances beyond their control.

Leading role was overplayed in the first two acts by Jean Carson, but in the third act she came through beautifully. Overplaying could have been due to opening night nerves, especially since this type of role is completely new to Miss Carson—definitely not type casting.

Plot is not a new one. It's been done many times before. Situation as developed shows little imagination, but the cast carries the show with all-round polished performances, and Dr. Greenberg's direction is top drawer.

Third act writing and staging brought the show to a beautiful climax with the entrance of Carson Alexander Parlan, a newcomber. Part was neatly played, and he looked like a dream. His crying scene was one of the best this reviewer has seen in years—played in a high key. The costuming here was especially interesting, striking a note of stark reality.

Mention should be made of Stan Parlan, a bit player, who deserves accolades for his performance as the father. He showed proper amount of anxiety and nervousness in two comedy relief scenes.

Show has good stock possibilities.

INFANT JOY
by WILLIAM BLAKE

"I have no name;
I am but two days old."
What shall I call thee?
"I happy am;
Joy is my name."
—Sweet joy befall thee!

Pretty joy!
Sweet joy, but two days old;
Sweet joy I call thee:
Thou dost smile:
I sing the while,
Sweet joy befall thee!

From *The Prelude*
by WILLIAM WORDSWORTH

Bless'd the infant Babe,
(For with my best conjectures I would trace
The progress of our Being) the Babe who sleeps
Upon his Mother's breast, who, when his soul
Claims manifest kindred with an earthly soul
Doth gather passion from his Mother's eye!
Such feeling pass into his torpid life
Like an awakening breeze, and hence his mind
Even (in the first trial of its powers)
Is prompt and watchful, eager to combine
In one appearance, all the elements
And parts of the same object, else detach'd
And loath to coalesce. Thus, day by day,
Subjected to the discipline of love,
His organs and recipient faculties
Are quicken'd, are more vigorous, his mind spreads,
Tenacious of the forms which it receives.
In one beloved presence, nay and more,
In that most apprehensive habitude
And those sensations which have been derived
From this beloved Presence, there exists
A virtue which irradiates and exalts
All objects through all intercourse of sense.
No outcast he, bewildered and depressed;
Along his infant veins are interfused
The gravitation and the filial bond
Of nature, that connect him with the world.
Emphatically such a Being lives,
An inmate of this active universe;
From nature largely he receives; nor so
Is satisfied, but largely gives again,
For feeling has to him imparted strength,
And powerful in all sentiments of grief,
Of exultation, fear, and joy, his mind
Even as an agent of the one great mind,
Creates, creator and receiver both,

Working but in alliance with the works
Which it beholds.—Such, verily, is the first
Poetic spirit of our human life;
By uniform control of after years
In most abated or suppress'd, in some,
Through every change of growth or of decay,
Pre-eminent 'till death.

The nurselings spare; nor exercise thy rage on new-born life.

—From DRYDEN's translation of VIRGIL's *Second Georgic*

REFLECTION ON BABIES

from *The Face Is Familiar*
by OGDEN NASH

A bit of talcum
Is always walcum.

(Editor's note: Actually, pediatricians today frown upon the excessive use of talcum because it can be harmful to the baby's lungs.)

A couple in Martinez, Colorado, named their newborn baby Robert J. They left the middle name open to permit him to adopt one of his own choice when he became old enough.

—*The New York Times Magazine*

THE FIRST BABY

from *Infant and Child in the Culture of Today* (1974)

by ARNOLD GESELL, FRANCES L. LIG, AND LOUISE BATES AMES

Husband and wife choose each other, but except when they adopt, they cannot choose their children. The parents cannot determine in advance the kind of children who will be born of marriage. That is the great adventure of life. The newborn infant is an individual in his own right, and must be accepted as such.

Indeed, the individuality of the infant is to a significant degree determined before birth; well before the fourth month of gestation the prenatal child has taken on certain fundamental features of the individuality that will become apparent in infancy. Through no process of maternal impression or of wishful thinking is it possible to determine in advance whether this child will be blonde or brunette, athletic or retiring; whether he will love the sea better than the mountains.

After the child is born, a parent with an overweening faith in the influences of environment may continue to harbor a preconceived image with excessive determination. In extreme instances there is a positive fixation upon a specific type of child. This fixation later impels the mother or father or both to attempt too strongly to make over the child in terms of this image. Matters grow still worse if the father has one ideal and the mother another. Such fixations are detrimental to the developmental welfare of the infant. From the very outset, parents must temper their wishes and school their affections. They must accept the infant for what he is. They should become consistently inquisitive about one permanent question, namely: *What kind of child is he—What is his true nature?*

This question is shrouded in darkness before birth, but will be ultimately answered in visible patterns of behavior. Even during the prenatal period the behavior characteristics of the future infant are undergoing preliminary development. So-called quickening is more than a mere index of life. It is the product of a patterned behavior response made possible by the maturing nervous system. The twenty-week-old fetus is already so far advanced in his bodily organization and in the sculpturing of his physiognomy that he is distinctly human in his lineaments, and assumes in the fluid medium of the uterus postures and attitudes not unlike those that he will display when he lies safely ensconced in his bassinet.

Although the mother's imagery cannot be too precise, the realization that the individuality of the child is in the making puts her in a better position to identify herself during the period of pregnancy with the developmental welfare of the child.

The impending crisis of the first birth is sometimes so magnified that the anxieties and fears of the mother prevent her from building up a natural, constructive outlook. The supervision of the obstetrician may relate itself too much to the birth episode alone. Expectant parents would greatly benefit from a prepediatric type of guidance, directed toward the postnatal career of the child. For example, it is probable that breast feeding would be more widely adopted in the interests of the child if both obstetricians and pediatricians encouraged the mother to nurse the child during his early months.

Such anticipations are especially important in the case of the first born child, when the mother has so many new orientations to accomplish. These orientations are physical or biological on the one hand, and cultural on the other. The attitude and expectancies of the mother during the period of gestation, therefore, have far-reaching implications for the early career of the forthcoming child.

The care and management of the child will depend not only upon the practical details of technique, but also upon the philosophy of the parents. The welfare of the child is best safeguarded by a developmental philosophy which respects at every turn the individuality of the child and the relativities of immaturity. The foundations of this philosophy are best laid before the baby is born.

BABY WORSHIP

from *Barchester Towers*

by ANTHONY TROLLOPE

"Diddle, diddle, diddle, diddle, dum, dum, dum," said or sung Eleanor Bold.

"Diddle, diddle, diddle, diddle, dum, dum, dum," continued Mary Bold, taking up the second part in this concerted piece.

The only audience at the concert was the baby, who however gave such vociferous applause, that the performers, presuming it to amount to an encore, commenced again.

"Diddle, diddle, diddle, diddle, dum, dum, dum: hasn't he got lovely legs?" said the rapturous mother.

"H'm, 'm 'm 'm 'm," simmered Mary, burying her lips in the little fellow's fat neck, by way of kissing him.

"H'm, 'm 'm 'm," simmered the mother, burying her lips also in his fat round short legs. "He's a dawty little bold darling, so he is: and he has the nicest little pink legs in all the world, so he has"; and the simmering and the kissing went on all over again, as though the ladies were very hungry, and determined to eat him.

"Well, then, he's his mother's own darling: well, he shall—oh, oh—Mary, Mary—did you ever see? What am I to do? My naughty, naughty, naughty, naughty, naughty little Johnny." All these energetic exclamations were elicited by the delight of the mother in finding that her son was strong enough, and mischievous enough, to pull all her hair out from under her cap. "He's been and pulled down all mamma's hair, and he's the naughtiest, naughtiest, naughtiest little man that ever, ever, ever, ever, ever—"

A regular service of baby worship was going on. Mary Bold was sitting on a low easy chair, with the boy in her lap, and Eleanor was kneeling before the object of her idolatry. As she tried to cover up the little fellow's face with her long, glossy, dark brown locks, and permitted him to pull them hither and thither, as he would, she looked very beautiful in spite of the widow's cap which she still wore.

"We'll cover him up till there sha'nt be a morsel of his little 'ittle 'ittle 'ittle nose to be seen," said the mother, stretching her streaming locks over the infant's face. The child screamed with delight, and kicked till Mary Bold was hardly able to hold him.

From *The Way of All Flesh*
by SAMUEL BUTLER

The birth of his son opened Theobald's eyes to a good deal he had but faintly realized hitherto. He had had no idea how great a nuisance a baby was. Babies come into the world so suddenly at the end, and upset everything so terribly when they do come: why cannot they steal in upon us with less of a shock to the domestic system? His wife, too, did not recover rapidly from her confinement; she remained an invalid for months; here was another nuisance and an expensive one, which interfered with the amount which Theobald liked to put by out of his income against, as he said, a rainy day, or to make provision for his family if he should have one. Now he was getting a family, so that it became all the more necessary to put money by, and here was the baby hindering him. Theorists may say what they like about a man's children being a continuation of his own identity, but it will generally be found that those who talk in this way have no children of their own. Practical family men know better.

About twelve months after the birth of Ernest there came a second, also a boy, who was christened Joseph, and in less than twelve months afterwards, a girl, to whom was given the name of Charlotte. A few months before this girl was born Christina paid a visit to the John Pontifexes in London, and, knowing her condition, passed a good deal of time at the Royal Academy exhibition looking at the types of female beauty portrayed by the Academicians, for she had made up her mind that the child this time was to be a girl. Alethea warned her not to do this, but she persisted, and certainly the child turned out plain, but whether the pictures caused this or no, I cannot say.

Theobald had never liked children. He had always got away from them as soon as he could, and so had they from him; oh, why, he was inclined to ask himself, could not children be born into the world grown up? If Christina could have given birth to a few full-grown clergymen in priest's orders—of moderate views, but inclining rather to Evangelicism, with comfortable livings and in all respects facsimiles of Theobald himself—why, there might have been more sense in it; or if people could buy ready-made children at a shop of whatever age and sex they liked, instead of always having to make them at home and to begin at the beginning with them—that might do better, but as it was he did not like it.

THE BABIES
from *Mark Twain's Speeches*

I like that. We have not all had the good fortune to be ladies. We have not all been generals, or poets, or statesmen; but when the toast works down to the babies, we stand on common ground. It is a shame that for a thousand years the world's banquets have utterly ignored the baby, as if he didn't amount to anything. If you will stop and think a minute—if you will go back fifty or one hundred years to your early married life and recontemplate your first baby—you will remember that he amounted to a good deal, and even something over. You soldiers all know that when that little fellow arrived at family headquarters you had to hand in your resignation. He took entire command. You became his lackey, his mere body-servant, and you had to stand around, too. He was not a commander who made allowances for time, distance, weather, or anything else. You had to execute his order whether it was possible or not. And there was only one form of marching in his manual of tactics, and that was the double-quick. He treated you with every sort of insolence and disrespect, and the bravest of you didn't dare to say a word. You could face the death storm at Donelson and Vicksburg, and give back blow for blow; but when he clawed your whiskers, and pulled your hair, and twisted your nose, you had to take it. When the thunders of war were sounding in your ears you set your faces toward the batteries, and advanced with steady tread; but when he turned on the terrors of his war-whoop you advanced in the other direction, and mighty glad of the chance, too. When he called for soothing-syrup, did you venture to throw out any side-remarks about certain services being unbecoming an officer and a gentleman? No. You got up and *got* it. When he ordered his pap bottle and it was not warm, did you talk back? Not you. You went to work and *warmed* it. You even descended so far in your menial office as to take a suck at that warm, insipid stuff yourself, to see if it was right—three parts water to one of milk, a touch of sugar to modify the colic, and a drop of peppermint to kill those immortal hiccoughs. I can taste that stuff yet. And how many things you learned as you went along! Sentimental young folks still take stock in that beautiful old saying that when the baby smiles in his sleep, it is because the angels are whispering to him. Very pretty, but too thin—simply wind on the stomach, my friend. If the baby proposed to take a walk at his usual hour, two o'clock in the morning, didn't you rise up promptly and remark, with a mental addition which would not improve a Sunday-school book *much,* that that was the very thing you were about to propose yourself? Oh! you were under good discipline, and as you went fluttering up and down the room in your undress uniform, you not only prattled undignified baby talk, but even tuned up your martial voices and tried to *sing!*—*Rock-a-by Baby in the Tree-top,* for instance. What a spectacle for an Army of the Tennessee! And what an affliction for the neighbors, too; for it is not everybody within a mile around that likes military music at three in the morning. And when you had been keeping this sort of thing up two or three hours, and your little velvet-head intimated that nothing suited him like exercise and noise, what did you do? You simple *went* on until you dropped in the last ditch. The idea that a *baby* doesn't *amount* to anything! Why, *one* baby is just a house and a front yard full by itself. *One* baby can furnish more business than you and your whole Interior Department can attend to. He is enterprising, irrepressible, brimful of lawless activities. Do what you please, you can't make him stay on the reservation. Sufficient unto the day is one baby. As long as you are in your right mind don't you ever pray for twins. Twins amount to a permanent riot. And there ain't any real difference between triplets and an insurrection.

Yes, it was high time for a toastmaster to recognize the importance of the babies. Think what is in store for the present crop! Fifty years from now we shall all be dead, I trust, and then this flag, if it still survives (and let us hope it may), will be floating over a Republic numbering 200,000,000 souls, according to the settled laws of our increase. Our present schooner of State will have grown into a political leviathan—a Great Eastern. The cradled babies of to-day will be on deck. Let them be well trained, for we are going to leave a big contract on their hands. Among the three or four million cradles now rocking in the land are some which this nation would preserve for ages as sacred things, if we could know which ones they are. In one of these cradles the unconscious Farragut of the future is at this moment teething—think of it! —and putting in a world of dead earnest, unarticulated, but perfectly justifiable profanity over it, too. In another the future renowned astronomer is blinking at the shining Milky Way with but a languid interest—poor little chap! —and wondering what has become of that other one they call the wet-nurse. In another the future great historian is lying—and doubtless will continue to lie until his earthly mission is ended. In another the future President is busying himself with no profounder problem of state than what the mischief has become of his hair so early; and in a mighty array of other cradles there are now some 60,000 future office-seekers, getting ready to furnish him occasion to grapple with that same old problem a second time. And in still one more cradle, somewhere under the flag, the future illustrious commander-in-chief of the American armies is so little burdened with his approaching grandeurs and responsibilities as to be giving his whole strategic mind at this moment to trying to find out some way to get his big toe into his mouth—an achievement which, meaning no disrespect, the illustrious guest of this evening turned *his* entire attention to some fifty-six years ago; and if the child is but a prophecy of the man, there are mighty few who will doubt that he *succeeded.*

WHAT HAPPENS TO YOUR NEWBORN BABY?

by AMELIA LOBSENZ

from *Today's Woman* (October 1951)

I saw my baby for the first time as we shared a stretcher taking us from the delivery room to the maternity wing. For a moment only, as a nurse held him up, I hazily glimpsed my son's wrinkled face and heard his cry. Then I fell asleep.

When I woke again I was in my room and Michael was gone. I knew, of course, that he was just a few hundred feet away, safe in a bassinet in the newborn nursery. But I was sure of nothing.

All the fears and worries of a new mother plagued me. Had he been born normal and healthy? Was the right baby marked with my name? Was he being washed and fed and kept warm? When would I see him?

The nurse who answered my buzz had a crisp voice. "Of course he's all right. Don't worry, that's probably some other baby crying." And she hurried along.

All new mothers worry and have these questions. For almost all of the crucial first seven days, a newborn baby is away from his mother—unless she has a rooming-in arrangement. I have been able to find out exactly what happens to a baby from the instant of birth to the moment he leaves for home.

The baby I saw born—he was later named Robert—was a seven-pound boy. Robert's first minutes of life were phenomenally busy. First he was dangled in mid-air, head down. When there was no responsive wail, the doctor pressed one finger on the infant's tongue. Backslapping and other shockers, I learned later, are no longer used. Immediately the baby yelled and expanded his lungs.

The obstetrician cut and dressed the umbilical cord, then examined Robert minutely. He counted fingers and toes, peered into his eyes and ears, poked and prodded his body. In accordance with state law, a nurse dropped Argyrol solution (some states require penicillin, others silver nitrate) into Robert's eyes as a precaution against infection.

One nurse footprinted Robert. Another circled each wrist with a beaded bracelet. The beads on one spelled out his mother's name, on the other her case number. To help make identification foolproof, two nurses and the doctor corroborated Robert's sex.

Robert's mother came out of the anesthetic for a moment. The nurse showed her the baby. "You have a son. A fine boy." The woman smiled, then closed her eyes. She was wheeled to her room. Robert was put in a heated crib, covered with sterilized blankets, and I followed the nurse carrying him down the hall. Though Robert was only fifteen minutes old, he was displayed for a moment behind a glass partition. Robert's father grinned. When Robert was brought into the newborn nursery all the nurses who weren't busy with other infants hurried up to see the newcomer.

"Well, look at little Buttercup," said one nurse.

I smiled at Miss Katherine Ginty, a pleasant motherly woman who is the supervisor in the nursery.

"We always give them nicknames," she said. "I suppose you've heard that hospital nurses at feeding time go down the aisles and stick a bottle in each mouth, then start from the first bassinet and take each bottle away, no matter how much the baby has drunk?

"Well, that's not true. We hold our babies in our arms when we feed them—and we feed them when they're hungry. We follow each baby's individual schedule. It means more bookkeeping for us, but it also means less crying."

I watched a nurse put Robert "around the pole." Every newborn is placed at first in a bassinet which forms part of a circle around a pole in the center of the nursery. There he's more easily observed. In these first hours, nurses keep an extra-careful watch on his condition.

The same nurse checked Robert's identification beads, put a name card on his bassinet, weighed and measured him, entered his name in the record book. Over his crib she adjusted a wire-protected lamp, to give him the extra heat he needed. The outside world is pretty cold after the snugness of the womb.

Then, placed on his side to allow a free flow of mucus from his nose and mouth, Robert was left to sleep. When he rested I inspected the nursery, where everyone who enters—nurses, doctors, cleaners—must have been chest X-rayed for tuberculosis and had a yearly health examination. I was scrubbed to my elbows in a germicidal solution, dressed in a sterile mask and gown, but I was still careful not to get too close to any of the babies.

The nursery had cream-colored ceiling tops, pale green walls and a gray tile floor. There were no curtains that would catch dust. The walls were covered with a sound-reducing material and the thermometer hovered around 77 degrees.

Thirty babies were lying in identical stainless-steel and plexiglas bassinets. Each bassinet is shaped like an inverted U so a baby can be rolled into his mother's room and above her bed without stirring from his own. One side of the plexiglas cover hinges open so a baby can be cared for without the nurse having to pick him up. In an attached cabinet are the infant's personal equipment: his individual lotion, thermometer, enough linen and diapers for a day.

In the nursery, the bassinets are at least six inches apart to help guard against spreading infection. Each time a nurse finishes a task for one baby, she washes her hands before touching another child. Nurses assigned to care for the newborn babies work nowhere else in the hospital, I found. The resident pediatricians and others on the nursery staff—dieticians, porters, nurses' aides—

are restricted similarly from all other wards as much as possible. Even nursery linens are laundered apart from those of the rest of the hospital.

In most hospitals, the nursery stands at the dead end of a wing corridor so it won't become a passageway to any other room. A nurse is always on duty to keep out visitors.

The door is one of the nursery's most difficult stations because so many friends and relatives want to see babies at odd times.

Only once, Miss Ginty told me, was this rule waived. The mother had borne six children. Each had died at birth or soon afterward and this seventh delivery had been a Caesarian. The mother couldn't make the trip to the nursery to see her child, nor was it considered safe to take the baby through the halls to her. So for six days, to reassure her that her long-desired son was alive and well, every one of her visitors was shown the baby, regardless of what time they came, so that they could report his progress.

Equally protected from infection is the formula room, where the bottle-fed babies' formulas are prepared.

Formula is made daily by five student nurses who work under Miss Stella's direction. I followed a trayload of formula-filled bottles back into the nursery. True to their built-in hunger clocks, many of the babies were awake, yowling. Each nurse double-checked the name on each bottle cap with the name on the end of the bassinet before picking up a baby to feed it.

I remembered how I had worried that my baby wasn't getting affection. Miss Ginty must have read my thought. She said:

"Baby nurses must love babies. Otherwise they could never stand the monotony of the nursery and the crying."

She showed me what the nurses call "the books"—a stack of ledgers which must be kept up to the minute. Each baby has his own book. In it are entered his weight (taken every other day), his temperature, a record of his bowel movements, his formula and feeding times. Any problems—they may range from too-frequent vomiting to red buttocks—are listed on a gripe sheet. The innocent-seeming symptoms that sometimes show up on this can give a doctor precious hours of warning of any potentially dangerous condition.

Finally, there is even a "wristlet book," checked thrice daily as the nurses inspect the identification bracelets on each child's arm to make sure they are securely attached.

Mealtime over, I went back to newborn Robert.

"He's ready to be cleaned up now," a nurse said. She turned him over, took his temperature. Then Argyrol was wiped from his eyes and his skin was cleaned with cotton and baby lotion. His hair was scrubbed with soap and water. Then he was placed in warm blankets, moved away from "the pole" and placed "in line" with the "older" babies. He was now ready to rest for twelve more hours.

Miss Ginty checked his chart before leaving him. She nodded. "His kidneys and bowels have functioned normally, his air passages are open."

"Why not feed him now?" I asked.

"It might cause dangerous vomiting," she explained. "We give him water twelve hours after birth, and his first formula at sixteen hours. From then on, he's fed on his regular schedule. Unless he's breast-fed, he won't be fed by his mother until the third day. From then on she will give him his ten A.M. bottle. That's her only chore while she's here."

I watched Robert go through a typical day. At 7:30 A.M.—when most of the mothers were eating their breakfasts and wondering whether anyone was looking after their babies—Robert was getting his "morning care."

He was washed with sterile cotton dipped in baby lotion. He was weighed, diapered (not with pins but with string tied about his waist as an extra safety measure), given a fresh shirt, sheet and blanket. His temperature was taken. He napped until 9:15 when, accompanied by his bottle, he set out in his traveling bassinet for his mother's room. There, for about forty-five minutes, he ate.

Back in the nursery he was turned on his right side and tucked in for sleep. "The stomach empties from left to right," a nurse explained. "In this position his food digests more easily. So we leave him on the right side for two hours, then turn him and leave him on the left until his next feeding."

At 7 P.M. Robert's father came to visit. Behind the glass door a nurse held up the swaddled infant while his father waved and clucked.

From *Jean-Christophe*
by ROMAIN ROLLAND

The new-born child stirs in his cradle. Although the old man left his sabots at the door when he entered, his footsteps make the floor creak. The child begins to whine. The mother leans out of her bed to comfort it; and the grandfather gropes to light the lamp, so that the child shall not be frightened by the night when he awakes. The flame of the lamp lights up old Jean Michel's red face, with its rough white beard and morose expression and quick eyes. He goes near the cradle. His cloak smells wet, and as he walks he drags his large blue slippers. Louisa signs to him not to go too near. She is fair, almost white; her features are drawn; her gentle, stupid face is marked with red in patches; her lips are pale and swollen, and they are parted in a timid smile; her eyes devour the child—and her eyes are blue and vague; the pupils are small, but there is an infinite tenderness in them.

The child wakes and cries, and his eyes are troubled. Oh! how terrible! The darkness, the sudden flash of the lamp, the hallucinations of a mind as yet hardly detached from chaos, the stifling, roaring night in which it is enveloped, the illimitable gloom from which, like blinding shafts of light, there emerge acute sensations, sorrows, phantoms—those enormous faces leaning over him, those eyes that pierce through him, penetrating, are beyond his comprehension! . . . He has not the strength to cry out; terror holds him motionless, with eyes and mouth wide open and he rattles in his throat. His large head, that seems to have swollen up, is wrinkled with the grotesque and lamentable grimaces that he makes; the skin of his face and hands is brown and purple, and spotted with yellow . . .

"Dear God!" said the old man with conviction. "How ugly he is!"

He put the lamp down on the table.

Louisa pouted like a scolded child. Jean Michel looked at her out of the corner of his eye and laughed.

"You don't want me to say that he is beautiful? You would not believe it. Come, it is not your fault. They are all like that."

The child came out of the stupor and immobility into which he had been thrown by the light of the lamp and the eyes of the old man. He began to cry. Perhaps he instinctively felt in his mother's eyes a caress which made it possible for him to complain. She held out her arms for him and said:

"Give him to me."

The old man began, as usual, to air his theories:

"You ought not to give way to children when they cry. You must just let them cry."

But he came and took the child and grumbled:

"I never saw one quite so ugly."

Louisa took the child feverishly and pressed it to her bosom. She looked at it with a bashful and delighted smile.

"Oh, my poor child!" she said shamefacedly. "How ugly you are—how ugly! and how I love you!"

Jean Michel went back to the fireside. He began to poke the fire in protest, but a smile gave the lie to the moroseness and solemnity of his expression.

"Good girl!" he said. "Don't worry about it. He has plenty of time to alter. And even so, what does it matter? Only one thing is asked of him: that he should grow into an honest man."

The child was comforted by contact with his mother's warm body. He could be heard sucking her milk and gurgling and snorting. Jean Michel turned in his chair, and said once more, with some emphasis:

"There's nothing finer than an honest man."

In the bed by his mother's side the child was stirring again. An unknown sorrow had arisen from the depths of his being. He stiffened himself against her. He twisted his body, clenched his fists and knitted his brows. His suffering increased steadily, quietly, certain of its strength. He knew not what it was, nor whence it came. It appeared immense,—indefinite, and he began to cry lamentably. His mother caressed him with her gentle hands. Already his suffering was less acute. But he went on weeping, for he felt it still near, still inside himself. A man who suffers can lessen his anguish by knowing whence it comes. By thought he can locate it in a certain portion of his body which can be cured, or, if necessary, torn away. He fixes the bounds of it, and separates it from himself. A child has no such illusive resource. His first encounter with suffering is more tragic and more true. Like his own being, it seems infinite. He feels that it is seated in his bosom, housed in his heart, and is mistress of his flesh. And it is so. It will not leave his body until it has eaten it away.

His mother hugs him to her, murmuring: "It is

done—it is done! Don't cry, my little Jesus, my little goldfish . . ." But his intermittent outcry continues. It is as though this wretched, unformed, and unconscious mass had a presentiment of a whole life of sorrow awaiting him, and nothing can appease him . . .

The bells of St. Martin rang out in the night. Their voices are solemn and slow. In the damp air they come like footsteps on moss. The child became silent in the middle of a sob. The marvelous music, like a flood of milk, surged sweetly through him. The night was lit up; the air was moist and tender. His sorrow disappeared, his heart began to laugh, and he slid into his dreams with a sigh of abandonment.

The vast tide of the days moves slowly. Day and night come up and go down with unfailing regularity, like the ebb and flow of an infinite ocean. Weeks and months go by, and then begin again, and the succession of days is like one day.

The day is immense, inscrutable, marking the even beat of light and darkness, and the beat of the life of the torpid creature dreaming in the depths of his cradle—his imperious needs, sorrowful or glad—so regular that the night and the day which bring them seem by them to be brought about.

The pendulum of life moves heavily, and in its slow beat the whole creature seems to be absorbed. The rest is no more than dreams, snatches of dreams, formless and swarming, and dust of atoms dancing aimlessly, a dizzy whirl passing, and bringing laughter or horror. Outcry, moving shadows, grinning shapes, sorrows, terrors, laughter, dreams, dreams . . . All is a dream, both day and night. . . . And in such chaos the light of friendly eyes that smile upon him, the flood of joy that surges through his body from his mother's body, from her breasts filled with milk—the force that is in him, the immense, unconscious force gathering in him, the turbulent ocean roaring in the narrow prison of the child's body. For eyes that could see into it there would be revealed whole worlds half buried in the darkness, nebulae taking shape, a universe in the making. His being is limitless. He is all that there is . . .

Months pass . . . Islands of memory begin to rise above the river of his life. At first they are little uncharted islands, rocks just peeping above the surface of the waters. Round about them and behind in the twilight of the dawn stretches the great untroubled sheet of water; then new islands, touched to gold by the sun.

So far from the abyss of the soul there emerges shapes definite, and scenes of a strange clarity. In the boundless day which dawns once more, ever the same, with its great monotonous beat, there begins to show forth the round of days, hand in hand, and some of their forms are smiling, others sad. But ever the links of the chain are broken, and memories are linked together above weeks and months. . . .

The River . . . the Bells . . . as long as he can remember—far back in the abysses of time, at every hour of his life—always their voices, familiar and resonant, have rung out . . .

Night—half asleep—a pale light made white the window. . . . The river murmurs. Through the silence its voice rises omnipotent; it reigns over all creatures. Sometimes it caresses their sleep, and seems almost itself to die away in the roaring of its torrent. Sometimes it grows angry, and howls like a furious beast about to bite. The clamor ceases. Now there is a murmur of infinite tenderness, silvery sounds like clear little bells, like the laughter of children, or soft singing voices, or dancing music—a great mother voice that never, never goes to sleep! It rocks the child, as it has rocked through the ages, from birth to death, the generations that were before him; it fills all his thoughts, and lives in all his dreams, wraps him round with the cloak of its fluid harmonies, which still will be about him when he lies in the little cemetery that sleeps by the water's edge, washed by the Rhine. . . .

The bells. . . . It is dawn! They answer each other's

call, sad, melancholy, friendly, gentle. At the sound of their slow voices there rises in him a host of dreams—dreams of the past, desires, hopes, regrets for creatures who are gone, unknown to the child, although he had his being in them, and they live again in him. Ages of memory ring out in that music. So much mourning, so many festivals! And from the depths of the room it is as though, when they are heard, there passed lovely waves of sound through the soft air, free winging birds, and the moist soughing of the wind. Through the window smiles a patch of blue sky; a sunbeam slips through the curtains to the bed. The little world known to the eyes of the child, all that he can see from his bed every morning as he awakes, all that with so much effort he is beginning to recognize and classify, so that he may be master of it—his kingdom is lit up. There is the table where people eat, the cupboard where he hides to play, the tiled floor along which he crawls, and the wall-paper which in its antic shapes holds for him so many humorous or terrifying stories, and the clock which chatters and stammers so many words which he alone can understand. How many things there are in this room! He does not know them all. Every day he sets out on a voyage of exploration in this universe which is his. Everything is his. Nothing is immaterial; everything has its worth, man or fly. Everything lives—the cat, the fire, the table, the grains of dust which dance in a sunbeam. The room is a country, a day is a lifetime. How is a creature to know himself in the midst of these vast spaces? The world is so large! A creature is lost in it. And the faces, the actions, the movement, the noise, which makes round him an unending turmoil! . . . He is weary; his eyes close; he goes to sleep. That sweet deep sleep that overcomes him suddenly at any time, and wherever he may be—on his mother's lap, or under the table, where he loves to hide! . . . It is good. All is good. . . .

These first days come buzzing up in his mind like a field of corn or a wood stirred by the wind, and cast in shadow by the great fleeting clouds . . .

The shadows pass; the sun penetrates the forest. Jean-Christophe begins to find his way through the labyrinth of the day.

It is morning. His parents are asleep. He is in his little bed, lying on his back. He looks at the rays of light dancing on the ceiling. There is infinite amusement in it. Now he laughs out loud with one of those jolly children's laughs which stir the hearts of those that hear them. His mother leans out of her bed towards him, and says: "What is it, then, little mad thing?" Then he laughs again, and perhaps he makes an effort to laugh because he has an audience. His mama looks severe, and lays a finger on her lips to warn him lest he should wake his father: but her weary eyes smile in spite of herself. They whisper together. Then there is a furious growl from his father. Both tremble. His mother hastily turns her back on him, like a naughty little girl: she pretends to be asleep. Jean-Christophe buries himself in his bed, and holds his breath. . . . Dead silence.

After some time the little face hidden under the clothes comes to the surface again. On the roof the weathercock creaks. The rain-pipe gurgles; the Angelus sounds. When the wind comes from the East, the distant bells of the villages on the other bank of the river give answer. The sparrows foregathered in the ivy-clad wall make a deafening noise, from which three or four voices, always the same, ring out more shrilly than the others, just as in the games of a band of children. A pigeon coos at the top of a chimney. The child abandons himself to the lullaby of these sounds. He hums to himself softly, then a little more loudly, then quite loudly, then very loudly, until once more his father cries out in exasperation: "That little donkey never will be quiet! Wait a little, and I'll pull your ears!" Then Jean-Christophe buries himself in the bedclothes again, and does not know whether to laugh or cry. He is terrified and humiliated; and at the same time the idea of the donkey with which his father has compared him makes him burst out laughing. From the depths of his bed he imitates its braying. This time he is whipped. He sheds every tear that is in him. What has he done? He wanted so much to laugh and to get up! And he is forbidden to budge. How do people sleep forever? When will they get up?

One day he could not contain himself. He heard a cat and dog and something queer in the street. He slipped out of bed, and, creeping awkwardly with his bare feet on the tiles, he tried to go down the stairs to see what it was; but the door was shut. To open it, he climbed on to a chair; the whole thing collapsed, and he hurt himself and howled. And once more at the top of the stairs he was whipped. He is always being whipped!

Oh, delightful memories, kindly visions, which will hum their melody in their tuneful flight through life! . . . Journeys in later life, great towns and moving seas, dream countries and loved faces, are not so exactly graven in the soul as these childish walks, or the corner of the garden seen every day through the window, through the steam and mist made by the child's mouth glued to it for want of other occupation. . . .

Evening now, and the house is shut up. Home . . . the refuge from all terrifying things—darkness, night, fear, things unknown. No enemy can pass the threshold. . . . The fire flares. A golden duck turns slowly on the spit; a delicious smell of fat and of crisping flesh scents the room. The joy of eating, incomparable delight, a religious enthusiasm, thrills of joy! The body is too languid with the soft warmth, and the fatigues of the day, and the familiar voices. The act of digestion plunges it in ecstasy, and faces, shadows, the lampshade, the tongues of flame dancing with a shower of stars in the fireplace—all take on a magical appearance of delight. Jean-Christophe lays his cheek on his plate, the better to enjoy all this happiness. . . .

He is in his soft bed. How did he come there? He is overcome with weariness. The buzzing of the voices in the room and the visions of the day are intermingled in his mind. His father takes his violin; the shrill sweet sounds cry out complaining in the night. But the crowning joy is when his mother comes and takes Jean-Christophe's hands. He is drowsy, and, leaning over him, in a low voice she sings, as he asks, an old song with words that have no meaning. His father thinks such music stupid, but Jean-Christophe never wearies of it. He holds his breath, and is between laughing and crying. His heart is intoxicated. He does not know where he is, and he is overflowing with tenderness. He throws his little arms round his mother's neck, and hugs her with all his strength. She says, laughing:

"You want to strangle me?"

He hugs her close. How he loves her! How he loves everything! Everybody, everything! All is good, all is beautiful . . . He sleeps. The cricket on the hearth cheeps. His grandfather's tales, the great heroes, float by in the happy night . . . To be a hero like them! . . . Yes, he will be that . . . he is that. . . . Ah, how good it is to live!

What an abundance of strength, joy, pride, is in that little creature! What superfluous energy! His body and mind never cease to move; they are carried round and round breathlessly. Like a little salamander, he dances day and night in the flames. His is an unwearying enthusiasm finding its food in all things. A delicious dream, a bubbling well, a treasure of inexhaustible hope, a laugh, a song, unending drunkenness. Life does not hold him yet; always he escapes it. He swims in the infinite. How happy he is! He is made to be happy! There is nothing in him that does not believe in happiness, and does not cling to it with all his little strength and passion! . . .

Life will soon see to it that he is brought to reason.

X

THE MOTHER

From *The Prophet*
by KAHLIL GIBRAN

And a woman who held a babe against her bosom
said, Speak to us of Children
And he said:
Your children are not your Children.
They are the sons and daughters of Life's
longing for itself.
They come through you but not from you,
And though they are with you yet they belong
not to you.

"IT IS MY BABY!"

from *Story of a Farm Girl*
by GUY DE MAUPASSANT

The next day Rose gave birth to a seven months' child, a miserable little skeleton, thin enough to make anybody shudder, and which seemed to be suffering continually, to judge by the painful manner in which it moved its poor little hands about, which were as thin as a crab's legs; but it lived, for all that. She said that she was married, but that she could not saddle herself with the child, so she left it with some neighbours, who promised to take care of it, and she went back to the farm.

But then, in her heart, which had been wounded so long, there arose something like brightness, an unknown love for that frail little creature which she had left behind her, but there was a fresh suffering in that very love, suffering which she felt every hour and every minute, because she was parted from her child. What pained her most, however, was a mad longing to kiss it, to press it in her arms, to feel the warmth of its little body against her skin. She could not sleep at night; she thought of it the whole day long, and in the evening, when her work was done, she used to sit in front of the fire and look at it intently, like people do whose thoughts are far away.

They began to talk about her, and to tease her about the lover she must have. They asked her whether he was tall, handsome and rich. When was the wedding to be, and the christening? And often she ran away, to cry by herself, for these questions seemed to hurt her, like the prick of a pin, and in order to forget these irritations, she began to work still more energetically, and still thinking of her child, she sought for the means of saving up money for it, and determined to work so that her master would be obliged to raise her wages.

The child was nearly eight months old, and she did not know it again. It had grown rosy and chubby all over like a little bundle of living fat. She threw herself on it as if it had been some prey, and kissed it so violently that it began to scream with terror, and then she began to cry herself, because it did not know her, and stretched out its arms to its nurse, as soon as it saw her. But the next day, it began to get used to her, and laughed when it saw her, and she took it into the fields and ran about excitedly with it, and sat down under the shade of the trees, and then, for the first time in her life, she opened her heart to somebody, and told him her troubles, how hard her work was, her anxieties and her hopes, and she quite tired the child with the violence of her caresses.

She took the greatest pleasure in handling it, in washing and dressing it, for it seemed to her that all this was the confirmation of her maternity, and she would look at it, almost feeling surprised that it was hers, and she used to say to herself in a low voice, as she danced it in her arms: "It is my baby, it is my baby."

ON NURSING CHILDREN
from *The Spectator* (December 12, 1753)

by ADDISON AND STEELE

Mr. Spectator,

As your Paper is Part of the Equipage of the Tea-Table, I conjure you to print what I now write to you; for I have no other Way to communicate what I have to say to the fair Sex on the most important Circumstance of Life, even the Care of Children. I do not understand that you profess your Paper is always to consist of Matters which are only to entertain the Learned and Polite, but that it may agree with your Design to publish some which may tend to the Information of Mankind in general; and when it does so, you do more than writing Wit and Humour. Give me leave then to tell you, that all the Abuses that ever you have as yet endeavored to reform, certainly not one wanted so much your assistance as the Abuse in nursing Children. It is unmerciful to see, that a Woman endowed with all the Perfections and Blessings of Nature, can, as soon as she is delivered, turn off her innocent, tender, and helpless Infant, and give it up to a Woman that is (ten thousand to one) neither in Health nor good Condition, neither sound in Mind nor Body, that has neither Honour nor Reputation, neither Love nor Pity for the poor Babe, but more Regard for the Money than for the whole Child, and never will take farther Care of it than what by all the Encouragement of Money and Presents she is forced to; like Aesop's Earth, which would not nurse the Plant of another Ground, altho' never so much improved, by reason that Plant was not of its own Production. And since another's Child is no more natural to a Nurse than a Plant to the strange and different Ground, how can it be supposed that the Child should thrive; and if it thrives, must it not imbibe the gross Humours and Qualities of the Nurse, like a Plant in a different Ground, or like a Graft upon a different Stock? Do not we observe, that a Lamb sucking a Goat changes very much its Nature, nay even its Skin and Wool into the Goat Kind? The Power of a Nurse over a Child by infusing into it, with her Milk, her Qualities and Disposition, is sufficiently and daily observed: Hence came the old Saying concerning an ill-natured and malicious Fellow, that he had imbibed his Malice with his Nurse's Milk, or that some Brute or other had been his Nurse. Hence Romulus and Remus were said to have been nursed by a Wolf, Telephus the son of Hercules by a Hind, Pelias the son of Neptune by a Mare, and Aegisthus by a Goat; not that they had actually sucked such Creatures as some Simpletons have imagin'd, but that their Nurses had been of such a Nature and Temper, and infused such into them.

Many instances may be produced from good Authorities and daily Experience, that Children actually suck in the several Passions and depraved Inclinations of their Nurses, as Anger, Malice, Fear, Melancholy, Sadness, Desire, and Aversion. This Diodorus, lib. 2 witnesses when he speaks, saying, That Nero the Emperor's Nurse had been very much addicted to Drinking; which Habit Nero received from his Nurse, and was so very particular in this, that the People took so much notice of it, as instead of Tiberius Nero, they call'd him Biberius Nero. The same Diodorus also relates of Caligula, Predecessor to Nero, that his Nurse used to moisten the Nipples of her Breast frequently with Blood, to make Caligula take the better hold of them; which, says Diodorus, was the Cause that made him so blood-thirsty and cruel all his Life-time after, that he not only committed frequent Murder by his own Hand, but likewise wished that all human Kind wore but one Neck, that he might have the Pleasure to cut it off. Such like Degeneracies astonish the Parents, who not knowing after whom the Child can take, see one to incline to Stealing, another to Drinking, Cruelty, Stupidity; yet all these are not minded. Nay it is easy to demonstrate, that a Child, altho' it be born from the best of Parents, may be corrupted by an ill-tempered Nurse. How many Children do we see daily brought into Fits, Consumptions, Rickets, etc. merely by sucking their Nurses when in a Passion or Fury? But indeed almost any Disorder of the Nurse is a disorder to the Child, and few Nurses can be found in this Town but what labour under some Distemper or other. The first Question that is generally asked a young Woman that wants to be a Nurse, Why she should be a Nurse to other People's Children; is answered by her having an ill Husband, and that she must make shift to live. I think now this very Answer is enough to give any Body a Shock, if duly considered; for an ill Husband may, or ten to one if he does not, bring home to his Wife an ill Distemper, or at least Vexation and Disturbance. Besides as she takes the Child out of mere Necessity, her Food will be accordingly, or else very coarse at best; whence proceeds an ill-concocted and coarse Food for the Child; for as the Blood, so is the Milk; and hence I am very well assured proceeds the Scurvy, the Evil, and many other Distempers. I beg of you, for the Sake of the many poor Infants that may and will be saved by weighing this Case seriously, to exhort the People with the utmost Vehemence to let the Children suck their own Mothers, both for the Benefit of Mother and Child. For the general Argument, that a Mother is weakened by giving suck to her Children, is vain and simple; I will maintain that the Mother grows stronger by it, and will have her Health better than she would have otherwise: She will find it the greatest Cure and Preservative for the Vapours and future Miscarriages, much beyond any other Remedy whatsoever: Her Children will be like Giants, whereas otherwise they are but living Shadows and like unripe Fruit; and certainly if a Woman is strong enough to bring forth a Child, she is beyond all Doubt strong enough to nurse it afterwards. It grieves me to observe and consider how many poor Children are daily ruined by careless Nurses; and yet how tender ought they to be of a poor Infant, since the least Hurt or Blow, especially upon the Head, may make it senseless, stupid, or otherwise miserable for ever!

But I cannot well leave this Subject as yet; for it seems to me very unnatural, that a Woman that has fed a child as part of herself for nine Months, should have no Desire to nurse it farther, when brought to Light and before her Eyes, and when by its Cry it implores her Assistance and Office of a Mother. Do not the very cruellest of Brutes tend their young ones with all the Care and Delight imaginable? for how can she be call'd a Mother that will not nurse her young ones? The Earth is called the Mother of all things, not because she produces, but because she maintains and nurses what she produces. The Generation of the Infant is the Effect of Desire, but the Care of it argues Virtue and Choice. I am not ignorant but that there are some Cases of Necessity where a Mother cannot give Suck, and then out of two Evils the least must be chosen; but there are so very few, that I am sure in a Thousand there is hardly one real Instance; for if a Woman does but know that her Husband can spare about three or six Shillings a Week extraordinary, (altho' this is but seldom considered) she certainly, with the Assistance of her Gossips, will soon persuade the good Man to send the Child to Nurse, and easily impose upon him by pretending Indisposition. This Cruelty is supported by Fashion, and Nature gives place to Custom.

Sir,

Your humble Servant

SHOULD BREAST-FEEDING BE ENCOURAGED?

by HUGH R. K. BARBER, M.D.

from *The Female Patient* (March 1977)

Before the end of World War II, breast-feeding was widely practiced. It began to lose popularity in the late forties and early fifties, but is becoming accepted once again. What are the arguments in favor of breast-feeding today?

This discussion includes both the psychologic aspects and the physiologic aspects—emphasizing recent work on the cellular component of milk and its possible immunobiological significance, which has stirred great excitement in the field of reproductive biology.

Psychiatrists and psychologists can comment objectively about the psychologic impact of breast-feeding on the infant and the entire family. My impressions and suggestions may have overtones of emotionalism, but I believe they are valid nonetheless.

From ancient times until recently, breast-feeding was a way of life. Babies whose mothers had died or were unable to nurse them were cared for by other lactating women. The so-called "wet nurse" had prestige. Without her, there could be no survival for infants without mothers. Services of a superior wet nurse who was endowed with the necessary physical and mental gifts of nature were sought after, and it was generally accepted that she should play a significant role in the physical and mental development of the child.

Breast-feeding epitomizes maternal devotion and the infant's feeling of security. It is one of the earliest expressions of total femininity preserved in art and literature. Some of the great art of the Renaissance shows the baby at the breast or about to nurse.

In modern times, before the total acceptance of bottle formula feeding, great emphasis was placed on the technique of breast-feeding. The baby was never put directly to the nipple, but was encouraged to root and find it. This stimulated a desire on the part of the baby for nourishment, and stimulated the let-down factor for milk ejection. Sucking stimulation is of paramount importance in the establishment of an adequate milk supply.

The physical course of lactation and a woman's emotions are closely related. The breast-feeding mother is different from the artificially feeding mother in several ways. Prolactin, which is known to produce maternal behavior in experimental animals, is also presumably present and operative in the breast-feeding mother. Oxytocin is liberated by the nursing mother, and this causes the uterus to contract rhythmically during breast-feeding. It may give sensuous pleasure, and some nursing mothers have a look of joyous contentment. Successful breast-feeding gives rise to the gentle and prolonged stroking of one of the most sensitive parts of the female body—the nipple—which also involves sensuous pleasure. There is interdependence between mother and baby. When the mother's breasts are distended with milk, there is physical relief in having the baby empty them; in turn, the baby's hunger pains are relieved. It is impossible for the bottle-fed baby to have the same relationship with his or her mother as does the successfully breast-fed baby. Insofar as the mother's whole body, as well as the baby's body, is involved in breast-feeding, the relationship is definitely different.

The physiologic and immunologic benefits contributed to the newborn by breast-feeding lend themselves to documentation more readily than does the psychologic impact.

Human milk contains many components which promote a "normal" bacterial colonization of the gastrointestinal tract, and also suppress the invasiveness of certain pathologic microorganisms. These qualities of breast milk may be of major importance for the newborn infant's defense against infection.

The increased use of disinfectants and antibiotics

has played a role in diminishing neonatal morbidity and mortality during a period in which there was a decreased incidence of breast-feeding. Recently, reports have suggested a changing pattern, with an increased frequency of colonization and infection caused by gram-negative bacteria.

Lately, it has been shown that secretory lgA is a major immunoglobulin in breast milk. Although, like other immunoglobulins, it is not absorbed across the gut membrane of the infant, it does provide protection at the surface membrane. Lactoferrin of breast milk inhibits growth of *Candida albicans* and has a strong bacteriostatic effect on *Escherichia coli.* Lysozyme (muramidase) has an antibacterial effect, and is found in breast milk in amounts up to about 2 mg/ml. A resistance factor against Staphylococci is present in human milk, but its protective role remains to be clarified.

Breast-feeding interferes with oral polio vaccination. There is a suggestion that breast-fed infants are less prone to respiratory infections and otitis media, and indirect evidence suggests that breast-feeding may protect against septicemia and meningitis in the newborn. The difference in incidence of enteric infections in breast-fed and bottle-fed infants is well known. In a study of a preindustrial society in Guatemala, it has been reported that diarrhea is uncommon in breast-fed infants, even though they are exposed to many organisms including Shigella, enteropathogenic *E. coli*, and Salmonella. Diarrhea occurred in these infants only after breast-feeding was stopped.

Beer and Billingham have focused attention on the immunological significance of the mammary gland. In pregnancy there is a nine-month maternal fetal relationship via the placenta. This provides a two-way exchange of cells; or, in popular terms, the fetus is chronically plugged into the placenta, with an exchange of cells and nutrients taking place across the placenta.

With parturition, the neonate becomes plugged into the breast, with the possibility of only one-way transfer of cells and nutrients, in the direction of the baby. The significance of lgA (secreted by the B cell, plasma cell) has been suggested. In addition, it has been shown that colostrum and milk are essentially suspensions of viable cells, predominantly leukocytes of hematologic origin, which are dispensed in a nutrient medium. In the milk of humans, cattle, and rats, the normal concentration of white blood cells is not greatly inferior to their concentration in the patient's peripheral blood. In addition to prominent lipid-laden macrophages and a few granulocytes, both T and B lymphocytes are present in significant proportions, and manifest various parameters of immunologic reactivity when isolated and studied *in vitro*.

Infants weighing 1,500 grams or less are immunologically incompetent. If they are to receive breast milk, it should be from their own mothers. Donor breast milk could result in a graft-versus-host syndrome—i.e., a runt syndrome—or even death.

A significant toll of human babies is taken by a disease known as necrotizing enterocolitis. Predisposing etiologic factors are prematurity, transient hypoxia, and disturbance of the splanchnic circulation, as a consequence of blood transfusion via the umbilical vein, infection and feeding. It has been shown that newborn rats die within a few days if they are formula-fed, but not if they are breast-fed. The protection may result from viable macrophages (which may be the first line of defense in breast milk) and/or lymphocytes in the breast milk. The equipping of an immunologically immature host with a variable number of mature, antigen-reactive cells is a form of adoptive immunization.

For mothers who are deciding whether to breast-feed, it should be pointed out that the observation that mothers who breast-feed their babies have less breast cancer has never been disproved.

Mother's milk is for babies and cow's milk is for calves. The important evidence strongly favors a return to breast-feeding, and it is hoped that the renaissance will be rapid and total.

From *The Good Earth*

by PEARL S. BUCK

Then, almost before one could realize anything, the woman was back in the fields beside him. The harvests were past, and the grain they beat out upon the threshing floor which was also the dooryard to the house. They beat it out with flails, he and the woman together. And when the grain was flailed they winnowed it, casting it up from great flat bamboo baskets into the wind and catching the good grain as it fell, and the chaff blew away in a cloud with the wind. Then there were the fields to plant for winter wheat again, and when he had yoked the ox and ploughed the land the woman followed behind with her hoe and broke the clods in the furrows.

She worked all day now and the child lay on an old torn quilt on the ground, asleep. When it cried the woman stopped and uncovered her bosom to the child's mouth, sitting flat upon the ground, and the sun beat down upon them both, the reluctant sun of late autumn that will not let go the warmth of summer until the cold of the coming winter forces it. The woman and the child were as brown as the soil and they sat there like figures made of earth. There was the dust of the fields upon the woman's hair and upon the child's soft black head.

But out of the woman's great brown breast the milk gushed forth for the child, milk as white as snow, and when the child suckled at one breast it flowed like a fountain from the other, and she let it flow. There was more than enough for the child, greedy though he was, life enough for many children, and she let it flow out carelessly, conscious of her abundance. There was always more and more. Sometimes she lifted her breast and let it flow out upon the ground to save her clothing, and it sank into the earth and made a soft, dark, rich spot in the field. The child was fat and good-natured and ate of the inexhaustible life his mother gave him.

XI

HOME VERSUS HOSPITAL DELIVERY

From *Cheaper by the Dozen*

by FRANK GILBRETH, JR. and
ERNESTINE GILBRETH CAREY

Mother had her first half-dozen babies at home, instead of in hospitals, because she liked to run the house and help Dad with his work, even during the confinements. She'd supervise the household right up until each baby started coming. There was a period of about twenty-four hours, then, when she wasn't much help to anybody. But she had prepared all the menus in advance, and the house ran smoothly by itself during the one day devoted to the delivery. For the next ten days to two weeks, while she remained in bed, we'd file in every morning so that she could tie the girls' hair ribbons and make sure the boys had washed properly. Then we'd come back again at night to hold the new baby and listen to Mother read *The Five Little Peppers*. Mother enjoyed the little Peppers every bit as much as we, and was particularly partial to the character named Phronise, or something like that.

When Dad's mother came to live with us, Mother decided to have Number Seven in a Providence hospital, since Grandma could run the house for her. Six hours after Mother checked into the hospital, a nurse called our house and told Dad that Mrs. Gilbreth had had a nine-pound boy.

"Quick work," Dad told Grandma. "She really has found the one best way of having babies."

Grandma asked whether it was a boy or girl, and Dad replied: "A boy, naturally, for goodness sakes. What did you expect?"

A few moments later, the hospital called again and said there had been some mistake. A Mrs. Gilbert, not Gilbreth, had had the baby boy.

"Well, what's *my* wife had?" Dad asked. "I'm not interested in any Mrs. Gilbert, obstetrically or any other way."

"Of course you're not," the nurse apologized. "Just a

moment, and I'll see about Mrs. Gilbreth." And then a few minutes later. "Mrs. Gilbreth seems to have checked out of the hospital."

"Checked out? Why she's only been there six hours. Did she have a boy or girl?"

"Our records don't show that she had either."

"It's got to be one or the other," Dad insisted. "What else is there?"

"I mean," the nurse explained, "she apparently checked out before the baby arrived."

Dad hung up the receiver. "Better start boiling water," he said to Grandma. "Lillie's on the way home."

"With that new baby?"

"No." Dad was downcast. "Somebody else claimed that baby. Lillie apparently put off having hers for the time being."

Mother arrived at the house about half an hour later. She was carrying a suitcase and had walked all the way. Grandma was furious.

"My goodness, Lillie, you have no business out in the street in your condition. And carrying that heavy suitcase. Give it to me. Now get upstairs to bed where you belong. A girl your age should know better. What did you leave the hospital for?"

"I got tired of waiting and I was lonesome. I decided I'd have this one at home, too. Besides, that nurse—she was a fiend. She hid my pencils and notebook and wouldn't even let me read. I never spent a more miserable day."

Lill was born the next day, in Dad's and Mother's room, where pencils and notebooks and proofs were within easy reach of Mother's bed.

HOME BIRTH

from *Safe Alternatives in Childbirth* (1976)

by FREDERIC M. ETTNER, M.D.

Conventional hospital obstetric practices in the U.S. have been founded, shaped, and influenced largely by cultural, economic and commercial pressures. Many of our accepted practices are not supported by scientific research and appear to be rooted more in hospital and medical professional tradition than human physiology.

Routine hospitalization for birth, promoting "just-in-case" and "exception-becoming-the-rule" obstetrical practices has not only promoted pathology in both mother and infant, but has enforced rigid separation of family members and long isolation of mother and infant from siblings. Home birth is the natural choice for those healthy women seeking an alternative incorporating healthy, not pathological practices.

HAVING A BABY AT HOME

from *American Baby Magazine* (July 1978)

by MYRYAME MONTROSE

Having a baby at home was a matter-of-fact occurrence not so long ago. As recently as 1950 only half the births in this country took place in a hospital; by 1975 that figure had risen to 99%, according to the American College of Obstetricians and Gynecologists (ACOG). Although home births are still commonplace in many countries, including some with better infant mortality rates than ours, the idea of having a baby at home is very controversial here in the U.S. Still, the number of home births in this country has been rapidly increasing in recent years, despite the fact that it can be difficult to impossible to find anyone—doctor or midwife—to attend the birth or even give prenatal care.

The medical establishment has taken a strong stand against all home births. They cite the risks of unpredictable, last-minute emergencies during labor and feel that because some women may be at risk, it is safer to have all births in a hospital setting. Those in favor of home birth as an alternative point out that it has never been conclusively proven that a hospital is the safest place to have a baby. They cite as potential hazards of hospital birth the use of pain-relieving drugs during labor; use of oxytocics to speed up contractions; routine use of fetal monitors, and so on.

The pros and cons of home vs. hospital births can be argued at great length—with studies, statistics and horror stories to support both sides. Ultimately there is no 100% "safe" way to have a baby. It is certain, however, that a lack of support from the medical community is making the option of home birth more dangerous than it need be. Couples who feel strongly about having their baby at home and who are willing to accept responsibility for the outcome should not have to forego essential prenatal care, childbirth education, competent medical assistance for the birth, and provision for hospital backup in an emergency.

Why a home birth?

The decision to have a home birth is a personal one, and there are many factors involved. However, all the home birthers I talked with had one thing in common—a desire to have control over the type of birth experience they would have and the willingness to accept fully the responsibility for the birth. As a group, home birthers tend to be well-educated and highly motivated. While they are aware that home birth is considered a risky business, they all had faith both in the birth process itself and in their chosen birth attendants.

At home you have control . . .

For many couples a major factor in deciding to give birth at home is the desire to control the specific circumstances of the birth. Unfortunately, for many couples this also means that they will have to go it alone.

Sue and John Crockett had their fourth child at home in 1975. Sue found an obstetrician who was willing to give her prenatal care, but who would not attend the birth. She could not find a midwife, nor would any of their friends or family consent to come. Everyone was too busy disapproving to provide any help. Sue and John decided, as so many other couples do, to go it alone.

They made this choice not because Sue had any horror stories to tell about her three hospital deliveries, but because they were convinced that a home birth would not only be more psychologically satisfying, but medically safer as well.

Sue admitted that the situation surrounding the birth was far from ideal. If there *had* been an emergency, John would have had to cope with Sue, the new baby, and their three other children. But, asks Sue, if doctors won't come to the home for the birth, can't they at least provide prenatal care and backup? "Home birth is here; by ignoring it, the medical community is just hiding its head in the sand."

What about a compromise, such as hospitals with one of the new homelike birthing rooms, I wondered? "No matter how homelike you make that room, you're still in the hospital," Sue maintains. "At home I felt free to do what I wanted to do. All the time I hear from women who had to compromise on the type of birth they wanted. At home *you* have control."

Sue and John are now involved in helping other couples who want to plan a home birth, as regional coordinators of the Association for Childbirth at Home, International. This organization's basic goal is to educate parents so they can make informed decisions about the birth of their baby. Says Sue, "The doctor only has the baby for a few minutes; you have it for the rest of your life. We are dedicated to the parents' rights to decide where and with whom they will give birth."

A spiritual beginning . . .

For many couples, the home seems the most natural place to offer a child a spiritual welcome and to celebrate the miracle of birth as a family.

"Through my religious beliefs I had come to the feeling that it was the most natural way, the way the mother had the greatest control," says Nancy R. as she describes her reasons for a home birth. "I had hoped my thinking would govern the process, as in Christian Science there is great mental preparation for having a baby—you endeavor to clear your thinking and become very relaxed and grateful. Many medical procedures, it seemed, jarred the kind of rhythm I was trying to establish. I read the Bible throughout my pregnancy, hoping to align myself with that sort of spiritual power."

Finding someone suitable to attend the birth was no easy task, as Nancy moved to California from New York when she was six months pregnant. "I went through many channels, both through my church and the medical establishment, before I found a woman in her 80s, a German doctor who had been delivering babies in Europe and in this country for about fifty years. She was willing to do a home birth if she felt that it was going to be uncomplicated."

Nancy's labor was not an easy one, yet she remembers that although it wasn't pleasant, "I felt in harmony with what was happening. In the case of something that's as natural as giving birth, if we get out of the way of what is happening as much as possible (except when it is truly pathological and you need some kind of assistance), that produces the best results."

The birth, says Nancy, was "the most wonderful thing. My husband was in tears because it was so beautiful. It was wonderful to feel that our child got that kind of spiritual beginning."

No hassles . . .

For some couples, the impetus for a home birth is the memory of an unhappy hospital experience.

Marilyn M. went to the clinic at a large New York hospital when she was expecting her first child. On each visit she was examined by a different doctor, and there was no way to predict who would actually deliver the baby—except that he was sure to be a stranger.

Once in labor, Marilyn was subjected to a barrage of medical procedures she now feels were unnecessary: drugs to speed up labor; an IV which inhibited movement; an episiotomy that healed so slowly she could still feel pressure from the stitches a year later. Marilyn continued to bleed for two months after delivery and had to return to the hospital for a D&C ("I've always suspected that maybe they didn't get all of the placenta out," she muses). But worst of all were the hospital rules which permitted Marilyn to hold and nurse her son only for brief periods.

Marilyn was determined to avoid the hospital next time if she could. She read up on home birth, and friends told her about a nurse-midwife who had a home birth service. Marilyn was reassured by the careful screening and professionalism of the midwife. And although she knew that there were arrangements for hospital backup, Marilyn was confident she wouldn't need it.

The birth itself, says Marilyn, was "so simple, no hassles. It was really a beautiful experience, and my husband got to cut the cord. There was no episiotomy, just two stitches, and I was fine by the second week. The baby was born at four in the morning. I stayed in bed an hour or so; then my husband helped me take a shower.

The midwife stayed for four or five hours to make sure the baby and I were O.K., and we all had breakfast together. It was a very peaceful thing."

Home birth practitioners point out that not all women can be considered candidates for home delivery. It is a viable option only for a woman with good health, an uncomplicated pregnancy and a positive attitude towards taking an active role in childbirth. Women with conditions such as diabetes, profound anemia, heart disease, or who are expecting twins or have a baby in breech position, are all considered high risk and should deliver in a hospital.

Having a midwife come to the home to attend the birthing woman is an ancient practice. What is new, however, is the advent of Certified Nurse Midwives, registered nurses with extensive training in managing a normal pregnancy and birth. While many CNMs operate within the hospital setting, there are a few who offer a comprehensive home birth service.

THE HOME BIRTH EXPERIENCE

by JANE DAVIS, C.N.M., LILY-SCOTT FORMATO, C.N.M., and JADE SINGER, Administrator, Home Birth Program, New York City

"We want to experience the emotional, physical and spiritual aspects of birthing in a loving, conducive atmosphere. We also want to have the opportunity to select the people with whom we want to share this joyous event—our son and a few close friends. A home birth seems to be the most natural and satisfying way to have a baby."

This is a quote written by parents planning their birth with the Home Birth Program. We are a group of private, certified nurse-midwives practicing in New York City, filling the needs of parents, like those quoted above, who want more from their childbirth experience than is traditionally offered in institutions.

The program is completely run by the nurse-midwives who control the acceptance of pregnant women, standards of maternity care, and cancellation and referral when necessary. We strongly believe that women have the right to choose where they have their babies. Women who are interested in home birth are asked to attend an introductory conference where they can meet the midwives and discuss questions in order to make a responsible and well-informed choice.

Women who choose home birth feel safer and more comfortable among friends and family in their own surroundings. Home birth is the safest for women who choose it when it follows thorough prenatal care and is carefully assisted by trained attendants. The midwives are always easily accessible to the mothers and know that establishing a relationship with mutual understanding is one of the most important aspects of their care. During prenatal visits, mothers get the individual attention that they need: information about their physiological development, reading material, emotional support, all given in a relaxed atmosphere without any time pressures. All women in the Home Birth Program have at least one visit with our nutritionist. They receive a diet history evaluation and nutritional counseling that respects and incorporates the eating habits and beliefs of the individual. There is an obstetrician consultant/backup who routinely checks the mother at thirty-seven weeks. If there is a serious problem during labor, the nurse-midwife will contact the obstetrician, who will assume complete care of the woman if hospital admission is necessary.

The midwives teach a series of childbirth classes for the mothers and those who will be present as coaches so that they can prepare together for the birth by learning breathing and relaxation techniques and more about their expected course of labor. These classes also serve to break the isolation of city life by bringing together parents sharing a common experience. The modern family is fragmented and mobile, and the traditional extended family system of supports is lacking; therefore, this opportunity for parents to share and support each other is essential.

Many women seek out the Home Birth Program after having had hospital experiences that they found cold, scary, alienating. They want to minimize their babies' exposure to tension, lights, strangers, and foreign germs. They say that they've experienced a great lack of control during their births; often the laboring woman is left alone and is then brought to a delivery room filled with strangers who may neglect her needs for the purpose of adhering to hospital procedures and schedules. In our highly advanced technological world of medicine, we have come to treat deliveries as an illness rather than as a natural process.

A woman giving birth at home has the advantage of knowing her birth attendant and the security of knowing that the attendant will stay with her all through active labor. She has the control and mobility she wants and the comfort of giving birth in the place that is her own life center, surrounded by those people with whom she has chosen to share this most precious moment. The impact of this ideal situation could only be that of helping the course of her labor and her concentration for delivery. She knows that the midwife will be there after the delivery, to give information and to help and to celebrate and not to intervene unnecessarily. Mother and baby will not be separated at perhaps their most important time together. After all, the delivery is accomplished by the mother herself, not the doctor or midwife. We can be there to attend and help, but it is the mother who has to do the work and she who has the right to make the choices.

STATEMENT OF POLICY ON HOME DELIVERIES

by THE AMERICAN COLLEGE OF OBSTETRICS AND GYNECOLOGY

Labor and delivery, while a physiologic process, clearly presents potential hazards to both mother and fetus before and after birth. These hazards require standards of safety which are provided in the hospital setting and cannot be matched in the home situation.

We recognize, however, the legitimacy of the concern of many that the events surrounding birth be an emotionally satisfying experience for the family. The College supports those actions that improve the experience of the family while continuing to provide the mother and her infant with accepted standards of safety available only in the hospital.

WHY GO TO A HOSPITAL?

from *Safe Convoy* (1944)

by WILLIAM J. CARRINGTON

As there were no hospitals where primitive women could be confined, they retired into the woods beside a stream or lake to have their babies. In the Sandwich Islands where native women were not as shy, childbirth was as public a performance as a wedding or a circus. With friends and neighbors gathered around, a woman had her baby while sitting on the lap of an elderly man midwife. There was primitive music and when the baby came, the proud father served whatever passed for hors d'oeuvres, cocktails, and cigars. Generally, however, public exhibitions and dramatized deliveries were unusual; privacy and seclusion were the rule. In fact, in almost every climate, regardless of longitude or latitude, pregnant women were isolated from society. Those who came near them were defiled, and everything they touched was contaminated. For example, in Cochin-China to this day delivery takes place in specially built huts which are burned to the ground after the lying-in period. The Japanese regarded the puerperal woman as unclean and provided her an isolated birth house of bamboo. In New Britain after a child is born, all of the men of the village have to be fumigated and rinse their mouths with a preparation of ginger.

In the United States the first hospital was founded in Philadelphia in 1751, thanks to Benjamin Franklin, but there were no accommodations for lying-in women. It was not until 1887 that the first maternity hospital in this country was established in New York. As late as the turn of the century only those women who needed surgical deliveries had their babies in hospitals. Confinement cases were not segregated but were placed in wards with other women who had all sorts of medical and surgical conditions. This practice prevails nowhere in the civilized world today, although in Chile where there has been no lag in other medical advancement, 53 percent of hospitals are without obstetric wards or departments . . . The best gauge of the civilization of a people is the care of women in confinement.

Hospital delivery is becoming increasingly popular because practically it is impossible to transform a room in a private home or apartment into a modern, aseptic surgically clean delivery room. One may go to endless bother and expense to prepare for any obstetric emergency and yet fall short of perfection. Not only do hospitals have every facility always at hand, but the trained staff of hospital doctors, supervisors, nurses and attendants on duty every moment of the night and day provides additional security that outweighs any argument for delivery at home.

A thrilling description of a home delivery is to be found in *The Citadel* but not all doctors possess the skill and perseverance of the fictional Andrew Monson, and not all patients are as fortunate as Mrs. Morgan of No. 12 Blaina Terrace.

It is true that many babies are born in private dwellings. It is also true that folks bathe in the ocean from unprotected beaches without drowning but there are currents, crosscurrents, and undertows that one may encounter unexpectedly. A well-trained crew of life-guards may be needed only on rare occasions. Obstetric emergencies are rare these days, but when one bobs up, the hospital can relieve the pain of childbirth, convalescence can be made more cheerful, the baby gets off to a better start under expert nursing care, and the stay in the hospital is a complete vacation from household management and drudgery. If a sincere attempt is made to rival hospital facilities by rearranging the home for delivery, the actual expense is greater than that incurred by going to a hospital. Even if no particular arranging is done and the baby is born under the trust-to-luck system, the cost almost equals that of hospital care when one considers such incidental expenses as nursing, laundry, drugs, and accessories.

In spite of all the advantages of hospital care, there are those who prefer to be delivered at home, and they do well there, under the care of the family physician and a trained or practical nurse as long as there are no serious complications.

HOME VERSUS HOSPITAL DELIVERY

from *Expectant Motherhood* (1940)

by NICHOLAS J. EASTMAN

The vast majority of maternity cases can be conducted at home with complete safety and a large number of women prefer to have their babies in the familiar surroundings of their own household.

The modern trend toward hospitalization for childbirth, a trend that is gaining ground every year, is a development of the last three decades. In the early years of this century it was well nigh impossible to persuade a respectable woman to enter a hospital for a normal delivery, since only the derelicts of woman-kind and the destitute sought hospitalization for such a purpose. The present popularity of the hospital, then, has been achieved against great odds and can only mean that hospital care has proved its value to hundreds of thousands of satisfied mothers.

It is often said that doctors are largely responsible for this change because of the great convenience that accrues to them. While this has doubtless been an important factor, the change could not have been brought about unless the mothers, themselves, had been in hearty accord. Women who have had one baby at home and another in the hospital almost always affirm that hospital delivery is more comfortable, more restful and, as a rule, only slightly more expensive. The bother and expense of preparing the rather complicated paraphernalia necessary for home confinement are avoided; the salary and board of the nurse are avoided and, as well, a considerable outlay for laundry; furthermore, a period of complete rest is assured without a responsibility in the world. But the most important of all is the safety offered by hospitals in the event any slight complication develops. Their laboratory facilities, their special apparatus, to say nothing of their greatest pillars of security, the staff of nurses and doctors, make modern hospitals the very safest place in the world to have a baby.

MEN IN WHITE

from *Safe Convoy* (1944)

by WILLIAM J. CARRINGTON

What about the men in white, internes and resident physicians? They may pop in at odd moments, ask questions and look at the chart. They may listen at the chest, or, mosquito-like, fly away to the laboratory with a drop of blood. These professional men are no longer students but are physicians who have spent more years in study and preparation than the members of any other profession. In the day of Dickens they may have been rough and ready like Bob Sawyer and Benjamin Allan, the young medico friends of Mr. Pickwick, "not reg'lar thoroughbred sawbones." But modern young medical men in their student days have to deliver more than a score of babies and assist with many others. These physicians who have just completed their studies have learned the latest methods, and keep older obstetricians on their toes. Their trained assistance saves patients many complications in the course of a year, and their skill in certain technics, together with the experience and riper judgment of their chiefs on service, makes an ideal combination for perfect obstetric care. Fortunate is the prospective mother who is under the care of Dr. Weelum MacLure from "Beside the Bonnie Briar Bush" with his wide experience and sympathetic understanding, assisted by a young Dr. Kildare with his modernity and dexterity.

We would encourage the development of a homelike atmosphere in hospitals rather than a total return to home deliveries. Hospitals can be improved by implementing family-centered care, permitting participation of the husband and allowing other family members to visit the mother if they desire. Continuity of care by the physician and the nurse is also essential, as are quiet, convenience and personal attention. The hospital stay should be as short as possible. A large proportion of the care of normal obstetric patients should be undertaken by nurse-midwives. Separation of hospital facilities into those for high-risk and those for low-risk patients should be also strongly considered. In this way, we should be able to achieve the advantages of technologic progress and still maintain the personal care and attention that are necessary for good obstetric practice.

—ATEF H. MOAWAD, M.D.
Journal of Reproductive Medicine (November 1977)

CHILDBIRTH CENTER RESPONDS TO DEMANDS FOR MORE FAMILY PARTICIPATION

from "Idea Forum," *Journal of the American Hospital Association* (September 1, 1976)

Having a baby these days does not always include the familiar race to the hospital. Indeed, a revolution is occurring in childbirth, and growing numbers of women are turning away from hospitals and having their babies at home—a practice that may not always be the safest for either the mother or the infant. More and more couples are demanding innovative practices generally not allowed in the hospital setting, such as skin to skin contact between parents and child, choice of delivery position, closeness of the family unit surrounding the birth, and lay midwives.

In an attempt to attract such couples back to an attended birth, the 58-year-old Maternity Center Association (MCA) has developed a demonstration project in New York City that provides comprehensive maternity care to low-risk families in a homelike, out-of-hospital setting. According to Ruth Watson Lubic, MCA general director, the center was not set up merely as an alternative to hospitals, but rather "to bring back into the system those families who had lost trust and refused to go to the hospital."

The purposes of the center, which is located in a six-story townhouse, are:

• To demonstrate that low-risk pregnancies and deliveries need not be managed in a traditional hospital setting.

• To eliminate, when appropriate, such routine procedures as strapping mothers to tables, immobilizing their legs in stirrups, and administering episiotomies and other routine procedures.

• To allow parents and babies to remain together for the entire stay and to permit them to go home within 12 hours.

• To give couples as much control as possible over the delivery of their child.

The Childbearing Center has been in operation since September 1975. After careful scrutiny, it was licensed by the State of New York and approved by Blue Cross. The center charges $750 for prenatal care, classes in preparation for childbirth and infant care, labor and delivery, and postpartum checkups. The fee is an estimate of the cost based on full operation of the center—500 families per year.

Medical care is provided by teams of nurse midwives

and obstetricians. There also are a consultant pediatrician and several midwife assistants on the staff. In addition, members of the visiting nurse service provide home visits following discharge.

The center is designed to be as homelike as possible while retaining the facilities to handle a medical emergency. In addition to two labor-delivery rooms, the intrapartum unit contains an examination room, a clean utility room with an autoclave, a soiled-utility room, and a team station with kitchen, bathrooms, and a shower-dressing room. An infant warmer and resuscitation equipment are kept in the unit as are oxygen and intravenous equipment. The center also has a family room and a garden that are used for the early stages of labor, an office, a reception and waiting area, a multipurpose room that is used for child care classes, and an additional examination room. A nearby hospital, which can be reached by ambulance in 11 minutes, provides back-up services in the event of a medical emergency.

Prospective candidates for the center are given a comprehensive physical examination and are evaluated for risk through the use of stringent criteria. Although there is no minimum age limit, a woman giving birth for the first time can be no older than 35. Women who have up to four children can be no older than 39, and women who have more than four children are automatically ineligible. A history of three or more miscarriages also is a barrier to participation. Finally, no family beyond the 20th week of pregnancy is accepted so that ample time is available for an extensive educational program.

A patient may be "risked out" for any irregularity that develops during the course of pregnancy including anemia, excessive weight gain, or the development of high blood pressure. Moreover, if the baby is more than two weeks postmature, the family is risked out.

Participants are required to attend classes during the second and third trimesters of pregnancy. Parent educators discuss topics such as the physiological and emotional reactions of the mother, feeding and sleeping patterns of the newborn, the role of the father or other support person, the physiology of labor and delivery, and the complications that might necessitate transfer to the hospital.

The infant never leaves its parents. Families remain in the center up to 12 hours after the birth and then return home. During the postpartum stay, the infant is given a pediatric examination in the presence of the parents. The family is seen by the visiting nurse within the first 24 hours of their return home and again on the third to fifth day postpartum. The mother and the baby return to the center on the sixth or seventh day and again for a five- to six-week checkup. Families also are expected to have initiated ongoing pediatric and gynecologic care of their choice before the birth.

According to Mrs. Lubic, an important aspect of the center is that it is being used as the basis of a research project to determine the degree to which risk criteria are sensitive predictors of who will have normal pregnancies and deliveries; to test the impact of the childbirth, infant care, and parent educational programs; and to find out what it really costs to have a baby. Data collection has been initiated, and a careful evaluation of the center is being implemented. The Maternity Center Association anticipates that following its current tests for safety, satisfaction, and economy, the model childbearing center will be adaptable for use in urban and suburban acute care settings and in rural areas.

MARTHA'S VACATION

by VARDIS FISHER

Martha stood by the great front door of the hospital, feeling very timid and alone. She pressed her homely face to a pane of glass and looked in; and then, seeing that her nose had stained the glass, she took a soiled handkerchief and tried to wipe the stain off. She was still briskly rubbing when the door was opened and a nurse in white stepped outside and looked at her.

"Oh!" cried Martha, abashed. Her fingers, working against her thigh, fed the handkerchief into a wad within her palm. She glanced guiltily at the pane of glass and then at the nurse. And the nurse looked at Martha's huge belly, at her worn shoes, at her round earnest face.

"You wish to see someone?"

"Uh-huh," Martha said. "I—"

"Will you come in?" The brisk manner of the nurse frightened Martha. She entered a gleaming hallway and looked about anxiously. The nurse said: "This way, please," and her voice was like the edge of a razor. She led Martha into an office that was one spotless gleam. "Wait here a moment."

The nurse left the office, her clothes alive with cleanliness, and Martha drew her breath on a great sigh. She looked at the chairs, but they were very clean and she dared not sit on them. She looked behind her to see if her shoes had tracked the floor. And she was standing there, trembling a little and feeling very lonely, when another nurse entered. The nurse seated herself at a desk.

"Will you sit down?" she asked.

Martha sank weakly to a chair.

"When do you expect your child?"

"I—" Martha stared, helpless. "I feel pains," she said.

"You do?" The nurse frowned and Martha was paralyzed. "Have you made arrangements here?"

"Huh-unh," Martha said.

"Who sent you here?"

"No one. I just come."

For a long moment the nurse looked at her. Her eyes, it seemed to Martha, were not friendly. They were clean cold eyes like her dress and the walls.

"Where is your husband?"

Martha looked down at the short hands lying in her lap.

"What is your name?"

"Martha Scott."

"Where are your parents?"

"I—I don't have none."

"You mean you're an orphan? How old are you?"

"Twenty-two."

"Do you work?"

"Yes, when I'n get work."

"What kind of work?"

"Oh, just anything. Just—just anything."

"And the father of your child, won't he marry you?"

Martha again stared at her hands. She hesitated; when she looked up to meet the steady gaze of the nurse, there was terror in her eyes. . . .

Martha felt better now. She was lying in a spotless bed and her pain was done. There was a strange smell in the room but everything else was very lovely and nice. Somewhere in this great building was her infant but she did not think of it; there was so much else to think of; the soft deep bed on which she lay, the clean fragrance of the bedding, the touch of cool linen on her hot flesh. There was a picture on the wall and she thought it was very nice, too: a young girl in a lovely place, with grass and running water and trees. In all her years she had never once seen running water.

When a nurse came, bringing her son, she took the tiny thing in her arms and laid it to her breast.

"How you feeling?"

"Just fine." Martha looked up and smiled. Never before had anyone asked how she felt. The people here were very nice. "I like it here," she said.

"Do you have enough to eat?"

"Oh, yes. It's very nice, the food is."

The nurse left the room and Martha suckled her child. The tiny sucking mouth gave her a little pleasure but not the deep pleasure George had given her. George had lain against her, his hungry mouth to her breast, his curly hair in her face, smelling of something sweet. She had been very happy then. Well, she was very happy now, in a different way. She might be here a long time—she wondered how long—having food brought to her bedside, having people smile at her and ask how she felt. She brushed her teeth now. The nurse had given her a new brush, taking it out of a sealed package, and powder that was sweet in her mouth. Afternoons, she chose from a bowl of fruit, taking a very little, not caring to take much.

"Is that all you want?"

"Yes, that's all."

"Honest?"

"Yes, honest." Martha looked up and smiled. "And thanks."

After a week passed she sat up in bed and tried to realize to its fullest the wonder of this place. There was no unpleasant smell in her room now. The nurse smelled as if she had just been starched and laundered; and so did the bed. She looked around her, thinking of her own dark hallway room. The pillows here were soft and she loved to bury her face in them and feel their cool cleanness; to move her head and feel the softness on the back of her neck. She loved to stretch out in this bed, thrusting with her naked legs into the cool recesses, remembering the hot world outside; reaching out with her arms and feeling the delicious chill; drawing the sheet, almost stiff with cleanliness and with a sweet smell, to her mouth and breathing of it.

The nurse had brought her some magazines. She did not read easily and she had to spell many of the words out and many of them she did not understand; but she felt her way through these love-tales and they thrilled her in a way George had thrilled her; a sudden rapture that came awake in her and moved in a flood to her heart. It was nice to lie here in a clean bed, with no work to do, and read of lovely things.

"Do you need more light?"

"No, ma'am. I'n see all right."

"Do you like these stories?"

"Yes, ma'am." Martha looked at her with eyes wide and bright. "They're awful nice, I think."

Every day a doctor came in. He was a tall man with a mustache and Martha thought he was very good-looking and very kind. He smiled at her and asked how she felt.

"Just fine," Martha said, her smile answering his.

"You look fit as a fiddle."

"I sure feel fine." Martha stretched luxuriously under the sheet. "I like it here," she said.

"You do? Most persons don't like a hospital."

"Oh, I do. I think it's awful nice. I could stay here a long time."

And when, one day, the nurse said: "You will leave tomorrow, you know," Martha stared at her and felt lost.

"Tomorrow?"

"Yes."

"Please, couldn't I stay a little while longer?"

"I'm afraid not. You see, other patients are coming all the time. You've been here two weeks, you know."

"I have! It seems like two days." She looked around her. "Like two hours," she said. "Couldn't I stay a little longer? . . . Couldn't I?"

"I'm afraid not." The nurse did not look at her.

"Wouldn't the doctor let me?"

"The doctor doesn't have anything to do with it."

"Oh," Martha said. She lay in silence, wondering. "If I could just stay one more day," she said, "it would be awful nice."

The next morning with the babe in her arms she

stood in a hallway and looked back at her room. She returned and looked in, and a nurse came and smiled and led her away.

Fifteen months passed and Martha stood again at the great front door of the hospital. She did not press her face to the glass and look in. She opened the big door and entered, and nurses hurried by on slim-slippered feet and did not look at her. She advanced a little, seeking the office where she had been questioned. The white nurse was there.

"Hello," Martha said.

"You wish to see someone?"

"Please. I'd like to see Miss Anderson. She's a nurse here."

The woman gave Martha a long and curious stare.

"Weren't you here once before?"

"Yes." Martha brightened and stepped into the office. "I'm Martha Scott," she said.

The nurse turned to records and searched among them. For a long moment she looked at one. She turned to Martha, her eyes unfriendly.

"And you're back again!"

Martha was radiant now. Her tired face smiled and her eyes filled with a happiness that was clean and bright.

"And, please," she said, "could I have the same room I had last time?"

XII

MIDWIVES AND BABY NURSES

MIDWIVES PAST AND PRESENT

from *Safe Convoy* (1944)

by WILLIAM J. CARRINGTON

The history of midwifery is ancient and honorable. Women delivered women in the valley of the Nile. All Arab and Persian confinements were presided over by midwives who made many contributions to the art. The ancient Jews had only their mejallah. When the Israelites were exiled, "The King of Egypt spoke to the Hebrew midwives of whom the name of one was Shiprath, and the other was Puah; and he said, When ye do the offices of a midwife to the Hebrew women, and set them upon the stools. . . ." (Exodus 1:15–16) The Greeks knew no obstetricians other than their maeentriae. Phanarete, the mother of Socrates, contemporary of Hippocrates, was a midwife, and Plato in his discourses refers to the profession with the highest respect. In the Middle Ages the famous Justine Siegunundin, court midwife of Brandenburg, after she was entreated by the wife of Georgel, wrote a book on the subject. About that time midwives began to use the rusty ergot blight which appeared on growing rye to control postpartum hemorrhage. Ergot is used to this day and has saved innumerable lives. A German midwife was brought to England to deliver Queen Victoria's first baby. On the Continent midwives are employed extensively today, but not so in England.

Many years ago in Great Britain there was intense rivalry between midwives and doctors, the women having the support of the public at large. John Stevens, in the name of the Society for the Suppression of Vice, denounced the "immorality" of employing men in the delivery room. A male midwife was compelled to tie one end of a sheet around his neck and the other end around the neck of the patient. Each could see the face of the other, but he had to fumble blindly beneath the sheet—all for the sake of false modesty in those days when women blushed easily.

There is a musty record under the date of 1662 of a Dr. Willoughby who was obliged to crawl into a darkened delivery room in order to help his own daughter who was a midwife. Mrs. Nihell, the famous Hay Market midwife, referred to William Smellie, the leading obstetrician of London, as "a great horse-godmother of a he-midwife." Shakespeare wrote in *Pericles*: "O Lucina, Divinest patroness and midwife gentle to those who cry by night." Today there is no trace of rivalry between midwives and members of the medical profession in England. They work there, as they always have worked in America, side by side in perfect harmony for there is a place for them both.

For more than a century after the colonization of the country, midwives delivered all babies. In New Amsterdam rules and regulations were laid down for them. In New England, some of them became famous; Anne Hutchinson, for example, who was killed by the Indians in Rhode Island after her exile from the Massachusetts Colony for religious fanaticism. And Ruth Barnaby, bless her soul, delivered babies for over fifty years and at the ripe old age of one hundred insisted on being vaccinated. In Salem, Margaret Jones was executed as a witch by some of those whose umbilical cords were tied by her own gnarled fingers. It was not until 1757 that a colonial physician became interested in obstetrics. In that year, William Shippen of Philadelphia, just returned from postgraduate studies in Europe, announced that he was specially qualified to care for premature and difficult births. From that day to this, lying-in care in America has been divided between midwives and physicians and without rivalry on the part of either group.

THE MIDWIFE

from *The Life and Opinions of Tristram Shandy*

by LAURENCE STERNE

In the same village where my father and my mother dwelt, dwelt also a thin, upright, motherly, notable, good old body of a midwife, who with the help of a little plain good sense, and some years' full employment in her business, in which she had all along trusted little to her own efforts, and a great deal to those of dame Nature,—had acquired, in her way, no small degree of reputation in the world:—by which *world*, need I in this place inform your worship, that I would be understood to mean no more of it, than a small circle described upon the circle of the great world, of four English miles diameter, or thereabouts, of which the cottage where the good old woman lived, is supposed to be the centre?—She had been left, it seems, a widow in great distress, with three or four small children, in her forty-seventh year; and as she was at that time a person of decent carriage,—grave deportment,—a woman moreover of few words, and withal an object of compassion, whose distress, and silence under it, called out the louder for a friendly lift: the wife of the parson of the parish was touched with pity; and having often lamented an inconvenience, to which her husband's flock had for many years been exposed, inasmuch as there was no such thing as a midwife, of any kind or degree, to be got at, let the case have been never so urgent, within less than six or seven long miles riding; which said seven long miles in dark nights and dismal roads, the country thereabouts being nothing but a deep clay, was almost equal to fourteen; and that in effect was sometimes next to having no midwife at all; it came into her head, that it would be doing as seasonable a kindness to the whole parish, as to the poor creature herself, to get her a little instructed in some of the plain principles of the business, in order to set her up in it. As no woman thereabouts was better qualified to execute the plan she had formed than herself, the gentlewoman very charitably undertook it; and having great influence over the female part of the parish, she found no difficulty in effecting it to the utmost of her wishes. In truth, the parson joined his interest with his wife's in the whole affair; and in order to do things as they should be, and give the poor soul as good a title by law to practice, as his wife had given by institution,—he cheerfully paid the fees for the ordinary's licence himself, amounting in the whole, to the sum of eighteen shillings and fourpence; so that betwixt them both, the good woman was fully invested in the real and corporal possession of her office, together with all its rights, members, and appurtenances whatsoever.

SARAH GAMP

from *Martin Chuzzlewit*
by CHARLES DICKENS

Her name, as Mr. Pecksniff gathered from a scrap of writing in his hand, was Gamp; her residence in Kingsgate Street, High Holborn. So Mr. Pecksniff, in a hackney-cab, was rattling over Holborn stones, in quest of Mrs. Gamp.

This lady lodged at a bird-fancier's, next door but one to the celebrated mutton-pie shop, and directly opposite to the original cats'-meat warehouse; the renown of which establishments was duly heralded on their respective fronts. It was a little house, and this was the more convenient; for Mrs. Gamp being, in her highest walk of art, a monthly nurse, or, as her signboard boldly had it, "Midwife," and lodging in the first-floor front, was easily assailable at night by pebbles, walking-sticks, and fragments of tobacco-pipe: all much more efficacious than the street-door knocker, which was so constructed as to wake the street with ease, and even spread alarms of fire in Holborn, without making the smallest impression on the premises to which it was addressed.

It chanced on this particular occasion, that Mrs. Gamp had been up all the previous night, in attendance upon a ceremony to which the usage of gossips has given that name which expresses, in two syllables, the curse pronounced on Adam. It chanced that Mrs. Gamp had not been regularly engaged, but had been called in at a crisis, in consequence of her great repute, to assist another professional lady with her advice.

NURSE-MIDWIVES

from *The American Journal of Nursing* (October 1975)

by RUTH WATSON LUBIC

It is my belief that nursing has failed to fulfill one of its potentials: teaching health care to women as well as ministering to the sick. Nursing, for the most part, has ignored the course so carefully charted by Florence Nightingale who said,

> Every woman . . . has, at one time or another in her life, charge of the personal health of somebody, whether child or invalid—in other words, every woman is a nurse. . . .
>
> If, then, every woman must, at some time or other of her life, become a nurse, i.e., have charge of somebody's health, how immense and how valuable would be

> the produce of her united experience if every woman would think how to nurse.
>
> I do not pretend to teach her how, I ask her to teach herself; and for this purpose I venture to give her some hints.

In fairness, it may be better to say nursing drifted off course. Why did this occur? Was it the siren call of professionalism that turned our heads, causing us to leave one of our basic roles as teachers of women and turn instead to self-concerns, both as individuals and as a group?

The time is ripe for us to realize that women now have prepared a milieu in which we can effectively implement our lost role. It is they to whom we should be indebted. On every side women speak out, saying they will manage their own care, and that of family members, ensuring health wherever possible. The following passage from a best-selling book published by the Boston Women's Health Collective is vigorously illustrative:

> Lots of changes are coming, and women's clinics and health centers will probably be part of them, but for most of us for a long time doctors and hospitals as they are now will be part of our lives. Just being enraged with the system shouldn't keep us from trying to get the very best medical care that money can buy right now, for the very least that we can pay, whenever we need it. But there is at present almost no way we can get perspective on the system or the care we receive, even in a women's clinic, without study. Which doesn't mean, as the doctors are fond of interpreting, that we all want to learn to become nurses or doctors or amateur specialists. For some of us that may be what we really want, but for others of us it is another matter, first of all that of having something to say about what happens to our bodies. Also, it is a hunger after those approaches and understandings that preserve health and prevent disease rather than a fascination with the drama of emergency creative care.

Childbearing Today

Nowhere are women more aware of and less patient with the "system" than in the field of their own reproductive functioning. Disenchantment with available services is demonstrated by the women's clinics which have grown up in many urban areas, most often to provide gynecologic and fertility control assistance. But perhaps a more dramatic response is seen in maternity care in the return to home deliveries, with or without professional assistance. This return, most prevalent on the West Coast, is widely documented in the media.

At first glance, it may seem paradoxical that awareness of health would lead away from institutionalized maternity care rather than toward it. But, as young people have informed themselves about childbirth, they have recognized its inherent normalcy and demanded a cooperative role in planning care. Routinized hospital practices have been illuminated as the ritual they often are.

Beginning in 1970, the Maternity Center Association became aware of an increase in requests for assistance in locating professionals who would attend at home deliveries. At the same time, we believed there was a subtle change in the character of the requests. Over the years our reputation for interest in nurse-midwifery, and the public mythology that nurse-midwives function primarily in home birth settings, caused us to receive a small but steady flow of requests. Often the seekers were people who had experienced home delivery in other cultures. Some were women and families who remembered Maternity Center Association's own home delivery service which had been staffed by nurse-midwives with obstetrical backup, but which had closed in 1958.

In 1970, however, those seeking assistance seemed much more vociferous in criticizing hospital practices and, at the same time, much more impatient with the lack of options available to them. We sensed that an unarmed revolution had begun.

We decided to poll maternal and child health nursing consultants in the country to see if others were experiencing a trend to do-it-yourself home deliveries. We found some were aware of the problem, but not all. Those in the Western states were seeing more of the phenomenon.

The Demand for Options

Late in 1971, an article appeared in *The New York Times* describing a local New York City group, which provided support and assistance for home-delivery-seeking families in the metropolitan area. Then, in September 1972, a meeting described in a report entitled "Meeting Consumers' Demands for Maternity Care" was held in Seattle at the University of Washington School of Nursing. According to that report, most, but not all, of the families seeking home deliveries could be described as "counter-culture." But, two years later, a 1974 study of 300 home birth families reports that only 10 percent of the study families could be considered "counter-culture." Ninety percent of the couples were "straight," middle class, attended college, owned their own autos and TV's, and often their own homes.

It is my hypothesis that "counter-culture" young people, in boldly demonstrating that home deliveries could be done without the dire results predicted by most professionals, provided an option for many other couples who, while dissatisfied with traditional care, believed they had no alternatives and would not themselves have initiated a move to home delivery.

Another interesting aspect to the changing scene has been the reappearance of the lay midwife. The "new" lay midwife is likely to be female, post high school but young, dedicated to humane pursuits, and self-taught in midwifery. Although her practice has not been legally sanctioned, she has come into being because "recognized" health professionals either will not or believe they cannot assist at home births without jeopardizing their own practices.

We see, then, that we are not dealing with a passive, accepting, unquestioning population but, rather, with knowledgeable young people who are willing to develop their own resources when the "system" refuses its support or when its offerings are seen as irrelevant, prohibitively expensive, or as imposing certain unacceptable risks. The following quote emanates from the Seattle meeting:

> Where risk was concerned, I, too, had to cross that bridge and ask myself the usual questions: what if the baby needed oxygen? what if I hemorrhaged? These possibilities were real, but not likely. That was the key. Another side of me asked, what if I go to the hospital, have a deformed baby and they keep it alive with all their equipment?
>
> So life is a great adventure. Everyone takes risks. Riding in an automobile is the worst risk of my daily life. In the end, I think a risk is made to gain an end well worth it. The unlikely medical emergencies were a small risk compared to the enormous reward and delight of having my baby at home.

Can Nurse-Midwifery Help?

I propose that these fraying threads of public disenchantment with the system and the demands of women to be equipped to ensure their own health and that of their families can be woven into a whole cloth of strength most effective through reaching women during the childbearing experience. I say this for a number of reasons.

First, education of mothers and families is the soul of nurse-midwifery practice, a dimension which causes it to differ qualitatively from an obstetrical approach to childbearing women. This fact, tied to the expertise of the nurse-midwife in the normal childbearing process, means that she has tended to be health oriented, not pathology oriented. These two facts, tied to her ability to teach the theoretical aspects of childbearing and rearing, and also provide practical suggestions in on-the-spot clinical situations, enhance her educational effectiveness.

But, more important, in my opinion, nurse-midwifery management of the entire childbearing experience offers an unusual opportunity for establishment of trust between care receivers and care givers. In this manner the validity and acceptance of teaching, which at times can be only theoretical and not applied until a future time, are ensured. Nurse-midwives, then, are *with* a family through one of its most exciting and gratifying life cycle events, sharing in the joy at the climax of the reproductive miracle as well as being supportive through the days of expectation and the trials of settling a newborn into the family.

Second, maternity care is prototypical preventive health care and, therefore, a natural entry point for providing the information that women and families are seeking. It has always been our experience at Maternity Center that families involved in the childbearing experience are eager for other health care information. "Lack of patient motivation," a phrase we professionals often use when our health teaching is ineffectual, is seldom a problem in prenatal classes, which are meticulously attuned to the interests and needs of families. What do women say on this topic? Again, from the Boston Women's Collective:

> Health will be the full-time responsibility of the patient, but not health as it is identified today, which is really synonymous with disease. The tools for prevention belong in the hands of the patients, as the tools for management of disease belong with the doctors. There should be programs in health information and education—even whole centers devoted to this purpose. . . . But what passes for health education today has little value. Courses taught by people who are part of the

> "health" system have rarely given really honest consumer information or unbiased weighing of advantages and disadvantages. For the most part they are highly partisan offerings designed to defend the system and frighten you. Most of these programs are concerned with several factors: what the disease or problem is, how to recognize it, how wide-spread it is, and how much money is still needed for research. And they usually offer one over-all answer: trust your hospital and get regular check-ups from your doctor.

It would thus appear that women are ready for and are seeking information. It also appears, however, that teaching is an exchange and not the giving of "truth" as we may happen to see it. The search is for direct, honest information and guidance; platitudes have no place in today's health education.

Third, nurse-midwifery's orientation toward enhancing the normal process and away from introducing interventionist techniques tends to increase the likelihood that women will trust nurse-midwifery care.

Alternative Models of Maternity Care

How do we know it can work—that women of all socioeconomic groups, who may be disenchanted with traditional care, will actually accept nurse-midwives?

In addition to an increasing number of group practices which include nurse-midwives as team members, we have several nationwide major programs which demonstrate acceptance of the nurse-midwife as an obstetrical team member by women of all socioeconomic levels.

At Roosevelt Hospital in New York, and at the University Hospital in Minneapolis, such nurse-midwifery services are successful and growing. Starting in 1970 in Springfield, Ohio, at the Community Hospital of Springfield and Clark County, the Maternal Health Service (now the Simpson Maternal Health Service) has unquestionably demonstrated women's acceptance of nurse-midwifery care backed up by obstetrical experts.

Probably the most exciting demonstration to date, particularly considering the responsible role of the patient in care decision-making, is the Booth Maternity Center in Philadelphia where, in a Salvation Army operated, free-standing maternity hospital, a small team of nurse-midwives and obstetricians provides care to a caseload of women which has almost trebled in three years. Women of all educational, social, economic, racial and marital backgrounds seek and use the facility. Kitty Ernst, CNM, Maternity Center staff cosultant on site at Booth, has expressed the philosophy as follows:

> "By getting the mother to participate in childbearing decisions, we help her build confidence in herself and her ability to do things—which I think is essential for motherhood. If you're going to raise children, you should start with a confidence base. We try to reinforce this rather than fragment it or break it down."

MIDWIFERY IN A HOSPITAL SETTING

by THOMAS F. DILLON, M.D., BARBARA A. BRENNAN, R.N., C.N.M., JOHN F. DWYER, M.D., ABRAHAM RISK, M.D., M.P.H., ALAN SEAR, PH.D., LYNNE DAWSON, M.P.H., R.N., RAYMOND VANDE WIELE, M.D.

There is controversy as to the better method of rendering obstetrical care to patients in this country. The plans that have been offered range from home deliveries on the one extreme to the medical center on the other with many different alternatives in between. The consumer perhaps more than in any other specialty raised a voice stating his preference. In the center of this controversy is the unending debate as to what role the nurse midwife should play in this health system. In an attempt to help solve the crisis we have presented a midwifery program for in-hospital care that emphasizes sensitive individualized and family centered care and at the same time preserves the concept of modern obstetrics. In this program the nurse midwife may care for patients from any sector of the community.

The history of midwifery in the United States has been well documented. While the profession antedates history and the work of the "midwife" is documented through the ages—it was the opening of the American School of Nurse-Midwifery in Harlem in 1931 that changed the course of this profession in the United States of America. Prior to this time midwifery was identified in many ways. Midwives worked with religious groups, with governmental agencies, with physicians as assistants and with institutions serving the underprivileged. With the development of "midwifery schools" the profession was re-identified. The participants were identified as fully trained registered nurses, and a relatively standard curriculum was adopted. All of this was, of course, an important change but it did not completely establish the role of midwifery in obstetrics in the United States. For now it was the nurse-midwife who was working in programs that ranged from physician assistants in private practice to rural or urban or maternity center types of operation. Thus it was at our institution from 1965 to 1974 wherein the nurse-midwives worked on the ward service helping the obstetricians care for a large group of obstetrical patients.

In 1974 we instituted an autonomous midwifery service [at Roosevelt Hospital in New York]. This was organized utilizing Hellman's criteria that were presented to the American College of Obstetrics and Gynecology in May 1964.

The prerequisites were:

1. A service large enough so that there will never be competition for patients.
2. A service well enough staffed so that a senior resident (or in our case an attending obstetrician or senior resident) is always assigned and/or present on the delivery floor.
3. A highly disciplined standard of obstetric care under the direct charge and responsibility of a single chief of staff.
4. One prerequisite added by us was to employ a group of well-trained nurse-midwives who were dedicated to this task.

In this strict environment five midwives began the practice of obstetrics on their private patients, and we set sail in a new vessel hoping to weld the charisma of the midwife with modern obstetrics as we know it in the nineteen-seventies. The midwives, operating in rotation, conducted office hours in the offices occupied by the full-time staff. They cared for and delivered their patients in a modern obstetrical suite with monitors, et al. Physician backup was available immediately at either attending or senior-resident level. In this experiment the consumer, and there are many, seems delighted to have total management by a midwife; knowing full well instant assistance is available.

WHAT IS TO BE DONE WITH THE CHILDREN?

from *The Republic*
by PLATO

The proper officers will take the offspring of the good parents to the pen or fold, and there they will deposit them with certain nurses who dwell in a separate quarter; but the offspring of the inferior, or of the better when they chance to be deformed, will be put away in some mysterious, unknown place as they should be.

. . . . They will provide for their nurture and will bring the mothers to the fold when they are full of milk, taking the greatest possible care that no mother recognizes her own child; and other wet-nurses may be engaged if more are required. Care will also be taken that the process of suckling shall not be protracted too long; and the mothers will have no getting up at night or other trouble, but will hand over all this sort of thing to the nurses and attendants.

ON THE CHOICE OF A WET-NURSE

from *Poem on Medicine*
by AVICENNA

If the child is to be fed by a wet-nurse, intrust him with only one of a certain age. Choose a wet-nurse of an average age, fleshy, with tight skin, of a well-balanced temperament, with a firm body, with voluminous breasts, whose head and eyes are clean, who has no internal illness, whose limbs and joints are robust, whose milk is neither too liquid nor too thick, white in color, sweet and pleasant to taste, with a good odor and homogeneous when one expresses it. Give her a sweet and fatty diet, fresh fish prepared in oil.

THE WET NURSE

from *The Autobiography of Dr. Robert Meyer* (1949)

Since it was fashionable at that time to have a wet nurse in a wonderful looking costume, I yielded to having one whom I loved. She loved me too and came to see me on my birthdays for many years. Her costume was that of the peasants in Hessen-Cassel where she wore it only occasionally on Sundays. But while in Hanover she wore it all the time to show off and to become acquainted with other maids. She had an illegitimate child which was in no way a disgrace in her home. To her people it was a legitimate child. She had to prove her fertility before she could get married because to have descendants was to a peasant an indispensable blessing. Besides, she had to earn her trousseau by nursing.

From THE BABY NURSE

by BEN AMES WILLIAMS

A waiting room is a fearful place. Millie had had some experience of waiting rooms and she dreaded them. She had been sitting in this particular waiting room at the employment agency for three days; a little woman, thin and taut, and just now curiously tremulous. Her eyes, inflamed and weary, looked blankly straight before her. And sometimes, for no apparent reason, they became suffused with tears; not merely misted with moisture, but drowned in a swimming, drenching flood which flowed over her lids and down her dry cheeks until she remembered to wipe away these evidences of the grief which racked her.

On the third day she found herself replying in a dull voice to the questions put to her by a woman who introduced herself by a name which Millie scarcely heard. She was not interested in the names of her mistresses; she had had so many of them. This woman's name might have been Brown or Jones. It happened to be Mrs. Smith.

Mrs. Smith asked question upon question, but Millie asked only one.

"Is the baby a boy or girl?"

"A little girl," Mrs. Smith replied. And Millie's ravaged face seemed to lighten faintly at the word.

"I like little girls best," she confessed.

They arranged for Millie to come next morning; and Millie was for the rest of that day a little more cheerful. Her aching grief found anodyne in the prospect of having another baby to love.

WOMEN OF HIGH CALLING

from *Safe Convoy* (1944)

by WILLIAM J. CARRINGTON

If the mother-to-be never has been in a hospital before, she may not understand nurses. They may seem too stiffly starched, efficient enough perhaps, but cold and unsympathetic. Nurses know full well that pregnant women need sympathetic kindness beyond the line of duty. The patient has the happiest and smoothest convalescence who treats her nurse as she would her own sister. The day has passed long since when patients regarded nurses as high-class servants. They are women of high calling of whom physicians are justly proud. The fact is that the modern trained nurse is an integral part of a trinity. Together with priest and physician, her prime mission is to heal both body and soul. When Charles Dickens painted a sombre word picture of Sairey Gamp, dirty, blustering, and foul of mouth, he brought before the mind's eye almost the only kind of nurse known before the disciples of Florence Nightingale tiptoed silently into the delivery room and went to work with deft fingers and stout hearts. If either a mother or a baby shows the slightest deviation from normal, it is an inspiration to watch a modern trained nurse go into action. Her efficiency is a joy to behold!

In the time of Hippocrates, 400 B.C., there were no trained nurses, only calloused souls like Dickens' Miss Prig of St. Barts, she of the male voice and whiskers.

COMPULSORY ROOMING-IN IN THE WARD AND PRIVATE NEWBORN SERVICE AT DUKE HOSPITAL

from *The Journal of the American Medical Association* (March 1951)

by ANGUS McBRYDE

Advantages to the Infant

A self-regulating schedule is advised for breast feeding, and every effort is made to facilitate this procedure. The mother can observe her infant's hunger rhythm and can nurse him whenever he is hungry. Thus, he gets as good care as a puppy and a kitten, who thrive nutritionally and psychologically better than many human offspring. The percentage of infants who are breast fed has been markedly increased by rooming-in (58.5 percent of the infants discharged are now breast fed as compared with 35 percent before the program began).

In addition to the reduced incidence of infections and the increase in breast feeding, the infant is better satisfied and cries less when he is near his mother. Not all crying represents hunger. It may represent discomfort or insecurity. Let us consider the newborn infant's plight. He comes into the world as a person who has been fed constantly by way of the placenta and has been kept warm with a blanket of soothing fluid about him. He arrives and immediately is surrounded by cold dry air. His last link with parasitic security is severed. He must now begin to breathe, eat and perform other functions for himself. In using the former nursery technic, we have tried to make him self-sufficient by immediately severing his maternal tie.

How has rooming-in aided him in adjusting to his new environment? First, by close physical contact with the mother whose warmth and firm clasp he needs. He should have the opportunity to suckle frequently and on demand. Obviously these things are needed when he wakes and demonstrates his desire for them. Only by having him constantly near the mother, where she can hear and satisfy his demands, can he be without discomfort or distress. We encourage the mother to feel that crying represents the infant's need for her, in terms of either warmth or food, and so the infant may be taken into her bed at any time. This apparently acts as a sedative for mother and child. He is left there until he is quiet and can easily be replaced in his crib. Aldrich has stated that strict adherence to rigid forms of child training and lack of affectionate treatment are factors resulting in aggressive, maladjusted children. We believe, with Moloney, that the early closeness of the parent-child relationship, as it is initiated in rooming-in, may be the first step in forming the proper close family relationship.

Advantages to the Mother

The advantages of rooming-in start with the satisfaction and delight of the mother in meeting her baby early instead of waiting the 24 to 48 hours often prescribed by obstetricians under the guise of rest. The rooming-in plan affords mothers an early opportunity to become acquainted with their babies and to handle them affectionately thus stimulating lactation.

There was almost universal approval of rooming-in by the mothers on our program, both primiparas and multiparas, especially if its advantages had been enthusiastically explained in advance. There was only an occasional maternal complaint of apprehension and sleeplessness during the first 24 hours when the infant did not rest well or had excessive mucus. Some mothers feel fatigued and emotionally spent and are concerned because of the infant's presence in the room, thus apparently increasing their responsibility. We are attempting to solve this difficulty by closer nursing supervision rather than by moving the infant to the nursery, which would defeat the purpose of isolation. Formerly, mothers (as well as fathers) on returning home were afraid to handle their baby and were bewildered and anxious about his perfectly normal reactions, such as sneezing and crying when he wanted anything from attention and food to a dry diaper. That the mother has more confidence in her ability to care for the infant is evidenced by a decrease of about 90 percent in the telephone calls from new mothers during their first week at home.

Visitors are limited to the father and grandparents, who are allowed to visit whenever they wish and may aid in the care of the infant so long as they wash their hands and are free of respiratory, skin and intestinal infections. The plan is very popular with the grandparents. The father is encouraged to help with the baby as much as possible so that he may become acquainted very early with the infant and his problems. Rooming-in has caused marked changes in the attitude of many fathers toward their babies; they begin to share the responsibility at once and therefore do not feel that care of the infant is completely in the mothers' province during the early months.

Origin of Newborn Nurseries

Those of us who have been interested in this rooming-in program believed that something new had been introduced into obstetrics and pediatrics. However, as pointed out recently by Strong in his excellent review of the history of rooming-in, practically all European hospitals, as well as those in Japan and China, have always had the rooming-in plan. At the Rotunda in Dublin, and other famous European maternity hospitals, nurseries were unheard of. La Fetra states that neither the New York Hospital nor the Nursery and Child's Hospital had a nursery in 1896. The New York Hospital in 1898 still had rooming-in. The Johns Hopkins Hospital was built without a nursery and did not have one until after 1890. (An attempt is now being made by Clifford to trace the origin of American nurseries and to discover the reasons for their introduction.) It was not until the turn of the century that hospital nurseries, with all their evils, became prevalent throughout this country. They were invented in the 1890's by nurses or obstetricians, or even possibly by pediatricians, although there were very few of them at that time. One reason suggested for the introduction of nurseries was the high incidence of maternal sepsis and the frequency of infections in the newborn. Now that obstetrics is less septic, rooming-in is safer than a nursery. It also is possible that prior to 1900 most of the mothers hospitalized for obstetric care were too ill to care for their infants, and a nursery was necessary. Today the great majority of obstetric patients are in good health.

Conclusions

Rooming-in is advantageous for infants, mothers, grandparents, pediatricians and hospital administrators. As they become more accustomed to the program, obstetricians and nurses also grow to like it. Making rooming-in compulsory and explaining its advantages in advance to the mother have averted many of the misunderstandings of the optional plan.

The nursing cost of the rooming-in program is less than that of a newborn nursery. No special equipment or modifications of rooms or wards is needed. The ordinary baby's bassinet with a storage cabinet beneath is all that is necessary.

There is nothing new in the world, and we are returning to a safer and saner method of caring for infants. Now that such a large percentage of infants are born in hospitals, it behooves all of us to make that process as safe and sane as possible. It is hoped that hospitals in the future will be built without nurseries for normal newborn infants who are born of healthy mothers.

BORROWED TIME IN THE NURSERY

from *Bliss*

by KATHERINE MANSFIELD

Nurse sat at a low table giving Little B. her supper after her bath. The baby had on a white flannel gown and a blue woollen jacket, and her dark, fine hair was brushed up into a funny little peak. She looked up when she saw her mother and began to jump.

"Now, my lovey, eat it up like a good girl," said Nurse, setting her lips in a way that Bertha knew, and that meant she had come into the nursery at another wrong moment.

"Has she been good, Nanny?"

"She's been a little sweet all the afternoon," whispered Nanny. "We went to the park and I sat down on a chair and took her out of the pram and a big dog came along and put its head on my knee and she clutched its ear, tugged it. Oh, you should have seen her."

Bertha wanted to ask if it wasn't rather dangerous to let her clutch at a strange dog's ear. But she did not dare to. She stood watching them, her hands by her side, like the poor little girl in front of the rich little girl with the doll.

The baby looked up at her again, stared, and then smiled so charmingly that Bertha couldn't help crying:

"Oh, Nanny, do let me finish giving her her supper while you put the bath things away."

"Well, M'm, she oughtn't to be changed hands while she's eating," said Nanny, still whispering. "It unsettles her; it's very likely to upset her."

How absurd it was. Why have a baby if it has to be kept—not in a case like a rare, rare fiddle—but in another woman's arms? "Oh, I must!" she said.

Very offended, Nanny handed her over.

"Now, don't excite her after her supper. You know you do, M'm. And I have such a time with her after!"

Thank heaven! Nanny went out of the room with the bath towels.

"Now, I've got you to myself, my little precious," said Bertha, as the baby leaned against her.

She ate delightfully, holding up her lips for the spoon and then waving her hands. Sometimes she wouldn't let the spoon go; and sometimes, just as Bertha had filled it, she waved it away to the four winds.

When the soup was finished Bertha turned round to the fire.

"You're nice—you're very nice!" she said, kissing her warm baby. "I'm fond of you. I like you."

And, indeed, she loved Little B. so much—her neck as she bent forward, her exquisite toes as they shone transparent in the firelight—that all her feeling of bliss came back again, and again she didn't know how to express it—what to do with it.

"You're wanted on the telephone," said Nanny, coming back in triumph and seizing *her* Little B.

XIII

OBSTETRICIANS

THE TRANSITION FROM MIDWIFE TO OBSTETRICIAN

from *Safe Convoy* (1944)

by WILLIAM J. CARRINGTON

The first handbook, *The Little Book for Women*, was written in Wurzburg, Germany, before Columbus discovered America. It was written by a man who probably never attended a woman in labor, for if he did it was in defiance of the law. As late as 1532, a doctor named Vertis was burned at the stake in Germany for disguising himself as a woman in order to help deliver a woman who was in desperate straits. The drudgery of caring for lying-in women was thrust into the dirty hands of untrained midwives to whom the government paid a yearly stipend, together with the grant of a cabbage patch, and immunity from taxation. In addition to these privileges, a midwife was not compelled to quarter soldiers, and her eldest son was excused from military duty.

Another handbook, the most famous of them all, was published in Strassburg, Germany, in 1513 by Easharios Roesslin under the euphemistic title of *The Garden of Roses for Pregnant Women and Midwives*. Roesslin wrote the book at the request of a woman, Catherine, Duchess of Brunswick, although it is almost certain that he had never as much as seen the birth of a baby. Several of the forty editions of his book were translated into Latin, French, Dutch and "Englysshe." The work was in no sense original, but rather a compilation, for midwives, of the writings of Hippocrates, Galen, and other old-time authorities.

In France men were not permitted into the delivery room until the time of Louis XV. How the ban was lifted is a sordid story. That philandering king had the feeling that doctors ought to know more than midwives and so, wanting nothing but the best for his mistress, Mademoiselle La Valliere, he engaged Dr. Boucher. But doubts assailed the monarch. Only after he had watched the proceedings from concealment behind heavy draperies, did he bestow his unqualified blessing on male midwifery. With royal approval, it soon became so fashionable, not only in France, but throughout Europe, that Dr. Clement was summoned from Paris on three occasions to deliver the wife of Philip V of Spain. For thirteen centuries physicians of Europe had been denied entrance into the delivery room but at long last the ban was lifted. At that, medical men were called in only on state occasions, or when there were complications. Ordinary midwifery remained beneath the pompous dignity of most doctors until the present generation. Nowadays, members of the medical profession look upon the practice of obstetrics as a high privilege; and the physician who is selected by an expectant mother feels that he has been honored when she places her life and that of her unborn baby in his hands.

It was Dr. Fraser who delivered Amber's son, for many of the court ladies were beginning to employ doctors rather than midwives—though elsewhere the practice was regarded as merely one more evidence of aristocratic decadence.

—KATHLEEN WINSOR, *Forever Amber*

DEVELOPMENT OF OBSTETRICS AS A MEDICAL SPECIALTY

from *Medical Reflections on Obstetrics and Gynecology*
Vol. I, No. 2 (March/April 1976)
by EVELYN RIVERS WILBANKS

The first male specialist in obstetrics is traditionally said to have been Soranus of Ephesus who practised in Rome in the first quarter of the second century, A.D. His *Gynecology*, originally written in Greek, became the chief source book for midwifery for the next 1500 years. It was addressed to the literate physician who needed special instruction to teach midwives.

Thus, the professionalization of the obstetrician reached a new milestone: a corpus of secret knowledge, written in a book, was taught by the physician as a superior form of competence to the less educated midwife. The next steps toward the institutionalization of knowledge were to attempt to control the qualification of the participants, and to permit access exclusively to qualified experts. The first two sections in Soranus' first book were expressly designed to help the physician to evaluate and upgrade midwives "to prevent fruitless work and the teaching of unfit persons." Proper qualifications included the character, mental ability, and the physical form of the aspiring midwife.

The second area in Soranus' work worth noting is his concern with normal childbirth as well as with the problematic. This obviously shows an increased participation in the care of healthy women, even though the physician's role was still primarily the instruction of midwives.

Soranus wrote about a third important aspect of obstetrics in Book III, "Whether women have conditions peculiarly their own." This problem reflects the basic human quest which occupied many classical thinkers: how men defined themselves in relation to women. In some Greek thought women were considered to be inferior males (Plato, *Timaeus*). Therefore it is easy to understand the concern of ancient physicians to ascertain whether the treatment of men and women should be the same or different. Soranus reviewed the literature and concluded that "there exist natural conditions in women peculiarly their own (as conception, parturition, and lactation if one wishes to call these functions conditions), whereas conditions contrary to nature are not generically different but only in a specific and particular way" [translation by Owsei Temkin].

By the end of the late classical period medical men interested in childbirth had become direct participants in obstetrics. While they did not actually deliver the baby except in trauma, they had collected their own knowledge, they had begun to learn the knowledge of the midwives, they were making efforts to set standards which they considered superior to prevailing practice, and they were beginning to be more aware of the patient herself. They had approached the role of the female midwife, and they were also in close proximity to women as the center of their concern.

What they wrote continued to have a limited value to practicing midwives. Most books were not within reach of the midwives, and few of them were able to read Greek or Latin. However, it is not correct to assume that there was no further development in the specialty before the sixteenth century. In eleventh century Salerno, a group of midwives, probably females in the families of professors of the medical school, practiced comprehensive care of women. Their wisdom was collected in written form under the name of Trotula. Although Trotula's identity has been lost in medieval traditions, historians generally agree on her existence. Her books were a compendium of ancient sources such as Soranus, and empirical observation and were respected by men in the medical profession.

The high standard of obstetrics at Salerno derives from the high quality of medical teaching in the medical school. Physicians set a new pattern for medical study and professionalization in the twelfth century. An apprentice system of learning was replaced by formalization of medical teaching. This pattern spread during the thirteenth century to other medical schools and was later followed by licensing of physicians in Italian cities. Inevitably the control of medicine began to settle in the hands of those with university training. The higher standards set by the teachers at Salerno was reflected in higher standards in obstetrical practice in the same community. But in the following centuries the university-trained physicians increased their control over who could study and what was taught.

The increase of physicians' control of obstetrics as an academic specialty is more than just a part of the growing professionalization of all knowledge. Another important factor in the later Middle Ages and early Renaissance was a change in the type of knowledge which men sought. Men's awakening interest in themselves as natural creatures led to a new consciousness of the natural world around and within them. This new perception included an increased awareness of the inter-relatedness of natural phenomena, a new understanding of facts they had already gathered. These new insights came at the same time that individual men were beginning to coordinate the mental and manual—the academic and practical—traditions of a field. In the Middle Ages the crafts were considered a subordinate area of activity to the intellectual.

From 1300 on men in northern Italy began to struggle with the problems involved in coordinating the eye, hand, and mind, and their writings are filled with the wonder and joy of the challenge. About 1400, the Florentine painter, Cennini, specifically declares his purpose to be to "make note of what he has tried out with his own hand." Some historians point to the figure of Brunelleschi as the point where art and science come together, since he worked out his theories in architecture and perspective by experimental means. Leonardo's work at the end of the fifteenth century indicates the influence which artists who studied human anatomy had on the development of medicine.

It is this co-ordination of mental and manual studies in the exploration of anatomy which was so important to the development of obstetrics. The medieval roles of Reader, Pointer, and Dissector came together for the first time in one man, Vesalius. He was able to see and perceive Galen's errors, and began to define more accurately the human body. While most bodies available for dissection were male, a very few female cadavers enabled Vesalius, Colombo, Fallopio, and Eustachius in the sixteenth century to study and compile an increasingly accurate anatomical knowledge of the female body. This knowledge gradually began to affect the work of physicians and surgeons.

A second aspect of men's awakening consciousness of themselves which influenced obstetrics was the awareness of how one human differed from another. Men came to see women as different from as well as like themselves in much more specific and individual ways than in the late classical period. Important in the development of this new relationship with women were the phenomena of the cult of the virgin and the courtly poetic tradition. They began in early twelfth century Southern France and soon spread through bordering regions with tremendous vitality, affecting other areas of life. The subsequent reaction, called the "querelles des femmes," which argued the faults and merits of women, was fed by clerical misogynists and waning knighthood. The sequence of events is less important to the development of obstetrics than the fact that the interest in women as separate creatures was becoming manifest in every sphere of human life including medicine.

Men began to write books exclusively for and about women in all areas of life. The invention of the printing press made the books more available after 1450 as the literate public increased. Men wrote about women's education, manners, cosmetics, etc., with some authors disparaging the new female license and others encouraging increasing freedom. Important to women themselves and to obstetrics as a specialty were the first books on midwifery for midwives which appeared in Northern Europe. . . .

Just as artists and anatomists had combined their mental and manual expressions, the two areas of obstetrics, the practical and the academic, began to converge during the mid-sixteenth century at the Hôtel-Dieu in Paris, especially in the work of Ambrose Paré (1510–90). While he was not a member of the academic college of surgeons, he was well-trained and gained tremendous practical experience in the public wards. His books written in French indicate first hand experience in deliveries. He developed the procedure of podalic version. While it may have been known in ancient times, Paré came to it through his studies of dissections. It was a practical manipulative technique which was based on knowledge gained through surgical training.

Another important event in the development of obstetrics is a book entitled *L'Heureux Accouchement* (1609), written by Jacques Guillemeau (1544–1612), a pupil of Paré. It shows the male midwife's awareness of not only the physiology of women's deliveries but also of the mother's mental-emotional condition. He attributed delay of delivery to women's fear of labor, and he urged the midwife to reassure her patient.

The close competitiveness of the male surgeons and female midwives in Paris is seen in the work of another of Paré's pupils at the Hôtel-Dieu, Louyse Bourgeois (1563–1636). She became the royal midwife to Marie de Medici, but she is important to the development of obstetrics as the first woman to write a text on midwifery for midwives. Although women were excluded by law from the University of Paris, they were still able to perform within a highly literate tradition and to set standards for their peers. Because of her fierce independence from male intervention, Louyse Bourgeois undoubtedly influenced the performance of male as well as female midwives.

By the seventeenth century, men were very active as

practicing midwives. Their increased intervention in obstetrics brought new manipulative techniques in the use of instruments. The crochet, perforator, speculum, and fillet had been in use since antiquity. They were used in traumatic cases and were dreaded by all. They were *not* factors leading to the success of men as midwives. The seventeenth century, however, was a mechanical age. It was a natural concomitant to the compelling spirit of the "scientific revolution"—men's belief that they could control themselves and their world. Instruments were developed to *facilitate* almost everything, especially movement and measurement. The most important single event in obstetrics in this period was the rediscovery of forceps.

The story of who first used forceps in the late sixteenth century is lost in confusion. More perplexing is the problem of why they should suddenly have become such a necessity. The references by Jacques Guillemeau in 1609 to fear and pain do show a new consciousness of the patient on the part of the physician, but it is possible that he was also indicating that women were experiencing increasing difficulties in delivery. It hardly seems logical that if fear and pain were of major importance in eleventh century Salerno obstetrics, that Trotula would not have had some wisdom to impart. Moreover, medical and popular literature in the late eighteenth and nineteenth centuries are full of examples of women from certain cultural groups who suffered little discomfort in childbirth. The omission of information in historical data concerning a problem does not prove it did not exist; but neither should one overlook the possibility that certain physical conditions which exist in one culture or period might be absent from others.

Certainly in seventeenth-century obstetrics, childbearing was a problem. Francois Mauriceau (1637–1709), one of the most influential men in establishing obstetrics as the province of male surgeons, wrote in his book, well known in several languages and editions, *Traité des maladies des femmes grosses* (1668), that pregnancy was a "tumor of the belly." Such an attitude reflects in part the person who wrote but perhaps indicates, in part, the conditions which he saw and treated.

Thus, the development of an instrument to improve difficult deliveries became the visible factor which tipped the scales toward the male attendant as the dominant person in the birthroom. The first name associated with the use of forceps is William Chamberlen. He brought them to England from France when he fled the Protestant persecutions in 1569 during the reign of Charles IX. The Chamberlen family kept the forceps secret for four generations. Their social and professional ambitions motivated them to hide the forceps to control the advantage of power they had. They probably worked beneath a sheet during deliveries.

Secrecy of professional knowledge was important from primitive times, and it was customary in the seventeenth century. Knowledge was the key to the universe; therefore if one owned a sizeable amount, one had a nest egg to be carefully guarded. Physicians as well as alchemists were known to have secret prescriptions and to sell secret formulas. How the Chamberlen forceps finally came to be used by other physicians is unknown. Their own set of forceps was buried beneath the floor of the family home in Essex where they were found in 1813. But around 1700 various kinds of forceps were in use in the Netherlands, France, and England.

Whatever their form, forceps were the most important secret the male midwives had found to gain status in their struggle for professionalization. Men became the regular anteroom attendants to royalty and nobility as well as the emergency aids to midwives in difficult deliveries. Female midwives did not relinquish their former power willingly and became very defensive in their battle to retain dominance.

In addition to the battle between the male and female midwives which continued on into the nineteenth century, a new battle arose in the seventeenth century between the men within the field of obstetrics. Surgeons like John Mowbray and William Harvey opposed intervention and the use of instruments in deliveries. They were criticized by the younger surgeons who acclaimed the forceps as a necessary tool for successful deliveries and a weapon against midwives.

William Harvey (1578–1657) was a strong voice for a reform which was to gain momentum in the eighteenth century. He advocated the idea of birth as a natural process. He denounced midwives who hurried labor by strong expulsive measures that actually injured mother and child. What he wrote had limited influence on his contemporaries because his ideas were buried in the last chapter of his second book, *De Generatione* (1651). But they influenced later generations of men fighting similar reform battles. More important to this study, his ideas indicate that men were telling midwives that they were losing the ability of assistance for lack of knowledge, not just for lack of instruments. In other words, physicians were saying that midwives were losing the *art* of midwifery.

Reform became more effective in the hands of William Smellie (1697–1763). It was the central motivation of his life. He began his surgical practice in Scotland with no degree or license. He observed a needless loss of lives in childbirth and set out to prevent it. He read about the forceps operation and sought further knowledge in London and Paris. Disappointed, he returned to London to work out his own methods and began a class to teach other male midwives in 1742. His bedside teaching was important for the practical involvement it offered the student. He used a dummy model, an improvement over the model used by Gregoire in Paris, to study the mechanical concept of the form in motion.

From these studies he wrote his *Theory and Practice of Midwifery* (1751) and *Anatomical Tables* (1754). These works revolutionized midwifery. For the first time the specialty of obstetrics had practical directions based on sound female anatomy and an understanding of the physiological mechanism of delivery. With an increased respect for women's bodies, Smellie urged caution and care in the use of instruments. He was the first to teach male midwives that forceps were to be used to assist natural though difficult childbirth.

Midwives themselves sought reform as a way to hold on to their practice in the eighteenth century. One Elizabeth Nihell, more verbose and vindictive than most, attacked Smellie in letters and pamphlets. She used the harm done by men's forceps as her main argument, little realizing the impact Smellie was making to improve that very problem. But the midwives could not shut the door of the delivery room. They did not have the training necessary to compete against the knowledge of anatomy, physiology, and mechanics of the male midwives.

Once men gained access to the delivery room with information and instruments which met the needs of women, they soon moved toward gaining respectability. The solid achievements which Smellie had begun were secured by William Hunter (1718–83). He moved in aristocratic circles and was attendant to Queen Charlotte. Hunter also received the advantage of the accumulated tradition of anatomy and physiology which are "cumulative" sciences, requiring years for facts to be gathered and associations to be made. Like Smellie, Hunter was a superb teacher, but he relied on the combined efforts of his brother, John, and Colin McKenzie to extend the impact of his school.

In his practice, William Hunter was even more conservative concerning instruments than Smellie and more thorough in his anatomical studies. He advanced the anatomical knowledge of the female further than ever before. After twenty-four years of painstaking study, he published the *Anatomy of the Human Gravid Uterus* (1774). It offered clarity in uterine anatomy and some physiological advances. His work was well accepted by his peers. He was never voted a member in the Royal College of Physicians, but pressures were building in the medical profession to accept male midwives.

The struggles between the male and female midwives and between the conservative and progressive male midwives were heightened by increased pressures from outside midwifery in the eighteenth century. Male midwives began to threaten the regular surgeons and physicians because of their new esteem. The anatomical knowledge contributed by Smellie and Hunter to this specialized branch of medicine gained scientific respect. It was a body of information which was difficult for the rest of the medical profession to ignore. Also, the popularity of male midwives with well-to-do women threatened the egos and purses of the physicians.

In order to oppose the new specialists the regulars withheld full professional status as long as possible and opened attack on the male midwives. The Royal College of Physicians, from its founding in 1660, had always degraded any form of surgery. Surgeons, therefore, formed their own college. Male midwives threatened both professional groups who retaliated by calling midwifery a trade or craft, dependent on touch, not art. The male midwife was also considered immoral. It was indecent and immodest for him to enter the birthroom. This professional battle continued to rage through the nineteenth century, although hospitals and universities were offering lectures and requirements in midwifery by the mid–1800's.

Women continued as attendants in the delivery room, but they were becoming secondary in professional status and in the eyes of the public. This is evident from popular as well as medical literature. They had lost prestige with the new status of the male midwife among his peers, they had less factual knowledge through their informal training, they had lost popularity with their patients who were requesting male specialists when they could be afforded, and with all this, they lost economic status. In France women continued to hold power longer as educated and accepted attendants in delivery. Certainly, the tradition of excellence in obstetrics in Paris contributed to their acceptance. Also, the more balanced social status between men and women in France as compared to most other European countries must have contributed to a climate of openness and enabled women to function as respected medical practitioners.

As male midwives gained status and respect, they consciously manipulated the control they were gaining as specialists. In addition to establishing a curriculum of midwifery, they began to support hospital settings for the specialty. The eighteenth century had been an important time in the development of hospitals which provided an institutional focus for training. As early as the eighth century the Hôtel-Dieu of Paris (founded in 652) had separate lying-in quarters in the basement. By the sixteenth century this was the center for training midwives as discussed earlier. Similar sections for women within hospitals were opened in Italy and Germany during the fifteenth and sixteenth centuries. But the first hospital for obstetrics was founded in Strasbourg in 1728, followed in 1745 by the second such establishment in Dublin, Ireland, the Hospital for Poor Lying-In Women which later became the Rotunda Hospital. The movement proliferated in the nineteenth century, and it was inevitable that this increase of institutional power in the hands of male midwives as administrators should contribute to their efforts of specialization.

By the nineteenth century obstetrics by its very nature and history had become one of the central areas in which men and women were examining their likenesses and differences as human beings, their proper and best suited roles of action, and their powers to challenge one another to viable balances. The basic issues were discussed most openly in Great Britain and America and permeated every sector of society. In other words, obstetrics became a sermon for a minister, a pamphlet for an educator, the subject for speeches, articles, and books in the liveliest of all medical specialties.

Male midwives were opposed not only by regular physicians and female midwives but by a newly awakened public who were aware of the implications. Their arguments included the following: 1) the natural likeness of female midwife to female patient best suited her for understanding and advising in delivery; 2) the midwives' methods of delivery were safer with less harm from the force of instruments and strong medicines; 3) women were the only morally acceptable attendants—male midwives threatened family stability; 4) men created fear by their manipulations which were adverse to the natural action of childbirth; and 5) men were mercenary, charging unjustifiably higher prices than midwives.

Male midwives countered these arguments with their own strategy. They attacked the ignorance and lack of institutional controls over the midwives, accusing them of no training and much conceit. They opposed the midwives' lack of moral fibre and character. The nineteenth century was an age of heroic medicine, and many practitioners felt the need to play a strong role in administering therapeutic bleeding and purges. This required not only superior medical training to that of the midwives—which justified their higher prices—but it also called for a man who displayed courage to administer to the needs of the "weak and helpless female." As one author wrote in 1851,

> Women actually prefer a male *accoucheur* to a female. They feel safer in his hands; they rely not only upon his superior knowledge, but upon his courage. They feel he would not flinch before duty, and would assume the greatest responsibility to save life. It is not generally so with female *accoucheurs*.

The fact was clear that women were choosing men as their attendants. It was a momentous decision in 1766 when Queen Charlotte asked for William Hunter to deliver her fourth child instead of the royal midwife, Mrs. Draper. No matter what their qualifications and technical prowess, male midwives gained their specialty because their patients chose them as most suited to their needs. These needs were met, in part, by the way men defined their role as men and women defined their role as women and, in part, by the knowledge and medical expertise.

The middle of the nineteenth century saw two important discoveries which gave visible weight in favor of the male midwives' technical prowess. The first was the discovery that puerperal fever was due to contagion. Oliver Wendell Holmes (1809–94) gave the rational arguments in an 1843 lecture in Boston, drawing on ideas of Edward Rigby (1841). Ignaz Philipp Semmelweis (1818–65) established the clinical testing and experimental studies from 1845 to 1861 which proved the issue. Their work met with much opposition, for it was difficult for men to accept their role in perpetuating such widespread death. But when they finally accepted the ideas, they won much popularity for the resulting lower maternal-fetal death rate.

The second important technical advance was the application of anaesthesia for an obstetrical maneuver by James Young Simpson (1811–70) in Edinburgh in 1847. Opponents like Charles Meigs, who decreed that woman's pain was ordained by God, lost their audiences when Queen Victoria received an anaesthetic during the delivery of her eighth child in 1853. Male midwives who controlled access to drugs were soon equated with the only competent attendants in delivery. The combination of anaesthesia and a lower rate of infection enabled physicians to develop operative obstetrics, to lower the death rate, and to overcome many of the fears of women.

Full professional status, establishing obstetrics as an independent specialty, is seen in the formation of obstetrical societies. On the national level, this is a relatively late phenomenon. The Royal College of Obstetrics and Gynaecology was not founded until 1929, and its counterpart, the American College of Obstetrics and Gynecology, in 1951. However, subspecialty groupings preceded these organizations in the nineteenth century. For example, in the United States the Boston Obstetrical Society was founded in 1861, followed in 1866 by similar groups in New York and Philadelphia, in 1876 by the Cincinnati Obstetrical Society, and in 1878 by the Chicago Gynecological Society. The American Gynecological Society was founded in 1876 and the American Association of Obstetricians, Gynecologists, and Abdominal Surgeons in 1888. Such organizations served to represent qualified specialists and to improve standards of teaching, selection, and practice.

Thus, the development of obstetrics as a specialty has involved constant change. In content, rational knowledge was added to intuitive knowing. Knowledge became something to collect, standardize, and carefully disseminate, and institutions were established to control and improve its quality. Even the locale changed where the most influential ideas were generated, moving from Greece to Italy to Northern Europe and to Great Britain and the United States, with ideas often being generated in peripheral areas and then worked out in practice in central medical areas. Certainly one of the most interesting changes occurs in the attendant-patient relationship. The ideas concerning who is best suited for management of delivery involve the cooperative relationship that is necessary between attendant and mother. The key factors which affect this relationship are the increased awareness by humans of themselves as individuals rather than collective entities and their increased concern for life and comfort in this world, not the life hereafter. Because of its central place in the perpetuation of the species, obstetrics has always and will continue to reflect the development of human beings as well as its own internal medical history.

The woman about to become a mother or with a new-born infant upon her bosom, should be the object of trembling care and sympathy wherever she bears her tender burden, or stretches her aching limbs. The very outcast of the streets has pity upon her sister in degradation, when the seal of promised maternity is impressed upon her. The remorseless vengeance of the law brought down upon its victims by a machinery as sure as destiny, is arrested in its fall at a word which reveals her transient claim for mercy. The solemn prayer of the liturgy singles out her sorrows from the multiplied trials of life, to plead for her in her hour of peril. God forbid that any member of the profession to which she trusts her life, doubly precious at that eventful period, should hazard it negligently, unadvisedly or selfishly.

—OLIVER WENDELL HOLMES

DR. SLOP

from *The Life and Opinions of Tristram Shandy*
by LAURENCE STERNE

Upon my honour, Sir, you have tore every bit of skin quite off the back of both my hands with your forceps, cried my uncle Toby—and you have crushed all my knuckles into the bargain with them to a jelly. 'Tis your own fault, said Dr. Slop—you should have clinched your two fists together into the form of a child's head as I told you, and sat firm.—I did so, answered my uncle Toby.—Then the points of my forceps have not been sufficiently armed, or the rivet wants closing—or else the cut on my thumb has made me a little awkward—or possibly— 'Tis well, quoth my father, interrupting the detail of possibilities—that the experiment was not first made upon my child's head-piece.—It would not have been a cherry-stone the worse, answered Dr. Slop.— I maintain it, said my uncle Toby, it would have broke the cerebellum (unless indeed the skull had been as hard as a granade) and turned it all into a perfect posset.— Pshaw! replied Dr. Slop, a child's head is naturally as soft as the pap of an apple;—the sutures give way—and besides, I could have extracted by the feet after.— Not you, said she.— I rather wish you would begin that way, quoth my father.

Pray do, added my uncle Toby.

And pray, good woman, after all, will you take upon you to say, it may not be the child's hip, as well as the child's head? 'Tis most certainly the head, replied the midwife. Because, continued Dr. Slop (turning to my father) as positive as these old ladies generally are—'tis a point very difficult to know—and yet of the greatest consequences to be known;—because, Sir, if the hip is mistaken for the head—there is a possibility (if it is a boy) that the forceps . . .

What the possibility was, Dr. Slop whispered very low to my father, and then to my uncle Toby.— There is no such danger, continued he, with the head.— No, in truth, quoth my father—but when your possibility has taken place at the hip—you may as well take off the head, too.

DR. CHAMBERLEN

from *Expectant Motherhood* (1940)

by NICHOLAS J. EASTMAN

In the early decades of the seventeenth century, a new and mysterious force was making itself felt in childbirth. It became known in London that in case a woman was experiencing a prolonged labor, delivery could be effected with incredible dispatch if any member of a certain family of physicians was called in and allowed to take charge. The name of the family was Chamberlen. One of the Doctors Chamberlen would appear with a bundle beneath his coat and proceed to hasten delivery under cover of a large sheet or blanket so that no one could see what he was doing; a great clanking of metal would be heard and forthwith the baby would be handed out from beneath the covers. Some more of clanking would occur and then Doctor Chamberlen, with his bundle carefully concealed under his coat, would be ready to collect his fee and depart. As a result of the metallic noises heard, and also because of the temporary marks which were sometimes left on the baby's head, the device by which the Doctors Chamberlen effected delivery became known as the "Hands of Iron"; and this was all that was known. For three generations—over a hundred years—this family of Chamberlens kept secret the instrument which has done more to abridge human suffering and to save human life than any other device in the whole range of surgical appliances. The "Hands of Iron," of course were the obstetrical forceps.

The modern obstetrical forceps consist of two separate blades with smooth inner surfaces curved to fit the sides of the baby's head. After the patient has been completely anaesthetized, the blades are inserted separately, first the left and then the right; they are next crossed and fitted together by an articulating device in such a manner that a gentle but firm grasp is obtained on the baby's head, which is then slowly extracted by means of moderate traction on the blades.

"Taking the baby with instruments" used to be regarded as an ominous procedure by the laity and the term still has a fearsome ring to many expectant parents. Today, the operation is carried out under such different conditions than formerly that it is almost a different procedure and warrants little concern. Nowadays, the majority of forceps delivery are performed when the baby's head is almost ready to be born and are done merely to relieve the patient of the last fifteen or twenty minutes of labor; the head is simply "lifted out" as it were, instead of being pushed out by the expulsive efforts of the mother. Whether it is best to expediate delivery in this manner depends upon the circumstances presented by the individual case and will be decided, of course, by the physician. Forceps are often used for other reasons; but the most important fact for the expectant mother and members of the family to know about these instruments is that they can be used safely only toward the end of labor, when the cervix has been fully dilated and when certain other prerequisite conditions are present.

XIV

OBSTETRICS-FROM PRIMITIVE TIMES TO THE ATOMIC AGE

PRIMITIVE OBSTETRICS

from *Safe Convoy* (1944)

by WILLIAM J. CARRINGTON

It is not known how many abnormal births fell to the lot of women before records were kept. The earliest archives were found in the tombs of the Pharaohs. On the walls are records of almost every phase of life, pictures of people with battle wounds, infantile paralysis and all sorts of diseases, but none of childbearing. Every conceivable article of furniture and all kinds of household implements have been unearthed except those that one might expect to find in a lying-in chamber. They had babies, all right, but how, we do not know. The earliest records were fragmentary, picked up here, there, and everywhere, from the ruins of ancient tombs and temples, crude drawings on the walls of caves, and from song and story, none accurate and complete. There is a majolica plaque, for example, which pictures a mother in bed with an attendant testing the temperature of the new-born infant's bath with her bare toe. Even as late as the Middle Ages there were no accurate records. Midwives kept no case histories, and doctors were not permitted to attend confinement cases. A German midwife was imported to bring the future Queen Victoria into the world, and Napoleon engaged Madame La Chappelle to deliver Marie Louise on a bed of crimson velvet under a canopy ornamented with gold. History records more of the frills and foibles than of obstetric technics in use at the time. The customs of the royal household were reflected in humbler homes but on a scale commensurate with the family budget. Until doctors replaced midwives in the eighteenth century there were no accurate case histories.

In spite of incomplete records, we are reasonably certain that early women had complications in labor, and that what preventive and corrective measures existed were crude and ineffective. The early Aztecs, for example, knew nothing to do for difficult delivery but to drag the woman along the ground, belly down. However, it must be admitted that there are valid reasons that lead to the belief that there may have been fewer abnormalities. Among primitive peoples food was not devitaminized by overpreparation. Early women did not weaken their abdominal muscles by wearing corsets, nor did they throw their pelvis out of alignment by teetering on high heels. She lived in the open and was more athletic than her civilized sister of today. Most important of all, there was no cross-breeding. No matter on what quarter of the globe she lived her people were all of one build, and the size of the baby conformed to the size of her pelvis. But when restless mankind began to explore strange lands and to push new trade routes into the uttermost islands of the seas, there were matings of misfits, which were followed by a host of obstetric difficulties heretofore unknown. If a complication arose, aborigines were shaken by the feet or tossed into a blanket. To frighten the baby out of its lair, North American Indian squaws were tied to a stake and almost run down by expert horsemen brandishing tomahawks and shrieking war whoops. In the islands of the South Seas, two husky midwives would seesaw astraddle the ends of a surfboard supported by the pregnant woman's abdomen. Something had to give way. In delayed labor it was an old Spanish custom for the midwife to place a hot plate on the abdomen over the womb and hit it with her fist. Italian midwives, less pugilistic, preferred the dried excrement of wild doves. Even in modern America, which we regard as enlightened, there are women who believe that the early stages of labor will be made easier if they wear their husband's breeches.

OBSTETRICS IN PRIMITIVE PEOPLES

by DUNCAN E. REID, M.D. and MANDEL E. COHEN, M.D.
from *The Journal of the American Medical Association*
(March 4, 1950)

There exists currently a widespread obstetric belief that modern civilized women have great difficulties during labor in comparison with women who have lived or do live in less industrialized societies. Statements are made such as "considering first the physical aspect of confinement and delivery among primitive peoples, we find a weight of evidence from many parts of the world to the effect that childbirth is easy and that the woman returns to her labor within a short time." In a publication devoted to the psychology of women one finds, "At any rate it is generally considered an established fact that the reproductive process in primitive women is simpler than that in women 'degenerated by civilization,'" or, from another publication, "Civilization and culture have brought influences to bear upon the minds of women which have introduced justifiable fear and anxieties concerning labor. The more cultured races of the earth have become, so much more the dogmatic have they been in pronouncing childbirth to be a painful and dangerous ordeal." Other writers, speaking of Eskimo women, said "They suffer little; they appear to be exempted from the curse of Eve and deliver their children with as little concern as is exhibited among the brutes," or, "Among primitive people, still natural in their habits and living under conditions which favor a healthy development of their physical organization, labor may be characterized as short, and easy, accompanied by a few aches and followed by little prostration." Statements of this type appear in great number.

However, if one examines the original sources on which such remarkable statements are based, it is clearly apparent that no data are recorded, and hence there is no scientific or factual foundation for these statements. In order to know the facts about childbirth in the less industrialized ethnic groups, such as those of Indians, Africans and South Pacific Islanders, among others, actual observations are necessary. The studies should include: (1) carefully recorded data of observations on a significant number of women in labor made by some one competent to assess obstetric problems; (2) careful study of pain in these groups of women during the course of their labor; (3) data describing the fetal and maternal mortality rates in these patients, and (4) follow-up studies giving data on the morbidity rate and the eventual medical, psychologic and social health, as well as the life expectancy, of both mother and child.

This would constitute a reasonable study and might well include some additional studies of a cross section of American women as well.

However, such reports as are available contain scarcely any observations pertaining to the birth process, and these observations are made up in a way which, unfortunately, has characterized so much of the anthropologic literature on this aspect of human reproduction, that is, by hearsay, anecdotes and, in some cases, possibly by bias and prejudice. We arrived at this rather forceful conclusion after reviewing the major works on the subject, papers by anthropologists, and, in addition, after examining the Cross Cultural Survey at the Institute of Human Relations at Yale University. (Dr. Seymour Romney aided in searching the literature.)

Only one study could be found with recorded observations of a series of women in labor, that of Hrdlicka, a physician, who reported on the labor and delivery of 67 Pima and Apache women. From his reports the incidence of prolonged labor was 21.7 percent. Labor of twenty or more hours from onset to completion of the birth process is defined as prolonged labor. This frequency is significantly higher (significance ratio 4.7) than the 1.8 percent which was the incidence of this syndrome in an attended group of patients at the Boston Lying-In Hospital. The only other quantitative data was about recovery from parturition and the fact that the Navajo mothers (15 cases) do not return to their household duties for about a week after an uncomplicated delivery. Hrdlicka concluded, "... the healthy Indian woman suffers ... quite as much and as long as does the normal white woman ..."

It is interesting to turn from the consideration of so-called primitive peoples to the consideration of groups of modern Americans who are less favored economically than others, specifically Negroes and Navajo Indians. The mortality rates of white and Negro mothers in the United States offer an opportunity to compare two groups, the white mother, with more scientific obstetric care, and the Negro mother, probably with more natural childbirth. Although there are many contributing factors, the fact that the maternal mortality in the Negro group is almost three times as high as that in the white group does not make one immediately enthusiastic about returning to more natural childbirth. Also, an estimated maternal mortality rate of 10 deaths per 1,000 live births has been reported recently for the Navajo Indians, an ethnic group often used for comparative purposes. These observations do not support the principle that primitive surroundings and more natural childbirth are conducive to better maternal welfare. It would seem instead to support the belief that there is a great need for a further expansion of modern obstetric hospital facilities and trained personnel.

In summary, it can be said that there are no reliable data to support the opinion that the "primitive peoples," whom we prefer to call peoples of less industrialized societies, have babies without pain and without difficulty. There are no data which suggest that pain during labor is an artificial product of culture and civilization or that primitive obstetrics is so satisfactory that it should be adopted by the modern American hospital.

SOME EARLY PREGNANCY TESTS
from *Expectant Motherhood* (1940)
by NICHOLAS J. EASTMAN

"Since the very dawn of civilization efforts have been made to devise a satisfactory test for pregnancy. The priest-physician of ancient Egypt, in the earliest writings handed down to us, tells of a test then in vogue based on the seeming ability of pregnancy urine to stimulate the growth of wheat and barley seed; the itinerant physician of classical Greece employed similar tests, while during the Middle Ages the omniscient physician merely gazed at the urine and in this way claimed to be able to diagnosticate not only pregnancy but many other conditions.

TABOOS AT CHILDBIRTH
from *The Golden Bough* (1890)
by SIR JAMES G. FRAZER

Among many peoples similar restrictions are imposed on women in childbed and apparently for similar reasons; at such periods women are supposed to be in a dangerous condition which would infect any person or thing they might touch; hence they are put into quarantine until, with the recovery of their health and strength, the imaginary danger has passed away. Thus, in Tahiti a woman after childbirth was secluded for a fortnight or three weeks in a temporary hut erected on sacred ground; during the time of her seclusion she was debarred from touching provisions, and had to be fed by another. Further, if any one else touched the child at this period, he was subjected to the same restrictions as the mother until the ceremony of her purification had been performed. Similarly in the island of Kodiak, off Alaska, a woman about to be delivered retires to a miserable low hovel built of reeds, where she must remain for twenty days after the birth of her child, whatever the season may be, and she is considered so unclean that no one will touch her, and food is reached to her on sticks. The Bribri Indians regard the pollution of childbed as much more dangerous even than that of menstruation. When a woman feels her time approaching, she informs her husband, who makes haste to build a hut for her in a lonely spot. There she must live alone, holding no converse with anybody save her mother or another woman. After her delivery the medicine-man purifies her by breathing on her and laying an animal, it matters not what, upon her. But even this ceremony only mitigates her uncleanness into a state considered to be equivalent to that of a menstruous woman; and for a full lunar month she must live apart from her housemates, observing the same rules with regard to eating and drinking as at her monthly periods.

From *The Book of Matthew,* 1:18–25

Now the birth of Jesus Christ was on this wise: When as his mother Mary was espoused to Joseph, before they came together, she was found with child of the Holy Ghost.

Then Joseph her husband, being a just man, and not willing to make her a publick example, was minded to put her away privily.

But while he thought on these things, behold, the angel of the Lord appeared unto him in a dream, saying, Joseph, thou son of David, fear not to take unto thee Mary thy wife: for that which is conceived in her is of the Holy Ghost.

And she shall bring forth a son, and thou shalt call his name JESUS: for he shall save his people from their sins.

Now all this was done, that it might be fulfilled which was spoken of the Lord by the prophet, saying,

Behold, a virgin shall be with child, and shall bring forth a son, and they shall call his name Emmanuel, which being interpreted is, God with us.

Then Joseph being raised from sleep did as the angel of the Lord had bidden him, and took unto him his wife:

And knew her not till she had brought forth her first born son: and he called his name JESUS.

From *The Man from Nazareth* (1949)
by HARRY EMERSON FOSDICK

There is no evidence in the Gospels, apart from the birth stories themselves, that any member of Jesus' family or any of his first disciples ever thought of him as virgin born. Mark, who gathered from Peter the facts of Jesus' life, does not mention it. In Matthew and Luke, where the birth stories appear, are two genealogies, so inconsistent that they cannot possibly be reconciled, both of which in tracing Jesus' lineage came down to Joseph, not to Mary. These genealogies are inconceivable except on the supposition that when they were prepared Joseph was thought to be Jesus' father. Indeed, in the Monastery of St. Catherine on the traditional Mount Sinai is an ancient Syriac translation of Matthew's Gospel, rendering, so scholars feel assured, an older manuscript of Matthew than any which we now possess, and ending the genealogy with its only logical conclusion: "Joseph begat Jesus." As for Luke, he quotes the genealogy he has before him, but destroys its meaning as a record of Jesus' lineage by his parenthesis: "Jesus . . . being the son [as was supposed] of Joseph."

The category of virgin birth was alien to Jewish thinking. The passage in Isaiah, in which the church, at the time Matthew and Luke were written, found prophecy of Mary's virginity—"Behold, a virgin shall conceive, and bear a son"—was taken not from the original Hebrew but from the mistaken rendering in the Septuagint, the Greek translation of the Old Testament, which even Paul and much more the later church commonly used. The original Hebrew says not "virgin," but "young woman." It was the Greek world in which virgin births were a common way of explaining unusual personalities. So Plato was said to be virgin born, and Alexander the Great, and Aesculapius, and Pythagoras and Simon Magus and Apollonius of Tyana, and many more. In the second century, when Justin Martyr stated the case, he even put Jesus' birth, for argument's sake, in the same category with such legends: "When we declare that the Word, who is the first-born of God, came into being without sexual intercourse . . . we do not report anything different from your view about those called sons of Zeus."

From *Medicine in the Bible* (1936)
by CHARLES J. BRIM, M.D.

"And the Lord blessed them and said to them, Be fruitful and multiply and replenish the earth."

To have a child is to be fruitful; to have more than

one child is to multiply; then only can the world be replenished. For the accomplishment of this end the Lord constructed *yiben*, women. Rashi understands this term to mean a lasting structure, sound and capable of supporting burdens—broader as it nears the base and narrower above—so that the woman shall be able to carry her child within her womb and the added weight shall not affect her body; he therefore reasons that a woman who is barren is not constructed soundly but is put together in a haphazard manner.

The early Hebrew women believed this to be the case, for Sarai, who was barren, *okoro*, pleaded with her husband, Abram, "to go into her maid, Hagar," who was very young so that she, Sarai, might, through such a noble deed (permitting Abram to become father of a child) be blessed with a child, *iboneh mimeno*—which means, to be reconstructed for childbearing. Her grandson's wife, Rachel, used the same phraseology in her plea for a child.

"After ten years of living together, Sarai, the wife of Abram, gave her maid Hagar to him for reproductive purposes, *ischo loi l'ischo*. Sarai, in this way, employed a so-called diagnostic test; she wished to ascertain who of the two was sterile. She found out soon enough. "He went into Hagar and she became pregnant." Rashi deduces from the text that conception took place from the one and only act of coitus, which proved the potency of Abram. Soon thereafter Hagar "lost her respect for her mistress," for sterility was looked upon as a shame.

Despite the care in the construction of "the mother of all living," she and all her descendants were cursed for her fatal error in the Garden: "In sorrow will you rear children, in pain will you bear them, and the stages of your labor shall be difficult and dangerous; yet, you will lust for your man. You will be passive. He will arouse you and become master over you."

The term pregnancy is used in a figurative sense in several scriptural passages. When the burden of caring for the Hebrews was thrust upon Moses, he exclaimed,

"Did I conceive, *hirisi*, this nation? Did I give birth, *y'lid-tihoo*, to it? Must I carry it in my arms like a nursemaid carries a nursling, *yonaik*?" Moses pleads with the Lord that the burden is too heavy, and he uses the feminine form of you, *ot*, instead of *oto*, for bearing, etc. is a feminine function.

A novel use of the expression, to give birth, occurs in the episode of Abimelech, who, together with the members of his household, was healed of impotence; "And they gave birth," *vayaildoo*. Rashi says this term means they were able to function again; the seminal fluid could again leave the urethral canal just like a fetus emerges from the genital canal—it is born.

A very expressive phrase occurs in Deuteronomy when Israel is accused of straying from the path of righteousness: "Thou hast forgotten the Lord who hath given thee birth, *m'cholelecho*," which Rashi interprets as "the God who has delivered thee from thy mother's womb." The word used here is the derivative form of *chil*, a chill; when a woman is in labor, the pains make her shake and shiver as if she is in a chill.

In most instances the Bible expresses the first stage of pregnancy as *vatahar*, which denotes that signs of pregnancy are already evident; this is followed by the term *vatailehd*, the stage of delivery. In the case of Zilpah, the youthful handmaid who became impregnated by Jacob, the word *vatahar* is not mentioned. Rashi says that her outward appearance in no way pointed to pregnancy until the time of her delivery had actually arrived. During the period of pregnancy the external features of the woman become altered. In the case of Tamar, "at the end of three months it was noticeable that she was pregnant, *horo*."

The normal duration of pregnancy is nine months. Mar Samuel, the Babylonian physician, reckons 271 to 273 days from the day of coitus. The Talmudic rabbis taught that fertilization of the ovum takes place within the first three days following sexual intercourse, and after this period, if fertilization does not take place, the sperms lose their potency and pregnancy will not ensue. For this reason the very orthodox Hebrews do not have intercourse on Wednesday, Thursday or Friday, to avoid the conception taking place on the Sabbath.

The book of Genesis is the book of Beginnings, and so it naturally deals with beginnings—births. The loves and lives of the early ancestors are vividly and fully described even as to details. Hagar's pregnancy is recorded to point out Abram's potency. This event is followed by Sarah's conception. "And the Lord remembered His promise as regards to Sarah, and it came to pass according to His words: Sarah conceived and gave birth to a son, *limoiyed*," which means at full term. In the case of Rebecca, the wife of Isaac, we are informed that "when the days of her conception had been completed [full term] she gave birth to twins." Referring to Tamar, the text states, "and it came to pass that in the time of her labor it was discovered that she had twins in her womb." From the difference in the wording of the textual description of Tamar's and Rebecca's pregnancies, Rashi deduces that the former's was not a full nine-month pregnancy.

Multiple Pregnancies

The first mother on earth was subject to multiple pregnancies. Rashi interprets the following passages as such: "And Eve conceived and she gave birth to Cain and another." Her next delivery consisted of triplets: "And Eve gave birth to a child, with his brother, with Abel." According to Rashi, most pregnancies in the early days were multiple. Lot's daughters and Jacob's sons, no mention of whose wives is recorded, seem to be outstanding illustrations to substantiate his belief. The children of Israel, while in Egypt, multiplied very rapidly, *vayischritzoo*—according to Rashi they had multiple pregnancies, as many as six at one time; he bases his assumption on the fact that the same word is used in connection with the lower forms of animal life, *scheretz*, which breed abundantly,—"and the crawling forms of animal life brought forth abundantly, *yischretzoo*." From this Rashi concludes that *vayischretzoo* refers to multiple pregnancies.

Cases of twin pregnancies are recorded and their detailed accounts are very interesting.

Rebecca, who had been barren for a number of years, finally became pregnant. She began to feel abdominal pains—*vayisroitetzoo habonim b'kirbo*, "and the fetuses moved about within her insides." And she said, if the pain of carrying is so great, why did I yearn so for a pregnancy?" So she went to the synagogue for a diagnosis. The diagnosis was "twins in her womb"—"two viable children will be separated from her womb; one will be stronger than the other; the older one will serve the younger." At full term, *vaymiloo yomeho loledess*, she gave birth to twins. "The first one came out red, and his body was covered with hair, and they called his name Esau" because Esau means ready-made, with hairy and other body developments which one would expect in an older child. "Then followed his brother, his hand grasping Esau's heel." According to Rashi, Jacob, the younger one, wanted to be the first-born, so he attempted to hold back the oncoming Esau by grasping at his heel; he felt that he should leave the womb first because he was the first one created during coitus—from the first drop of the seminal fluid. To explain this statement, Rashi gives the following illustration: take a small, narrow tube, and put into it two small marbles one after the other. Shake them out, and the marble that went in last comes out first while the one that was put in first comes out last. Even after the children had grown up, the younger one felt that birthright was his. Rashi says that the parents called Esau the first-born but the Lord called Jacob the first-created.

The description of Tamar's twin birth is even more interesting. Here is the first recorded account of shoulder and hand presentation.

"As she was having her labor pains, a hand presented itself; and the midwife took and bound a scarlet thread upon the hand and said, This one came first. But the hand was withdrawn and behold, his brother came out without waiting for a labor pain, and the midwife asked, Why do you rush out so?"

There is one word in this description which has caused a great deal of discussion; *peretz*. The Aramaic translation of this term is a tear, a rip. In the forceful expulsion of the fetus, he tore the perineum. In I Sam. 6:8, "God made a rent upon Uzzah and smote him, whereupon David called the name of the place Peretzuzzah." In the text of Genesis the word is used in the same sense of tearing. In another passage this word is used to denote an increase, *vayiphrotz*. By tearing the perineum the vaginal outlet became enlarged. For this, he was called Peretz. "And afterward came his brother that had the scarlet thread upon his hand, and he was named Zorach," which means bright (referring to the bright red thread around his wrist).

In the case of Rebecca the first-born was a normal occiput presentation, and the second was a hand presentation, both from the same amniotic cavity. In Tamar's case the first was a shoulder-and-hand presentation, which was interfered with by the oncoming head of the other. In both cases the diagnosis of twins was made before delivery.

Early Forms of Delivery

In the early days delivery took place upon the lap of an attendant, a member of the household, the husband or any other relative. "Bilha was in labor and gave birth upon the lap of Rachel"—*birkay*, the lap. Joseph was the last of the ancient Hebrews upon whose lap delivery took place. "And Joseph saw Ephraim's children of the third generation . . . they were born on the lap, *birkay*, of Joseph. This explains a custom among the Jews which exists even to this day: At the eighth day after birth the male child is circumcised and, as part of the ritual, an elder is selected, usually the grandfather, who sits upon a chair and holds a pillow upon his lap; upon this pillow the newborn babe is placed. The operation of circumcision is performed and the pillow with the child upon it is lifted from the lap and placed in bed beside the mother.

In the land of Egypt the lap gave way to the delivery stool. In Pharaoh's edict to the midwives he specified "when you deliver Hebrew women and you notice upon the stools, *ovnoyim*, a male child . . ."

Midwives were employed at a very early period, even before the Hebrews settled in Egypt. Rachel employed a *m'yolledess* and Tamar was also attended by a *m'yolledess*. The word for midwife varies and depends upon the nature of the delivery. She is a *m'yolledess* when she is called to attend a difficult labor, *m'yolled*. In uncomplicated labors, *moilid*, she is termed a *moilidess*. Women who had no training and were not recognized as professional midwives were called *chayoss*, because they were like the animals (*chayos*) of the field who attended to their own afterbirths.

The two outstanding professional midwives of Egypt, *m'yoldoiss*, because they were specialists in their line and were especially called in to attend all difficult labors, were Shifro and Pooah. Shifro was Yochebed, the mother of Moses. She was called Shifro because she trimmed and cleaned the newborn baby—*shifro*, to trim; Pooah was Miriam, Moses' sister. She was called Pooah because she played and spoke lovingly—*pooah*—to the baby. *Pooah* also means to whisper—she whispered into the woman's ear words of encouragement to ease her labor pains and to facilitate the delivery.

The idea of maternity hospitals may seem far-fetched for the Bible, but we must bear in mind that at that time Egypt was at the height of her civilization and institutions abounded within her territory. Everything was moving at top speed; and the Hebrews were multiplying very rapidly. The Hebrew midwives were being kept very busy. Because they disregarded Pharaoh's edict about first-born males, "God was good to the midwives; He built for them houses."

The Hebrew women were more prolific than their native Egyptian sisters. When Pharaoh noted the rapid increase of the Jews he reprimanded the Hebrew midwives, whose answer to him was, "but the Hebrew women are not as the Egyptian women, for they deliver themselves before the arrival of the midwife." The Egyptian women lived a gay and carefree life—they dressed in stylish clothes, attended to their toilettes, and were corrupted by the national ritualistic orgies of their perverted sexual worship. The Jewish women, on the other hand, were wives of workers in the cities and toilers in the fields or assistants in small shops, and lived according to the orthodox ritual of their ancestors. They lived a more natural and healthier life; hence their deliveries tended to be less difficult and less complicated. This splendid physical condition of the Jewish lying-in woman added greatly to a normal pregnancy, labor, and delivery, including the postpartum period.

There were occasional cases recorded of premature births. The vast majority were full term, *vayimloo yomeho loledess*. According to Rashi, Tamar gave birth to a premature set of twins. The great lawgiver, Moses, was a premature baby. His birth is described as follows:

His mother "conceived and gave birth to a son; when she examined him—(she was the foremost midwife in Egypt)—she found him to be normal and she hid him for three months." The Egyptians had known of her pregnancy and the secret-service men in the employ of Pharaôh had spied upon her, for there was a royal decree to do away with all male births. They had counted upon nine months; but the child was born early in the seventh month of pregnancy. The mother feared for the viability of the child, so she kept him in a crude, home-made incubator box and "watched him thrive" (the text says "she looked after him and saw that he was good"). She was thus enabled to hide the baby for three months, at the end of which period (the nine months were now up) "she could not hide him any longer." She expected a visit any day now from the government officials, so "she prepared a box of . . ." and the story of Moses in the bulrushes being picked up out of the waters of the Nile by Pharaoh's daughter is a notable page in history.

The Offspring

The offspring is called *p'ri ha-butten*, the fruit of the womb. The young of the animals is denoted by the term *sch'gar*, used in a derivative sense: that of expelling the contents of the womb. In one instance the offspring is referred to as a root: "If there be among you a root that grows into gall and wormwood," meaning an evil person.

Wet Nurses

While there is no law in the Torah regarding the nursing of newborn babes by the mother, the later Talmudists prefer this to the employment of wet nurses, to whom reference in the Pentateuch occurs very frequently.

A wet nurse is a *maynekess*, derived from *saynik*, to give suck. *T'nikayhoo* means to give suck to babies. Deborah was the *maynikto* of Rebecca. This term is even applied to animals. Milch-camels are referred to as *g'malim maynikoss*. In Egypt the wet nurse held an important position in the household. The Bible allots space to the announcement of the death of Deborah, Rachel's wet nurse. The Egyptian wet nurses were well renumerated for their services, for they treated the child as if it were their own, *halichi*. There is a legend that when the Egyptian princess discovered the baby Moses among the bulrushes she called in several Egyptian wet nurses, but he refused their breasts because he did not with to contaminate his lips, which were to be holy for his future conversations with the Lord, who gave him orders to deliver the children of Israel out of their bondage.

The age for weaning was fixed in Babylonia and Egypt at three years. The Chinese also followed this custom. From the Bible we learn that Hannah nursed her baby for three years.

When Isaac was born to Abraham and Sarah, who were very much advanced in years, a feast was celebrated to which all the nursing mothers of the village were invited. To silence rumors that the child was not Sarah's, the mother volunteered to nurse, *hayniko*, all the babies present. And Sarah said, "Who would have foretold to Abraham that (his old) Sarah could give suck to babies? See, it was I that bore him a son in his old age." "When the child grew up, he was weaned, *yigomahl*, and Abraham made a great feast on the day that Isaac was weaned." Rashi tells us this event took place at the end of the baby's second year.

Parturition

Rules for the postpartum period were laid down in Leviticus with a view to regulating the habits of the lying-in women. The text specifically states that "a woman who had been pregnant, *sazria*, and had been delivered of a male child is unclean for seven days, the same length of time assigned to a menstruating woman. Rashi tells us that from the wording of the text he assumes that this includes a stillbirth, such as a macerated fetus, *yoldosoi mochooy*, as well as a viable premature baby.

"On the eighth day shall the flesh of his foreskin be circumcised." She shall then count 33 more days during which period she is excluded from holy and ritualistic functions. She may live with her husband during this period, even though some blood may still show, *bidmay tohro*.

If the birth be a female child, she is unclean for 14 days (observing during this period all the rules and regulations pertaining to menstruation). She shall then count 66 more days before she be permitted to partake of holy and ritualistic functions.

At the expiration of the "male" or "female" days she shall offer as a sacrifice a lamb one year old, *ohlo*, and a young pigeon or turtledove for a sin offering, *chatoss*, and the priest shall accept them as an atonement sacrifice and she shall be cleansed from the issue of her blood. If she cannot afford a lamb, then two young pigeons or two turtledoves may serve instead.

Birth, like menstruation, was regarded as something rendering the woman unclean, hence she was to be set apart, *niddo*, for a period of seven to fourteen days as far as intercourse was concerned, and 40 to 80 days as far as ritualistic functions were concerned.

The placenta or afterbirth is termed *schilyo*, and described as "the afterbirth which hangs down between her legs, *schilyo ha-yohtzais mibain rogleho*.

CHILDBIRTH THROUGH THE AGES

by SOLVEIG EGGERS

from *Private Practice* (October 1973)

The position of women in a society is said to be an indication of that society's advancement. The treatment accorded women in childbirth is an excellent gauge of woman's status and a society's nature. An example is the favorable situation of parturient women during the heights of Egyptian, Greek and Roman civilization. Bearing children during the Middle Ages was, in comparison, quite unpleasant, if not fatal.

A certain distinction can be made between "primitive" and "civilized" women of past times. Due to their lives of hard work, bearing children did not entail for primitive women the "labor" that plagued more pampered creatures. Primitive women were blessed with the "natural childbirth" for which many modern women diligently prepare only to find that it's not so natural after all.

The primitive woman's greatest fear was that her baby was in an abnormal position transversely across the pelvis, making childbirth impossible. On the other hand, she escaped the childbed fever that travelled from bed to bed with helping hands in more civilized times.

In most cultures women have sought isolation during childbirth, as they have during menstruation. The Sandwich Islands were an exception where the blessed event took place in public, with the woman seated on the lap of an elderly man who acted as midwife.

Superstition frequently demanded a period of purification following childbirth, which had a beneficial effect because of the rest accorded the mother. The women of Siam might experience unimaginable evil, it was believed, if they did not expose the back and the abdomen alternately to a blazing fire at a distance of two feet for thirty days.

A most tenacious belief held that labor pains were voluntarily caused by a temperamental unborn child and that it was up to those attending the birth to coax the baby from the womb with all manner of promises. The method of podalic version, whereby the ill-positioned baby is placed in the appropriate head down position, was discovered in ancient times and periodically forgotten and rediscovered through the ages. More often employed were instruments especially designed to destroy the baby in the case of an impossible birth. In better times physicians performed this task, but during the Middle Ages frequently clumsy and inept midwives butchered both mother and child in this manner.

The physicians of Hippocrates' (400 B.C.) time had a knowledge of anatomy and medicine, which was passed on to midwives, a well organized group under their supervision. During medieval times midwives, like prostitutes, were under the supervision of priests. The ancient Greeks reportedly knew about podalic version and, at the risk of being called a "he-grandmother," the physician attended difficult births, a practice which prudery banned in later times. The *Susruta*, a book describing the ancient method of midwifery, stipulates that a woman be delivered by four aged and knowing women whose "nails were well trimmed." Later the law of Athens required that a midwife be beyond childbearing age, but that she must have born a child.

During the Christian era there were no regulations for midwives, a fact which later gave rise to stories such as that of Dickens' Sairey Gamp, a notorious butcher of women. In 1580 in Germany herdsmen and others who wielded the knife were banned from attending childbirth and during the 16th century a school for midwives was established at the Hôtel-Dieu.

Childbirth in ancient times was often a mixture of neglect and brutality. The methods for hastening labor were rough, to say the least, and some were still used in Europe only 400 years ago. According to medical historian Dr. Howard W. Haggard, in his book *Devils, Drugs and Doctors* the woman:

> was picked up by the feet and shaken, head down, or rolled and bounced on a blanket, or possibly laid on the open plain in order that a horseman might ride at her with the apparent intention of treading on her, only to veer aside at the last moment, and by the fear thus inspired, aid in the expulsion of the child. Again, she might be laid on her back to have her abdomen trod upon, or else be hung to a tree by a strap passed under her arms, while those assisting her bore down on a strap over her abdomen.

After the dignified ladies, who served as midwives in ancient Greece, had lifted and dropped their patient a sufficient number of times to cause birth, their next task was to present the baby to the father. If he refused to acknowledge the baby by lifting it, it was the midwife's duty to "expose" it on a mountainside.

The use of beds for childbirth did not begin until the 17th century at the suggestion of the great French obstetrician, Mauriceau. The most ancient childbirth implement is probably the obstetrical chair, which is mentioned in the Old Testament: "When you do the office of the midwife to the Hebrew woman, and see them upon the stools . . ." This was Pharaoh's command to the midwives to slay all Jewish male infants.

After the destruction of Corinth in 146 B.C. Greek medicine migrated to Rome where it continued to develop, although hampered to some extent by the Roman system of medical deities. "The midwife should be no believer in spirits," wrote Soranus of Epheseus, the great humanitarian of the second century A.D.

Soranus reintroduced podalic version and brought a kindness of treatment of childbearing women that was to be forgotten until Eucharius Roeslin wrote a book on obstetrics in 1513, which was largely based on Soranus' writings. In his concern for the well-being of the mother, Soranus went so far as to advocate abortion if the mother's life was in danger:

> There is a disagreement: for some reject destructive practices, calling to witness Hippocrates, who says: "I will give nothing whatever destructive; and deeming it the special province of medicine to guard and preserve what nature generates." Another party maintains the same view but makes this distinction, namely, that the fruit of conception is not to be destroyed at will because of adultery or of care for beauty, but is to be destroyed to avert danger appending to birth, if the womb be small and cannot subserve perfection of the fruit, or have hard swellings or cracks at its mouth, or if some similar condition prevail.

During the "ages of faith" that followed Soranus' period the obsession with driving out the devil prevented all rational thought about the true causes of pain and disease. The teachings of hygiene handed down by the ancient Jews were forgotten. So was all knowledge of anatomy as medical learning was submerged in a sea of pestilence and superstition.

Haggard refers to the Middle Ages as:

> The most unfortunate period in the history of womankind. . . . complete ignorance prevailed without the intuitive skill of the primitive period and without the knowledge of previous civilizations. Women were deprived of the aid, however poor, of the male physician, and at the same time the penalties of urban civilization were making childbirth more and more hazardous. The practice of the Middle Ages presents the accumulated evils of previous periods aggravated by ignorance and barbarism.

A certain Dr. Wertt of Hamburg is said to have donned women's clothing in order to observe childbirth firsthand. He was found out and burned to death for his trespass.

The "penalties of urban civilization" included disease-bearing sewage in the streets of medieval towns and the existence of such pernicious institutions as the Hôtel-Dieu, a charitable hospital established in Paris between 641 and 649 as "a place for God's hospitality," in the words of its founder, Saint Landry, Bishop of Paris. This brand of hospitality proved fatal to many of its residents, especially to childbearing women and their babies. Max Nordau describes conditions at the Hôtel-Dieu:

> In one bed of moderate width lay four, five, or six persons beside each other, the feet of one to the head of another; children beside gray-haired old men; indeed, incredible but true, men and women intermingled together. In the same bed lay individuals affected with infectious diseases beside others only slightly unwell; on the same couch, body against body, a woman groaned in the pangs of labor, a nursing infant writhed in convulsions . . .

The body was neglected in favor of the soul during the Middle Ages. In the thirteenth century the Dominican monk Albertus Magnus (Albert von Bollstadt 1193–

1280) wrote a guidebook for midwives. Different from the ancient guidebooks, this one did not focus on improving treatment of the mother or the child, but was concerned mainly with keeping the baby alive long enough to baptize it.

Strange instruments, such as the baptismal syringe, were invented for insertion in the womb in case the mother died before the birth or if the birth was impossible. In 1280 the Council of Cologne decreed that on sudden death of a woman in labor her mouth was to be kept open with a gag long enough so that the child would not suffocate while being removed by operation.

The three most important advances with regard to childbirth are podalic version, the forceps and Caesarean section. The French surgeon Ambroise Paré (1510–1590) reintroduced podalic version and the use of the method spread throughout Europe, marking another upswing in the lot of childbearing women. Paré obtained his surgical training at the Hôtel-Dieu, an experience which motivated him to do what he could to alleviate suffering. As surgeon to four kings of France he introduced his childbirth methods to the courts.

It was long thought that Caesarean section derived it name from the manner in which Julius Caesar was born. In truth, however, the operation was not performed on living women in those days and Caesar's mother, Julia, lived for several years after Caesar's birth. In 715 B.C. the king, Numa Pompilius, codified the Roman law or *lex regia* under which it was ordered that all babies of women who die in advanced pregnancy must be removed by incision of the womb in order that mother and baby could be buried separately. In Caesar's time the *lex regia* became *lex Caesare* and the operation became Caesarean section.

Paré, like the Greeks, believed that during childbirth the pelvis separated in the middle and opened out permitting the exit of the baby. Because of this misunderstood anatomy, Paré opposed Caesarean section, not realizing that podalic version did not solve the problem of the woman with too small a pelvis to give birth. Caesareans were performed on living women during the 17th century but, due to the lack of anesthesia and means for controlling hemorrhage, it was not a popular operation.

The reluctance with which obstetrical forceps were introduced temporarily damaged the reputation of medicine that Paré's humanitarianism had done so much to elevate.

In the 16th century two sons of a Huguenot physician, both named Peter Chamberlen, devoted their lives to midwifery and invented the obstetrical forceps. The invention was kept a secret, as the Chamberlens hoped to dominate the field of midwifery, and passed on to two generations of Chamberlens until it reached Hugh Chamberlen, a charlatan and a dabbler in politics.

Hugh Chamberlen travelled about selling the family secret for high fees, and it was not until the 18th century when his son, also named Hugh, permitted the secret to leak out to such an extent that the forceps soon came into general use. La Motte, obstetrician of Volgens, expressed the views of the time toward those who behaved as did the Chamberlens: "He who keeps secret so beneficial an instrument as the harmless obstetrical forceps deserves to have a worm devour his vitals for all eternity . . ."

Although Paré laid the groundwork for a new branch of medicine—obstetrics—it was to be a long time before the treatment of childbirth was separated from the field of surgery. A prominent German physician in the 18th century was said to have employed instruments "twenty-nine times in sixty-one births." The surgeons, moreover, couldn't resist using bloodletting in both normal and abnormal births—for different reasons, of course. The strong reaction that arose in England to any interference with childbirth had the initial result that such instruments as the forceps fell temporarily into disrepute and disuse and the eventual result that obstetrics became a medical branch separate from surgery.

When a certain Dr. William Smellie established in the 18th century a school in London for teaching midwifery, his competitor, Mrs. Nihell, the Hay Market midwife, called him "a great-horse-godmother of a he-midwife." Today's term—obstetrician—is definitely more prestigious.

In primitive cultures today, assisting at childbirth is still women's work, and those who perform the task retain the air of power, arrogance and superstition that categorized the colleagues of Sairey Gamp. In the novel *Beast of the Haitian Hills* Phillippe and Pierre Marcelin describe the life of the Haitian peasants. Among them is Sor Ti-Ma, the village midwife:

> She soon arrived, puffing and blowing in her haste. She was a big Negress with an authoritative face, whose imposing corpulence commanded respect. She was covered with heavy rolls of fat, which bulged under her showy clothes, clearly proving that she lived in honorable abundance and had never suffered hunger.
>
> Conscious of her own importance, she hardly deigned to acknowledge the greetings of those present. She walked majestically straight to the bed of the woman in childbirth. She carried with her the articles of her profession in a palm-straw sack, which contained various medicinal herbs, amulets and a kitchen knife, well sharpened, to cut the umbilical cord.

Earlier Sor Ti-Ma had warded off evil by binding around the expectant mother's belly a dried umbilical cord and by placing upon her a poultice of starch, the white of an egg and elm bark.

Another, more positive, flashback to the past can be seen in the interest of many modern women to practice "natural childbirth." An indication of how far removed women are from the natural childbirth of the past is the fact that it takes nine months of breathing exercises, physical exercises and practice in relaxation to *minimize* labor pains to the point where the women can stay awake in the delivery room.

The major difference between then and now is the fact that women need not follow the command from Genesis, "in sorrow shalt thou bring forth children," for a lack of means to prevent pain and difficulty.

CAESAREAN SECTION
from *The Rochester Post* (September 13, 1895)

We have heard of an operation very unusual in its cause and results which was performed by the Drs. Mayo, at St. Mary's Hospital last evening. A lady from near Byron who had been in the hospital for three weeks, awaiting the birth of a child, was relieved by the Caesarean section, which consists of cutting into the cavity of the abdomen and extracting the child, and is so named because tradition says the great Caesar was born this way.

The result of the operation in this case was not only the birth of the child, which weighted nine pounds, but also the removal of a tumor weighing twenty pounds. The mother and child are both doing nicely. The case is the first of the kind ever known in this part of the world.

From *Brave New World* (1932)
by ALDOUS HUXLEY

"I shall begin at the beginning," said D.H.C. [Director of Hatcheries and Conditioning] and the more zealous students recorded his intention in their notebooks:

Begin at the beginning. "These," he waved his hand, "are the incubators." And opening an insulated door he showed them racks upon racks of numbered test-tubes. "The week's supply of ova. Kept," he explained, "at blood heat; whereas the male gametes," and here he opened another door, "they have to be kept at thirty-five instead of thirty-seven. Full blood heat sterilizes." Rams wrapped in theremogene beget no lambs.

Still leaning against the incubators he gave them, while the pencils scurried illegibly across the pages, a brief description of the modern fertilizing process; spoke first, of course, of its surgical introduction—"the operation undergone voluntarily for the good of Society, not to mention the fact that it carries a bonus amounting to six months' salary"; continued with some account of the technique for preserving the excised ovary alive and actively developing; passed on to a consideration of optimum temperature, salinity, viscosity; referred to the liquor in which the detached and ripened eggs were kept; and, leading his charges to the work tables, actually showed them how this liquor was drawn off from the test-tubes; how it was let out drop by drop onto the specially warmed slides of the microscopes; how the eggs which it contained were inspected for abnormalities, counted and transferred to a porous receptacle; how (and he now took them to watch the operation) this receptacle was immersed in a warm bouillon containing free-swimming spermatozoa—at a minimum concentration of one hundred thousand per cubic centimetre, he insisted; and how, after ten minutes, the container was lifted out of the liquor and its contents re-examined; how, if any of the eggs remained unfertilized, it was again immersed, and, if necessary, yet again; how the fertilized ova went back to the incubators; where the Alphas and Betas remained until definitely bottled; while the Gammas, Deltas and Epsilons were brought out again, after only thirty-six hours, to undergo Bokanovsky's Process.

"Bokanovsky's Process," repeated the Director, and

the students underlined the words in their little notebooks.

One egg, one embryo, one adult—normality. But a bokanovskified egg will bud, will proliferate, will divide. From eight to ninety-six buds, and every bud will grow into a perfectly formed embryo, and every embryo into a full-sized adult. Making ninety-six human beings grow where only one grew before. Progress.

"Essentially," the D.H.C. concluded, "bokanovskification consists of a series of arrests of development. We check the normal growth and, paradoxically enough, the egg responds by budding."

Responds by budding. The pencils were busy.

He pointed. On a very slowly moving band a rack-full of test-tubes was entering a large metal box, another rack-full was emerging. Machinery faintly purred. It took eight minutes for the tubes to go through, he told them. Eight minutes of hard X-rays being about as much as an egg can stand. A few died; of the rest, the least susceptible divided into two; most put out four buds; some eight; all were returned to the incubators, where the buds in their turn budded; and having budded were suddenly chilled, chilled and checked. Two, four, eight, the buds in their turn budded; and having budded were dosed almost to death with alcohol; consequently burgeoned again and having budded—bud out of bud out of bud—were thereafter—further arrest being generally fatal—left to develop in peace. By which time the original egg was in a fair way to becoming anything from eight to ninety-six embryos—a prodigious improvement, you will agree, on nature. Identical twins—but not in piddling twos and threes as in the old viviparous days, when an egg would sometimes accidentally divide; actually by dozens, by scores at a time.

"But, alas," the Director shook his head, "we *can't* bokanovskify indefinitely."

Ninety-six seemed to be the limit; seventy-two a good average. From the same ovary and with gametes of the same male to manufacture as many batches of identical twins as possible—that was the best (sadly a second best) that they could do. And even that was difficult.

"For in nature it takes thirty years for two hundred eggs to reach maturity. But our business is to stabilize the population at this moment, here and now. Dribbling out twins over a quarter of a century—what would be the use of that?"

Obviously, no use at all. But Podsnap's Technique had immensely accelerated the process of ripening. They could make sure of at least a hundred and fifty mature eggs within two years. Fertilize and bokanovskify—in other words, multiply by seventy-two and you get an average of nearly eleven thousand brothers and sisters in a hundred and fifty batches of identical twins, all within two years of the same age.

"And in exceptional cases we can make one ovary yield us over fifteen thousand adult individuals."

Beckoning to a fair-haired, ruddy young man who happened to be passing at the moment, "Mr. Foster," he called. The ruddy young man approached. "Can you tell us the record for a single ovary, Mr. Foster?"

"Sixteen thousand and twelve in this Centre," Mr. Foster replied without hesitation. He spoke very quickly, had a vivacious blue eye, and took an evident pleasure in quoting figures. "Sixteen thousand and twelve; in one hundred and eighty-nine batches of identicals. But of course they've done much better," he rattled on, "in some of the tropical Centres. Singapore has often produced over sixteen thousand five hundred; and Mombasa has actually touched the seventeen thousand mark. But then they have unfair advantages. You should see the way a negro ovary responds to pituitary! It's quite astonishing, when you're used to working with European material. Still," he added, with a laugh (but the light of combat was in his eyes and the lift of his chin was challenging), "still, we mean to beat them if we can. I'm working on a wonderful Delta-Minus ovary at this moment. Only just eighteen months old. Over twelve thousand seven hundred children already, either decanted or in embryo. And still going strong. We'll beat them yet."

"That's the spirit I like!" cried the Director, and clapped Mr. Foster on the shoulder. "Come along with us and give these boys the benefit of your expert knowledge."

Mr. Foster smiled modestly. "With pleasure." They went.

In the Bottling Room all was harmonious bustle and ordered activity. Flaps of fresh sow's peritoneum ready cut to the proper size came shooting up in little lifts from the Organ Store in the sub-basement. Whizz and then, click! the lift-hatches flew open; the bottle-liner had only to reach out a hand, take the flap, insert, smooth-down, and before the lined bottle had had time to travel out of reach along the endless band, whizz, click! another flap of peritoneum had shot up from the depths, ready to be slipped into yet another bottle, the next of that slow interminable procession on the band.

Next to the Liners stood the Matriculators. The procession advanced; one by one the eggs were transferred from their test-tubes to the larger containers; deftly the peritoneal lining was slit, the morula dropped into place, the saline solution poured in . . . and already, the bottle had passed, and it was the turn of the labellers. Heredity, date of fertilization, membership of Bokanovsky Group—details were transferred from test-tube to bottle. No longer anonymous, but named, identified, the procession marched slowly on; on through an opening in the wall, slowly on into the Social Predestination Room.

"Eighty-eight cubic metres of card-index," said Mr. Foster with relish, as they entered.

"Containing *all* the relevant information," added the Director.

"Brought up to date every morning."

"And co-ordinated every afternoon."

"On the basis of which they make their calculations."

"So many individuals, of such and such quality," said Mr. Foster.

"Distributed in such and such quantities."

"The optimum Decanting Rate at any given moment."

"Unforeseen wastages promptly made good."

"Promptly," repeated Mr. Foster. "If you knew the amount of overtime I had to put in after the Japanese earthquake!" He laughed good-humoredly and shook his head.

"The Predestinators send in their figures to the Fertilizers."

"Who give them the embryos they ask for."

"And the bottles come in here to be predestinated in detail."

"After which they are sent down to the Embryo Store."

"Where we now proceed ourselves."

And opening a door Mr. Foster led the way down a staircase into the basement.

The temperature was still tropical. They descended into a thickening twilight. Two doors and a passage with a double turn insured the cellar against any possible infiltration of the day.

"Embryos are like photograph film," said Mr. Foster waggishly, as he pushed open the second door. "They can only stand red light."

And in effect the sultry darkness into which the students now followed him was visible and crimson, like the darkness of closed eyes on a summer's afternoon. The bulging flanks of row on receding row and tier above tier of bottles glinted with innumerable rubies, and among the rubies moved the dim red spectres of men and women with purple eyes and all the symptoms of lupus. The hum and rattle of machinery faintly stirred the air.

"Give them a few figures, Mr. Foster," said the Director, who was tired of talking.

Mr. Foster was only too happy to give them a few figures.

Two hundred and twenty metres long, two hundred wide, ten high. He pointed upwards. Like chickens drinking, the students lifted their eyes towards the distant ceiling.

Three tiers of racks: ground floor level, first gallery, second gallery.

The spidery steel-work of gallery above gallery faded away in all directions into the dark. Near them three red ghosts were busily unloading demijohns from a moving staircase.

The escalator from the Social Predestination Room.

Each bottle could be placed on one of fifteen racks, each rack, though you couldn't see it, was a conveyor travelling at the rate of thirty-three and a third centimetres an hour. Two hundred and sixty-seven days at eight metres a day. Two thousand one hundred and thirty-six metres in all. One circuit of the cellar at ground level, one on the first gallery, half on the second, and on the two hundred and sixty-seventh morning, daylight in the Decanting Room. Independent existence—so called.

"But in the interval," Mr. Foster concluded, "we've managed to do a lot to them. Oh, a very great deal." His laugh was knowing and triumphant.

"That's the spirit I like," said the Director once more. "Let's walk round. You tell them everything, Mr. Foster."

Mr. Foster duly told them.

Told them of the growing embryo on its bed of peritoneum. Made them taste the rich blood-surrogate on which it fed. Explained why it had to be stimulated with placentin and thyroxin. Told them of the *corpus luteum* extract. Showed them the jets through which at every twelfth metre from zero to 2040 it was automatically injected. Spoke of those gradually increasing doses of pituitary administered during the final ninety-six metres of their course. Described the artificial maternal circulation installed on every bottle at Metre 112; showed them the reservoir of blood-surrogate, the centrifugal pump that kept the liquid moving over the placenta and drove it through the synthetic lung and waste-product filter. Referred to the embryo's troublesome tendency to anaemia, to the massive doses of hog's stomach extract and foetal foal's liver with which, in consequence, it had to be supplied.

Showed them the simple mechanism by means of which, during the last two metres out of every eight, all the embryos were simultaneously shaken into familiarity with movement. Hinted at the gravity of the so-called "trauma of decanting," and enumerated the precautions taken to minimize, by a suitable training of the bottled embryo, that dangerous shock. Told them of the tests for sex carried out in the neighborhood of Metre 200. Explained the system of labelling—a T for the males, a circle for the females and for those who were destined to become freemartins a question mark, black on white ground.

"For of course," said Mr. Foster, "in the vast majority of cases, fertility is merely a nuisance. One fertile ovary in twelve hundred—that would really be quite sufficient for our purposes. But we want to have a good choice. And of course one must always leave an enormous margin of safety. So we allow as many as thirty per cent of the female embryos to develop normally. The others get a dose of male sex-hormone every twenty-four metres for the rest of the course. Result: they're decanted as freemartins—structurally quite normal (except," he had to admit, "that they do have just the slightest tendency to grow beards), but sterile. Guaranteed sterile. Which brings us at last," continued Mr. Foster, "out of the realm of mere slavish imitation of nature into the much more interesting world of human invention."

He rubbed his hands. For of course, they didn't

content themselves with merely hatching out embryos: any cow could do that.

"We also predestine and condition. We decant our babies as socialized human beings, as Alphas or Epsilons, as future sewage workers or future . . ." He was going to say "future World controllers," but correcting himself, said "future Directors of Hatcheries," instead.

The D.H.C. acknowledged the compliment with a smile.

They were passing Metre 320 on Rack 11. A young Beta-Minus mechanic was busy with screwdriver and spanner on the blood-surrogate pump of a passing bottle. The hum of the electric motor deepened by fractions of a tone as he turned the nuts. Down, down . . . A final twist, a glance at the revolution counter, and he was done. He moved two paces down the line and began the same process on the next pump.

"Reducing the number of revolutions per minute," Mr. Foster explained. "The surrogate goes round slower; therefore passes through the lung at longer intervals; therefore gives the embryo less oxygen. Nothing like oxygen-shortage for keeping an embryo below par." Again he rubbed his hands.

"But why do you want to keep the embryo below par?" asked an ingenuous student.

"Ass!" said the Director, breaking a long silence. "Hasn't it occurred to you that an Epsilon embryo must have an Epsilon environment as well as an Epsilon heredity?"

It evidently hadn't occurred to him. He was covered with confusion.

"The lower the caste," said Mr. Foster, "the shorter the oxygen." The first organ affected was the brain. After that the skeleton. At seventy per cent of normal oxygen you get dwarfs. At less than seventy eyeless monsters.

"Who are no use at all," concluded Mr. Foster.

Whereas (his voice became confidential and eager),

if they could discover a technique for shortening the period of maturation what a triumph, what a benefaction to Society."

"Consider the horse."

They considered it.

Mature at six; the elephant at ten. While at thirteen a man is not yet sexually mature; and is only full-grown at twenty. Hence, of course, that fruit of delayed development, the human intelligence.

"But in Epsilons," said Mr. Foster very justly, "we don't need human intelligence."

Didn't need and didn't get it. But though the Epsilon mind was mature at ten, the Epsilon body was not fit to work until eighteen. Long years of superfluous and wasted immaturity. If the physical development could be speeded up till it was as quick, say, as a cow's, what an enormous saving to the Community!

"Enormous!" murmured the students. Mr. Foster's enthusiasm was infectious.

He became rather technical; spoke of the abnormal endocrine co-ordination which made men grow so slowly; postulated a germinal mutation to account for it. Could the effects of this germinal mutation be undone? Could the individual Epsilon embryo be made to revert, by a suitable technique, to the normality of dogs and cows? That was the problem. And it was all but solved.

Pilkington, at Mombasa, had produced individuals who were sexually mature at four and full-grown at six and a half. A scientific triumph. But socially useless. Six-year-old men and women were too stupid to do even Epsilon work. And the process was an all-or-nothing one; either you failed to modify at all, or else you modified the whole way. They were still trying to find the ideal compromise between adults of twenty and adults of six. So far without success. Mr. Foster sighed and shook his head.

Their wanderings through the crimson twilight had brought them to the neighborhood of Metre 170 on

Rack 9. From this point onwards Rack 9 was enclosed and the bottles performed the remainder of their journey in a kind of tunnel, interrupted here and there by openings two or three metres wide.

"Heat conditioning," said Mr. Foster.

Hot tunnels alternated with cool tunnels. Coolness was wedded to discomfort in the form of hard X-rays. By the time they were decanted the embryos had a horror of cold. They were predestined to emigrate to the tropics, to be miners and acetate silk spinners and steel workers. Later on their minds would be made to endorse the judgment of their bodies. "We condition them to thrive on heat," concluded Mr. Foster. "Our colleagues upstairs will teach them to love it."

"And that," put in the Director sententiously, "that is the secret of happiness and virtue—liking what you've *got* to do. All conditioning aims at that: making people like their unescapable social destiny."

In a gap between two tunnels, a nurse was delicately probing with a long fine syringe into the gelatinous contents of a passing bottle. The students and their guides stood watching her for a few moments in silence.

"Well, Lenina," said Mr. Foster, when at last she withdrew the syringe and straightened herself up.

The girl turned with a start. One could see that, for all the lupus and the purple eyes, she was uncommonly pretty.

"Henry!" Her smile flashed redly at him—a row of coral teeth.

"Charming, charming," murmured the Director and, giving her two or three little pats, received in exchange a rather deferential smile for himself.

"What are you giving them?" asked Mr. Foster, making his tone very professional.

"Oh, the usual typhoid and sleeping sickness."

"Tropical workers start being inoculated at Metre 150," Mr. Foster explained to the students. "The embryos still have gills. We immunize the fish against the future man's diseases." Then, turning back to Lenina, "Ten to five on the roof this afternoon," he said, "as usual."

"Charming," said the Director once more, and, with a final pat, moved away after the others.

On Rack 10 rows of next generation's chemical workers were being trained in the toleration of lead, caustic soda, tar, chlorine. The first of a batch of two hundred and fifty embryonic rocket-plane engineers were just passing the eleven hundred metre mark on Rack 3. A special mechanism kept their containers in constant rotation. "To improve their sense of balance," Mr. Foster explained. "Doing repairs on the outside of a rocket in mid-air is a ticklish job. We slacken off the circulation when they're right way up, so that they're half starved, and double the flow of surrogate when they're upside down. They learn to associate topsy-turvydom with well-being; in fact, they're only truly happy when they're standing on their heads."

From *Mr. Adam* (1946)
by PAT FRANK

I was inquiring, I told the red-headed girl in the office, about the possibility of reserving a room in the maternity section, say about June 20th. The girl dipped into a filing cabinet. She came back to the counter, shook her head, and smiled. "Too bad," she said. "We're booked solid for June 20. Now if it was just two days later—"

"You mean," I said, feeling my stomach knot up inside me, "that you have plenty of space for the twenty-second?"

"For the twenty-second," she said, "we don't have a

single reservation. As a matter of fact, we don't have any at all beyond June 21." The redhead frowned. "That is peculiar," she said. "That is very peculiar. Funny I didn't notice it before."

"Thank you very much," I said, and I left, and noticed as I walked out into the snow that she was telephoning, and that the frown had not gone from her face.

I went to the AP office and called five other hospitals. Then I walked into J. C. Pogey's inner sanctum, unannounced. I certainly was shaken, and I suppose I must have been white with fright and foreboding, because when J. C. saw me he said: "For Christ's sake what's the matter?"

I fell into the leather chair by his desk, and tried to light a cigarette. "It may be the most frightful thing!" I said. "The most frightful thing!"

"What?"

"No babies. No babies after June 21."

J. C. Pogey is a very old, and patient, and infinitely wise man who has been the New York manager since, it is believed, the Administration of Taft. In that time all the most startling events of history have flowed through his ancient and delicate fingers, so what must have appeared to him as the spectacle of a reporter going wacky could not be expected to move him over-much. He said, gently, "All right, Steve, take it easy and tell me the tale."

I started with my knee, and went through the whole chronology. When I had finished he did not speak for a time, but rubbed his bald head behind the ears with his thin thumbs—a sort of manual method he employed to induce rapid cerebration.

Finally he said: "It may be, of course, the most terrible and certainly the most important story since the Creation. We must make the most thorough check, and yet we must not reveal what we're after, or do anything that will bring premature publication. It may be simply an extraordinary coincidence—but I'm afraid not."

"That's pretty pessimistic," I said.

J. C. swung his high-backed chair until it faced the window, and he looked out upon the spires of the city, soft gold in the winter sun, and it seemed that he looked through and beyond. "If I were God," he said, "and I were forced to pick a time to deprive the human race of the magic power of fertility and creation, I think that time would be now."

We decided that I should check the story, as far as possible, by telephone. We didn't want to send any more queries or cables than necessary, because when you start sending queries you get a lot of other people excited, and the story is likely to get beyond your control.

I armed myself with telephone directories for twenty big cities. I started by calling a hospital in Boston. I didn't say it was the AP calling. I just said I was a prospective father. The Boston hospital was booked up for June 21, like those in New York, but I was somewhat relieved when they said they had a few reservations for the last week in June.

"I don't think that is important," J. C. warned. "I think you'll find it is just a miscalculation by some Boston doctor. That's bound to happen."

I called Rochester, Philadelphia, Miami, and New Orleans, and then desperately swung west to San Francisco. The situation was identical. I called Chicago, St. Louis, and Omaha, and then tried some small towns in the South. So far as I could discover, our July birth rate was going to be zero.

"Maybe it's only the United States," I suggested.

"Try Montreal and Mexico City and B.A. and Rio," J. C. ordered.

I found I was hungry, and that it was night, and we sent out for sandwiches and coffee, and I began combing the Western Hemisphere. Things didn't change.

"This isn't proving anything," I said at midnight. "Maybe there isn't any shortage of hospital space. The only people who really know about this are the obstetricians."

"All right," said J. C., "call some obstetricians." I knew, by the way he said it, that his mind was set. A night fog had rolled over the city, and a Europe-bound liner was moaning its way to sea. He kept staring out into the night as if he expected to see something.

I only knew one obstetrician, Maria Ostenheimer, a friend of Marge, who lived around the corner on Fifth Avenue. While I dialed her number, I noticed that J. C. was scribbling on an outgoing message form.

Dr. Ostenheimer was awake, and by the noise, she was having a party. I said, "Maria, I've got something serious, and very confidential to ask you."

"Marge was over here, and she left a half-hour ago," Dr. Ostenheimer said. "She came over here alone, and she left alone, and I think you're a pig to even suspect—"

"No! No! No! This is nothing like that," I interrupted. "This is strictly business, and damn vital business."

"If you're going to have a baby," she said, "it'll be both a relief and a surprise, because nobody else is having babies." Her voice was just a bit hysterical, I thought.

"That's what I called about," I said, "this business of no babies."

There was a pause, and I knew she had shut the door to her rumpus room, because the party noises ceased. "What do you know about it?" she asked.

"I know that the hospitals aren't getting reservations in the maternity wards after June 21. That's not only here, but all over the country, all over other countries too."

There was no sound from the other end of the phone, and I thought for a moment that Maria might have fainted. But then she said, in a hushed, tense voice: "Stephen, at first I thought it was me. At first I thought somebody was spreading vicious lies about my work, and that I was being secretly blackballed. You know I've got a big practice, Stephen, and then suddenly, a few months ago, no new patients came. I start in the beginning with prenatal care, you know, Stephen."

"You only accept a limited number of patients each month, but that quota is always filled, right?"

"That's right. Well, it's awfully hard, going to a colleague and announcing that you're not getting any new patients, and I kept quiet until a few days ago, and then Dr. Blandy—he's got a big practice in Westchester—dropped in to see me, and I felt that the same thing was worrying him, and all of a sudden he told me, and I told him that the same thing had happened to me. We've talked to six others—I suppose together they're the top obstetricians in Manhattan—and we're having a meeting next week to investigate."

"You keep it quiet," I said, thinking of the story, although when I look back on it now a news beat seems very small potatoes, and indeed almost irrelevant. "You keep quiet about this, but I'll want to see you about it later."

I hung up, and turned to J. C. "I think," I said, "that the world has had it!"

"Perhaps not the whole world," said J. C. "Perhaps only the Western Hemisphere." He handed me the message form. It read:

URGENT PRESS FYI ONLY FYI USING UTMOST DISCRETION ASCERTAIN WHETHER ANY SUDDEN DROP BIRTHRATE EXPECTED LOCALLY JUNE OR JULY STOP REPLY

"We'll send this immediately," he said, "to Pat Morin in Paris, and Boots Norgaard in Rome, and Frank O'Brien in Istanbul, and Goldberg in Budapest, and Eddy Gilmore in Moscow. And of course to the London Bureau."

J. C. put the worn serge of his elbows on his desk and massaged his head behind the ears. "All night," he said, "I kept thinking of something General Farrell said after he witnessed the first atomic bomb explosion in New Mexico. He said, if I remember the words correctly, that the explosion 'warned of doomsday and made us feel that we puny things were blasphemous to dare tamper with the forces heretofore reserved to the Almighty.' "

I recalled a kindred phrase, after Hiroshima was atomized, about civilization now having the power to commit suicide at will. I thought about it, and I thought of the Mississippi disaster, and the thing began to come clear to me, and I yelled: "When was it that Mississippi blew up? Wasn't it in September?"

J. C. straightened. "That's it, of course!" he said. "The Mississippi explosion was September the twenty-first. Nine months to the day! Nine months to the very day!"

THE MILKY WAY CONFERENCE

An Atomic Age Play in One Act

from *The Saturday Review of Literature* (August 2, 1947)

by EMANUEL MARTIN GREENBERG, M.D.

CHAIRMAN:

(*Impatiently.*) Go on, go on!

APE-MAN:

Well, gentlemen, I shall be very brief. My people realize how futile it is to try to make you listen to a mere one million voices. We're through with asking you. From now on *we're telling you. . . .* (*Laughs and insults from representatives, rap of gavel.*)

Our scientists have perfected a new "birth accelerator." With this weapon, the ape-man's period of gestation, instead of your nine months, will be *two weeks*. If we decide to multiply at maximum capacity, we will soon overrun Mars by sheer force of numbers. Unless we get our rights, we will unleash this new biological weapon and conquer by propagation.

THE ARTIFICIAL UTERUS (U.S. Patent No. 2,723,660)

from *International Record of Medicine and General Practice Clinics* (MD Publications, Inc., 1956)

by EMANUEL MARTIN GREENBERG, M.D.

The artificial uterus is intended to replace the natural uterus when the latter expels an embryo prematurely at the fifth or fourth month of gestation or sooner. This often happens in such obstetric disorders as spontaneous or habitual abortion and eclamptic toxemia of pregnancy. In certain severe cases of Rh incompatibility, it might, in the future, conceivably be advisable actually to take the embryo from the mother and place it in the artificial uterus. After achieving further maturity in the artificial uterus, the young miscarriage would be transferred to an ordinary incubator and from there, eventually, to the crib.

This new organ complex, the artificial uterus, is dependent upon two other artificial organs, namely, the artificial kidney and the artificial heart-lung. The artificial uterus also depends upon the integrity of the embryo, umbilical cord, and placenta as one unit. The umbilical cord is not cut and the embryo is not separated from the placenta; this is the crux of the thesis of the artificial uterus.

The combination of a highly advanced type of incubator plus the new concept of the *fetus-cord-placenta* as one unit, utilizing a circulating blood stream that is constantly being oxygenated, purified, and nourished, constitutes the artificial uterus—what is hoped will become a salvager of miscarriages and abortions.

The placenta, or afterbirth, which is made up of tissue from both mother and embryo, is an organ that permits the mutual exchange of blood components; in the artificial uterus, as in the natural womb of the mother, the maternal blood and the fetal blood do not mix.

At first it was thought that the umbilical cord would shrivel up outside of the uterus. However, a segment of umbilical cord was placed in normal saline in a glass vial and remained perfectly intact, clear, and glistening for more than six months.

In addition, to prove the ability to transport nutrients and waste products through and from its vessels, the following experiment was performed. It demonstrates the ability of the placenta and umbilical cord system to permit ionic absorption and transfer to the embryo extra utero.

White rats were cesareanized on the seventeenth day of gestation under intraperitoneal barbiturate anesthesia. The embryos were delivered by hysterotomy, the surgeon being careful not to injure the umbilical cord and placenta attachment. The placentas were immersed in a lake of radioactive sodium in a watch glass for five minutes. The placentas and cords were then cut off and the embryos exposed to the Geiger counter. An appreciable amount of radioactivity was demonstrated to be present in the fetus.

The extrauterine passage of sodium ions through the placental capillaries and the umbilical vein to the body of the fetus demonstrates one of the component mechanisms upon which the function of the artificial uterus depends.

What are the fetal requirements that should be supplied by the artificial uterus?

1. Continuous flow of blood to and from the fetus.
2. Blood carrying nutrients and oxygen and removing carbon dioxide and waste products.
3. Even temperature (simulating intrauterine temperature).
4. Relative freedom from environmental shock injury.
5. Expansible chamber or a chamber large enough to accommodate a full-term child.
6. Bacteriologic sterility.

The artificial uterus that answers these requirements is an advanced type of incubator designed to salvage the fetus prematurely passed as a "miscarriage" by the mother prior to the age of viability. The fetus may also be taken from the mother by cesarean section in certain cases of Rh incompatibility, of eclampsia (if removal of the fetus is indicated before the period of viability), and in cases of threatened abortion if there is a history of habitual abortion or of sterility. The artificial uterus attempts to imitate the natural uterus in the following ways:

1. The umbilical cord is not severed; the baby, placenta, and umbilical cord are considered as one unit and are removed by cesarean section. When delivery has taken place from below, rapid manual removal of the placenta without severing the cord is recommended if possible.
2. The baby is placed in a fluid medium chemically and physically simulating the amniotic fluid.
3. The "uterus" is expansible or large enough to accommodate an embryo that would increase in size.
4. The "uterus" is uniformly heated.
5. The placenta is placed in a blood chamber and its cotyledons are bathed in blood just as truly as if they were in the maternal sinusoids. The maternal

blood from the uterus enters the intervillous space through a central arterial sac; there are only a few such sacs per cotyledon.

The pressure of the blood ejected from the terminal sacs is about 40 mm. of mercury and the blood is sprayed from the terminal sac through the intervillous space toward the fetal surface like water from the end of a fire hose.

The fetal blood and maternal blood actually do not mix.

As Arey states, "The blood of the mother and that of the fetus circulate in totally independent and separate channels. The relation of the chorionic villi and its vessels to the maternal blood which bathes the villi is much like that of the blood vessels of the hand to the water in a tub when the arm is immersed. A more precise comparison is furnished by the intestinal villi and the fluid content of the gut cavity during digestion. In the case of both chorionic and intestinal villi there is no direct contact or mixture between the external fluid and the blood of the villus, but their only communication is through diffusive interchange."

6. The placental blood chamber is connected to an artificial kidney and an artificial heart-lung, thereby bringing nutrient material and oxygen to the placenta and affording a means of waste product excretion. The placental blood chamber may instead be connected with the blood system of the embryo's own mother by connection with an artery and vein of the mother.
7. Employment of aseptic technique and the use of antibiotics.

The artificial uterus would be transparent, so that the development of the fetus could be observed from day to day. An electrically conductive, transparent "glass skin" could be applied to the outside to maintain the desired level of heat. Experimentation in the use of the artificial uterus will emphasize the normal but nonviable fetus in the 200 to 450 Gm. range.

The perfection of the artificial kidney and the artificial heart-lung is patiently awaited, for upon these will the success of the artificial uterus so much depend.

The artificial uterus thus comprises a synthesis of two artificial organ mechanisms—plus the new concept of fetus-cord-placenta integration into one unit in direct imitation of the natural state.

This is based on the belief that the young fetus is not ready to use its lungs, heart, or digestive tract and must depend upon its own placenta and umbilical cord for nutrient sustenance and gaseous interchange. Direct cannulization of the umbilical artery and vein may make it possible to by-pass the placenta, although in early embryos with correspondingly young and feeble hearts, it would seem logical to retain the placenta, thus imitating as much of the natural state as possible.

PROCREATION WITHOUT SEX

from *Physician's World* (May 1973)

by ALBERT ROSENFELD

In civilized society, sex and procreation have traditionally been joined in holy wedlock. Though lapses were never uncommon, all our religious upbringing and public schooling have trained us to think of sex as properly restricted to the marriage bed—and then mainly for the traditionally accepted purpose of propagating family, race and species.

In recent years, with the advent of the sexual revolution and the rise of contraceptive technology, more and more people of all ages have felt freer and freer to have sex for fun rather than family. It is no news, then, that sex has long since filed for divorce from procreation. What *is* news is that the divorce may well turn out to be uncontested: procreation may be able to get along very well without sex!

Already artificial insemination is common practice. Though its legal and ethical status remains fuzzy, thousands of American children are born in this fashion every year. The sudden popularity of vasectomy, timed as it was with advances achieved in sperm-freezing techniques, has led to the establishment of commercial sperm banks. True, some recent studies cast doubt on the effectiveness of sperm that has been frozen and stored for longer than three years. Nonetheless, should additional sperm-freezing and storage techniques be developed that would overcome any longevity problems, it would raise the prospect that children may be born many years after the sperm has been deposited. Indeed, they might be born years after the father's or donor's death, bringing us into a strange era of posthumous parenthood.

But artificial insemination, whether the sperm is fresh or frozen, whether contributed by the husband or by an anonymous donor—or even, as has been suggested, by *known* donors selected for their presumably desirable genetic characteristics—is only the first small step in the coming revolution in reproductive biology.

We hardly realize, on a conscious level, the extent to which our personal morals, our theological tenets, our marital and child-rearing customs, and many of our seemingly unrelated laws and social institutions are built on the Eternal Verities—i.e., the procreative Facts of Life. But in a day when the verities grow less veritable and profoundly less eternal even as we watch, as the facts of life lose their capitalized immutability, all our taken-for-granted concepts about sex, marriage, family and child-rearing are in for a wrenching reappraisal.

A mere catalogue of the procreative possibilities is

enough to dizzy the mind. Until now, the creation of a new human being required the bringing together of sperm and egg, joined by the sexual union of a Mama and a Papa—who, it was assumed, would stay on to nurture the newborn through its long period of juvenile vulnerability. We have lately begun to tamper freely with what nature seems to have intended. Birth control is a key phrase of our time.

We practice many kinds of birth control—some of it to *induce* fertility, as in the case of hormones administered to coax forth eggs from reluctant ovaries; but most of it designed to *prevent* fertility, to keep sperm and egg apart.

A Procreative Revolution

The newer kinds of control—those closest to us in time—bring together sperm and egg without the sex act; first inside, then outside the human body into a Huxleyan era of in vitro embryology. In the later stages of the procreative revolution, sperm will not be needed at all; and finally neither sperm nor egg will be required as we move into the futuristic realms of cloning and genetic engineering.

A physician of the future, when he is called upon to advise young men and women who may or may not want to become parents—or, if they do, are not sure what kind of parents they may want to become—will have an impressive spectrum of options to offer and explain. Because this future may come to pass, in large part, in our own lifetimes, today's physician—if he is not already pushing retirement age—is well advised to keep track of them.

Conception Control

We usually use the phrase birth control in a quite restricted sense to mean *conception* or *fertility* control. Virtually every non-specialized physician has already had occasion to offer advice about, or to prescribe, one or more of the variety of alternatives now at hand. He is probably familiar, too, with much of the research in progress, such as the so-called "morning after" pill, and hormonal implants that may last for months or even years.

Most of the existing methods, and much of the new research directions, involve doing something to the female, or having her do something to herself. Some researchers are now seriously investigating what can be done with the male. But one prominent researcher in reproductive biology, Robert Nes of Drexel University in Philadelphia, believes a man's total personality is considerably more vulnerable than a woman's to hormonal tampering. (Dr. Nes is working toward a pill that would be individually tailored to a given woman's needs—thus minimizing side effects—so that she could order a special pill just as she now orders a certain size of shoe or glove.)

Birth control will, very soon now, begin to take on expanded meaning. The new definition is best illustrated by citing and describing some of the future patient's procreative options.

Artificial insemination and *sperm banks*, already mentioned, are present realities, and seem certain to become more commonplace as their legal and ethical ambiguities are elucidated. Experimental work in animals strongly suggests that donor eggs, too, can be implanted in women who might need or desire them. Since they, too, can be frozen (though techniques are much less advanced than is the case with sperm), *artificial inovulation* and *egg banks* cannot be too far off.

Fertilization in vitro has been achieved in a number of laboratories. Soon such an artificially fertilized egg is likely to be implanted into a human female and permitted to develop to term as if it were her own natural baby. Best guess as to who will first achieve this is the Cambridge (England) team of Robert Edwards and Richard Gardner.

Though no one has yet been able to carry an *in vitro* embryo very far along the road to babyhood, there do exist new reasons (e.g., the rise of the science of fetology, and the increasing concern about the quantity of congenital defects that might be avoided if the fetus were visible and accessible) for hurrying along the engineering breakthroughs necessary to the attainment of the full-term *in vitro* baby. Prospective mothers in the not impossibly distant future may well be able to have their babies "carried" for them in laboratory prenurseries. Many old-fashioned types will deplore this practice as dehumanizing, while others will applaud it as a marvelous labor-saving device, one more step on the road to liberation from the bondage of female biology.

Superovulation is the artificial bringing-down of more than one egg from the ovary via the administration of hormones. It has been achieved inadvertently in human females through overdosage in the treatment of infertility; hence the increased incidence of multiple births in recent years. In cattle, superovulation has been carried out by design. E. S. E. Hafez of Wayne State University in Detroit has routinely been able to induce the release of 100 eggs at a time from a calf's ovaries, then fertilize them all with a single artificial insemination. In a few days the tiny embryos can be flushed out and reimplanted, one at a time, into other cows.

Dr. Hafez does not anticipate much human demand for this technique, unless certain females were to possess characteristics so superior as to be prized by other would-be parents. Can one imagine a hundred eggs from such a woman, inseminated by the sperm of a superior male? Or perhaps inseminated by the sperm of a hundred different superior males? Hafez does not consider it absurd to envision prospective mothers shopping for their future babies in a medical commissary in the form of already *prefertilized embryos*, frozen, a few days old, and being furnished with a description of the offspring's probable genetic characteristics.

Parthenogenesis, also known as virgin birth, is a

phenomenon that occurs naturally in certain lowly orders of the animal kingdom (rotifers, insects, crustaceans). It can also be induced artificially—and fairly easily at that—in animals (sea urchins, frogs, rabbits) in whom it does not normally take place. In such case the egg, without benefit of sperm, doubles its own supply of chromosomes. Hence the offspring will have only the mother's genetic traits—and will be a female. This technique could easily enough be applied to human eggs. Indeed, Dr. Landrum Shettles of the Columbia-Presbyterian Medical Center believes it may even happen spontaneously in rare cases. Moreover, it would not be unusually difficult to remove the egg's nucleus altogether and substitute a double supply of the father's chromosomes. This would constitute *androgenesis*. The child would have only the father's genetic instructions and could be either male or female, depending on whether or not a "y" chromosome had been included in the mix.

It is hard to see why patients would ask doctors for this option, unless they were excessively narcissistic and wanted only their own characteristics to appear in the child, or were virulently anti-male or anti-female, perhaps desiring a truly unisexual society.

Neither Sperm nor Eggs

In *cloning*, or tissue-culture reproduction, we dispense not only with the sex act, but with sperm *and* egg as well. The theoretical possibility is that we can take a cell from almost anywhere in the adult body and make available once more all the genetic information in the cell's nucleus—as Dr. Frederick C. Steward has done with carrots and tobacco plants at Cornell. This information should comprise the entire manual of genetic instructions that existed in the original fertilized egg—passed on from cell to cell with each division, but never again used in its entirety.

With all that information available again, the cell

would *behave* like a fertilized egg cell—would behave as if sperm and egg had been brought together all over again; and from this cell (so we suppose) a new human being, an identical genetic twin of the cell donor, could be grown. It could be implanted in a woman and grown conventionally; or, when *in vitro* technology is perfected, developed outside the human body.

There is no reason why, if it turns out that a new being can be grown from one cell, a hundred identical beings could not be grown from a hundred cells. The moral, social, theological, political and philosophical implications of a world where cloning has become routine would be almost beyond imagining. But imagine them we must, for it would be foolish to rule it out as too fanciful and futuristic for our concern.

Genetic Engineering

This is even truer of *genetic engineering* when it becomes available. The surmise is that one day we will know not merely how to read the genetic code but how to "write" in it. Thus we could correct any genetic errors (some real progress has been made in this direction), make additions or deletions to the DNA, or even write out entire sets of genetic instructions in advance, specifying whatever characteristics we consider desirable. (Who decides which characteristics *are* desirable?) It has been estimated that a thimbleful of synthetic DNA would be enough to repopulate the earth! Man in control of his own further evolution, if any, is a fearful thing to contemplate—but also a challenge to the creative imaginations of physicians and patients alike. (That includes everybody, doesn't it?)

From *In His Image: The Cloning of a Man* (1978)
by DAVID RORVIK

It was hypothesized that if a very dexterous and clever technician, a master microsurgeon, really, could take the nucleus of a body cell—any body cell, practically—and somehow get it undamaged into an egg cell whose nucleus had been removed or inactivated—also without damage—there would be an excellent chance that the total replicative machinery of the body cell would be "switched on" and that it would thus proceed to divide and differentiate, re-creating, in a sense, the individual from whom it had been taken in the first place. If ever a person could be said to be a chip off the old block, it would be this duplicate offspring. . . .

Max [the "father"] was secretive about his plans for Sparrow [the mother surrogate]. He talked of marrying her; he also talked of adopting her. At this writing I am not sure whether he ever did either. He said that this need not concern me, that in the event of his death, provided the offspring was still legally a minor, I and others would be apprised of all pertinent details. In any case, there was no doubt that whether he lived or died, both Sparrow and the child would ultimately know the full truth.

From what he said to me on one occasion, I was left with the impression that he foresaw and perhaps even desired a lifelong relationship between Sparrow and his copy, one that might more closely approximate that of man and wife than of mother and child. It was thus important to him that they be assured they were in no way related. The difference in years between them would be substantially less than the difference between Sparrow and Max. And if Sparrow did fall in love with Max, which seemed certainly to be a possibility if not already a fact, it did not seem unreasonable to guess that some day she might similarly love his copy, once Max was gone and the boy had grown up.

It was decided well in advance of delivery that Mary would be retained by Max after the birth of the child. She was devoted to Sparrow—and to Max—though I wondered how the two women would ultimately divide their duties. Perhaps, I thought, Mary would end up the primary maternal influence and Sparrow would evolve into something more remote and thus, at the same time, more accessible as a future romantic interest. But Sparrow was very strong, with a mind of her own. Of one thing I was certain: it would be intriguing, whatever happened.

The pregnancy advanced uneventfully. For that we were all most grateful. We had all assumed, and I think Max himself had always intended, that the baby would be delivered at the hospital, where it had been conceived. Then, "at the last minute," as Darwin [the doctor] put it, Max decided that the child must be born in the United States. Although he did not tell me exactly why, I could see many advantages in Max's heir being born an American citizen. . . .

Max had made arrangements whereby Darwin could deliver the baby in a small hospital. The decompression unit made the trip, too, and the plan was to deliver without anesthesia. Both Max and Sparrow had read some books on the subject and were converts to natural childbirth; Max said he did not want his heir coming into the world "drugged."

Sparrow was moved into a motel room, very plain but in the vicinity of the hospital, and I was at last able to join the group. We made jokes about being holed up, in hiding, and so forth. It was a tense period, particularly for Darwin, who did not travel so well and found California in December—at least as viewed from a rather inelegant motel—not at all to his liking.

Sparrow's contractions started a couple of days earlier than expected. Max called me from the hospital in the early morning hours. The others were already there, he said; the contractions had come on so rapidly and so strongly that they had all rushed off, leaving me behind.

I dressed and drove my rented car to the hospital, where Sparrow was already in decompression, looking quite content.

Two hours and forty minutes after she had began decompressing, by Mary's calculation, Sparrow was ready to deliver. The second stage of labor—which neither Max nor I witnessed, having been forbidden by Sparrow to do so—was over in a matter of minutes. The baby presented head first, without difficulty, appeared immediately normal, cried robustly and was given a near-perfect Apgar score by Darwin. (The Apgar Scoring System, developed by Dr. Virginia Apgar of the National Foundation—March of Dimes, is now almost universally used to evaluate a newborn infant's health, taking into account such things as muscle tone, color, and reflexes.)

Max had wanted to film the birth, but Sparrow objected. It would be immodest, she said. But she did permit Max to place a tape recorder in the delivery room to catch the baby's first cry. Max was permitted into the delivery room a short time after the baby was born, and I was allowed in about twenty minutes after that.

Sparrow said that she wished the baby had come at Christmas—still two weeks away. Max was delighted that it had happened in 1976—his contribution to the Bicentennial, he said. Darwin was beaming. Mary looked almost beatific. Max was sitting on the edge of Sparrow's bed. She was holding the baby in a small blanket to her breast.

It was not, I thought, exactly the nuclear family. But it was a thrilling sight, this old man, this young girl, this strange baby. I wondered what this wrinkled little creature could see. I wondered what he might know. I wondered if he would be brave.

Afterword

One year after the birth described in this book, Max's primary concern continues to be for his privacy and for the privacy of his new "family." Max, Sparrow, and the child are together—and well. Blood analyses and other tests involving various histocompatibility factors have demonstrated to Max's complete satisfaction that the child is indeed his clonal offspring. I have some reason to believe that Sparrow has now been apprised of the origin of the baby to which she gave birth.

HUMAN CLONING: REALITY OR RIPOFF?

from *Medical World News* (April 3, 1978)

NEW YORK—Was it a stunning scientific breakthrough or an April Fool hoax? True or false, the claim made last month by a lay writer that he had arranged for a man to be cloned stirred tempests in the waters of biomedical research, science politics, and public opinion. Here are sample reactions:

- "We're publishing David Rorvik's book on the cloning of a human as nonfiction on the strength of Mr. Rorvik's credentials," says the marketing director for J. B. Lippincott Company's trade division, Arthur Stiles.
- "I went on TV to kill that damn claim; it can turn society antiscience," says Nobelist James D. Watson of double-helix fame. "I don't know of anyone I'd have less confidence in than David Rorvik."
- "I'd favor a four-year moratorium on research in human cloning or even development of techniques for doing it," says citizens' lobbyist Jeremy Rifkin of the Washington-based Peoples Business Commission. He adds: "I'd favor stopping recombinant DNA research at this point."

Leading biomedical researchers surveyed by MWN were unanimous in denouncing, as scientific malpractice, Rorvik's unsupported boast that he had brokered and witnessed the cloning of a sexagenarian millionaire who wanted to perpetuate his own genes in his offspring. Yet none dismissed the feat as downright impossible. Mammalian cloning is feasible in theory, they point out, though still technically far beyond the ability of developmental biologists.

Without waiting for the book to come out—or the evidence—three scientists went into federal court here to join in a lawsuit lodged by the Peoples Business Commission seeking investigation of, and controls over, a broad area of human genetic research. These same scientists, geneticists Jonathan Beckwith of Harvard and Ethan R. Signer of MIT and biologist Liebe F. Cavalieri of the Sloan-Kettering Institute for Cancer Research have become known to the public for their active opposition to recombinant DNA research.

The lawsuit, filed under the Freedom of Information Act, calls on all branches of the federal government, including the CIA, to release all information concerning public funding for "the general subject of research involved in asexual reproduction in mammals, including human beings, specifically: cloning, in-vitro fertilization, embryo implantation."

"It's the height of hubris," said Rifkin, "for a government agency . . . to be going ahead without any knowledge on the part of the public. There ought to be a four-year moratorium on all such scientific investigation," he added, "so that citizens get a chance to learn, and choose, where their tax dollars are going."

Harvard's Beckwith, in his affidavit joining the lawsuit, added "new screening methods for genetic defects" as another field to be scrutinized and presumably curbed.

Should scientists oppose a ban on human cloning? Says Dr. Robert G. McKinnell, professor of zoology at the University of Minnesota and U.S. pioneer frog cloner: "I think the likelihood is so remote, it would be something like making a ban on landing a man on Mars next week."

By Rorvik's account, it was on or about April 1, 1976, that a sexagenarian American millionaire, at a clandestine laboratory in a distant clime, had his somatic cells fused with a previously fertilized enucleated human ovum to yield, nine months later, a baby boy now 15 months old. But all during 1976 Rorvik was writing a monthly newsletter for the Alicia Patterson Foundation on "the politics of cancer." It was in these newsletters, declares James Watson, that Rorvik "viciously misquoted" him to make the Nobel biochemist appear to be in favor of Laetrile.

Rorvik's new cloning book is dedicated to Laetrile's principal promoter, a sexagenarian Canadian entrepreneur named Andrew McNaughton, who last year pleaded guilty to the felony of conspiring to transport smuggled pills and vials of the contraband substance into the U.S. and is now on two years' probation.

Dr. Watson, in a TV interview, rated as "less than one in a billion" the chance that some scientist, in secret, had surmounted the formidable technical obstacles that so far have foiled the cloning of any animal—man, mouse, or even frog—from an adult somatic cell. The few frogs that have been cloned, researchers point out, derive from embryonic somatic cells, not the adult nuclei alleged to have been used by Rorvik's secret scientist.

"It won't float!" exclaims geneticist V. Elving Anderson, scoffing at Rorvik's protest that he will never reveal the persons and places involved, "to protect the child from harmful publicity and other participants from certain controversy." To make such a claim and withhold all proof in itself is socially harmful, says Dr. Anderson, who is associate director of the Dight Institute of Human Genetics at the University of Minnesota. Its public backlash "hurts people and discredits science," he says, adding, "Rorvik and Lippincott are both stupid if they think they can protect the identity of the cloned child; it will come out—if he really exists."

A full-page Lippincott ad in *Publishers Weekly* acclaims Rorvik's unsupported story as "the scientific investigative report of the century." To express his concern, in late February Dr. Anderson phoned and then wrote the Philadelphia-based medical division of J. B. Lippincott Company, which publishes a prestigious list of clinical journals and textbooks. The Minnesota scientist urged Lippincott to demand scientific evidence for the book's human cloning claim or label it science fiction. As of mid-March, Anderson had had no reply.

Queried by MWN, company president Joseph Lippincott insisted that the firm's medical division had nothing to do with the cloning book, which was accepted for publication by the Adult Trade Division. Stiles, that division's marketing director, confirmed, "The medical-division people may have an opinion, but we didn't ask for their views or permission."

Rorvik's five-page prepublication press release bases his over-all cloning claim on several refutable assertions:

- Rorvik: "Among those who have predicted that human cloning would occur long before most scientists expect are Nobel Prize winners Joshua Lederberg [and] noted geneticist Kurt Hirschhorn . . ." who heads the department of genetics at Mount Sinai Medical Center here. Says Dr. Lederberg now: "In 1962—quite a few years ago—I did feel that cloning was a hypothetical possibility. It had been demonstrated in frogs, and at the time I was unaware of the fundamental obstacles. I was wrong in 1962." The Stanford Nobelist reproaches the author for insinuating that he, Lederberg, still believes cloning to be imminent or that he advocates it for human beings. "As for making a cloned human," says Dr. Lederberg, "who needs it?" Dr. Hirschhorn states: "Mammalian cloning experiments have not succeeded, are not feasible. Rorvik's statements are fiction, and people like to believe science fiction."
- Rorvik: "My painstaking search of the literature

reveals only one paper in the English language that reports upon an effort to clone a mammal. . . . in the December 25 issue of *Nature* [the year, 1976, was omitted from the press release] . . . authored by Dr. J. D. Bromhall at Oxford University . . . [who was] able to create three seemingly normal rabbit embryos through the cloning process. His research effort, however, was not geared up for implantation of these embryos into surrogate mothers."

Bromhall's paper clearly characterizes those "seemingly normal embryos" as being merely nonviable morulae (clusters of 18 to 26 cells) representing four or five cleavages during 42 hours of incubation. Moreover, they were not at all analogous to the adult human clone claimed by Rorvik, since the donor nuclei came from embryonic cells, themselves in the morula stage. Bromhall (whom Rorvik says he consulted) never tried "to clone a mammal," only to test the ability to introduce a somatic nucleus into an egg.

• Rorvik: "A refinement of existing cell-fusion techniques was used in the first successful cloning of a man—a feat achieved by a team with millions of dollars at its disposal." For background, he refers readers to "the cell-fusion papers" of half a dozen known research teams, including "Roger Laddo [Rorvik's misspelling of Roger L. Ladda] of the Walter Reed Army Institute of Research . . . Dr. Hilary Koprowski of the Wistor Institute of the University of Pennsylvania [correct spelling: Wistar; not part of any university] . . . Dr. Christopher E. Graham of Oxford University."

Dr. Graham: "When you introduce an embryo nucleus, you know nothing of the character of the [donor] embryo; for true cloning, one must use an adult-cell nucleus. In published work, there is no evidence this problem has been overcome in mammals." Even if that outstanding problem were solved, explains the Oxford lecturer in zoology, there would still remain at least 15 formidable obstacles, from "inducing the donor nucleus to divide as fast as the egg nucleus" to "the quite difficult problems of reintroducing the egg into a foster mother's uterus."

Rorvik dismisses all these hurdles as merely Bromhall not being "geared up for implantation."

"We are now asked by an experienced writer of fiction as well as fact to believe that all of these obstacles have been cleared at a single bound," declares the NIH director of the office for protection from research risks, embryologist Donald T. Chalkley. "Not one scintilla of evidence is available to support these claims," points out Dr. Chalkley, and adds: "To mount a full-scale and federal investigation at this stage could do little more than provide free publicity for the author and the publisher."

CLONING: DON'T POUR BABY OUT WITH THE HOGWASH

Editorial by DORSEY WOODSON

from *Medical World News* (April 3, 1978)

Cloning is in the news, but is it in the cards? Highly unlikely, says every scientist at work in the field of asexual reproduction. Yet the naked boast of a lay writer that he saw a human being cloned has commanded prime time and space in the news media. It also sent several scientists from other fields into federal court, along with a Washington-based citizens' lobby, to seek disclosures, congressional hearings, and bans or moratoriums on research in cloning and human genetics generally. The same lobby and some of the same scientists earlier raised a similar alarm over the hazards of research in recombinant DNA. That line of work would create new forms of life, some perhaps dangerous. Cloning by definition would merely perpetuate an existing life's genetic makeup.

As MWN views the furor over human cloning, the real and present danger lies in pouring out the baby with the hogwash.

Unlike Dr. Frankenstein's secret sanctum, cloning research is not carried out in hidden laboratories by monomaniacal scientists seeking to immortalize some genius, dictator, or millionaire. Rather, the investigators in this country and Europe who are experimenting with the still-elusive techniques of making a frog, mouse, or rabbit grow from a nonsexual progenitor cell are seeking clinical payoffs in such areas as understanding (so as some day to control) the malignancy process, wound healing, and organ regeneration.

Last year, biologist Peter Hoppe at the Jackson Laboratory in Bar Harbor, Maine, succeeded in producing full-grown homozygotic diploid uniparental mice, by removing either the sperm or the egg pronucleus immediately after fertilization and implanting in a foster uterus. "This is a giant step toward true cloning," says Hoppe, "which would be a fantastic cancer research tool. We could determine whether malignancy is a property of the cell nucleus or cytoplasm, or both, and attempt to reverse malignant transformation."

There is no cloning research per se; almost all high-technology biological investigation of cells can and will spin off techniques to serve the eventual purpose of cloning mammals.

To prevent the sidetracking of such vital research by uninformed public opinion—horrified at human-cloning science fiction coming true here and now—means that scientists must communicate what they are up to. They must be candid and patient in explaining the nature of their work.

Like atomic energy and moon landings, mammalian cloning is inevitable. When it does happen, it will not be a scientific or medical issue but a moral and legal one, calling for the informed consent of the body politic. Until then, the progress should be watched and discussed—not disrupted and delayed.

THE FIRST "TEST TUBE BABY"

from The New York *Daily News* (July 27, 1978)

by EDWARD EDELSON

The birth of the world's first "test tube baby"—a child who was conceived outside a woman's body—sent waves of joy and wonder around the world yesterday as scientists hailed it as a momentous medical achievement. The jubilation was tempered, however, by warnings over the morality and ethics of producing human life in the laboratory.

The cheers in England for the proud mother and father—Lesley Brown, 30, and John Brown, 38—were shared by tens of thousands of other childless couples for whom the birth opened a new era of hope.

For the Browns, it was a girl—a perfectly normal child weighing 5 pounds and 12 ounces—born by Caesarean operation nine days prematurely at the general hospital in Oldham, England, because Mrs. Brown was suffering from toxemia, a mild form of blood poisoning.

"It came out crying its head off and breathing very well," said Dr. Patrick Steptoe, the obstetrician who worked to achieve such a laboratory pregnancy for 12 years. "It was a beautiful, normal baby."

The Browns named their daughter Louise.

Hospital personnel described Brown as "crying his

eyes out" after he learned that he had fathered a daughter.

They said that Brown ran down hospital corridors hugging people and shouting: "I've got a girl! I've got a baby daughter!"

EPILOGUE

From *Song of Myself*

by WALT WHITMAN

A child said, "What is the grass?" fetching it to me
with full hands;
How could I answer the child? I do not know what it is
any more than he.
I guess it must be the flag of my disposition, out of
hopeful green stuff woven.

Or I guess it is the handkerchief of the Lord,
A scented gift and remembrancer designedly dropt,
Bearing the owner's name somewhere in the corners,
that we may see and remark, and say "Whose?"
And now it seems to me the beautiful, uncut hair of
graves.

Tenderly will I use you, curling grass.
It may be you transpire from the breasts of young men;
It may be if I had known them I would have loved
them;
It may be you are from old people, and from women,
and from offspring taken soon out of their mothers'
laps.

What do you think has become of the young and old
men?
And what do you think has become of the women and
children?

They are alive and well somewhere;
The smallest sprout shows there is really no death . . .
All goes onward and outward—nothing collapses.